Zuma Exposed

Zuma Exposed

Adriaan Basson

Jonathan Ball Publishers
JOHANNESBURG & CAPE TOWN

First edition published in trade paperback in 2012 by
JONATHAN BALL PUBLISHERS
A division of Media24 (Pty) Limited
PO Box 33977
Jeppestown
2043

Reprinted once in 2012

Paperbook ISBN 978-1-86842-538-9
eBook ISBN 978-1-86842-540-2

Cover design by Michiel Botha, Cape Town
Design and typesetting by Triple M Design, Johannesburg
Colour section and graphics by MR Design, Cape Town
Printed and bound by CTP Books, Cape Town
Typeset in 12.5/15 pt Walbaum LT Std

Twitter: www.twitter.com/JonathanBallPub
Facebook: www.facebook.com/pages/Jonathan-Ball-Publishers/
298034457992
Blog: http://jonathanball.bookslive.co.za/

To the brave and selfless whistleblowers
who believe we can be better.

'My capacity to be offended had been eroded cumulatively and decisively by Zuma's conduct before he became president of the ANC and president of South Africa, and ever since.'

Professor Njabulo S Ndebele
City Press, 17 June 2012

Contents

Acronyms and Abbreviations

ADS   African Defence Systems

AMSA   ArcelorMittal South Africa

ANC   African National Congress

CCMA   Council for Conciliation, Mediation and Arbitration

COPE   Congress of the People

Cosatu   Congress of South African Trade Unions

DA   Democratic Alliance

DPP   Director of Public Prosecutions

DSO   Directorate of Special Operations (the Scorpions)

FPB   Film and Publication Board

ICT   Imperial Crown Trading 289 (Pty) Ltd

MEC   Member of the Executive Council

MP   Member of Parliament

NDPP   National Director of Public Prosecutions

NEC   National Executive Committee of the ANC

NIA   National Intelligence Agency

NPA   National Prosecuting Authority

PSC   Public Service Commission

SABC   South African Broadcasting Corporation

SACP   South African Communist Party

Sadtu   South African Democratic Teachers Union

SAPS   South African Police Service

SARS   South African Revenue Service

SCA   Supreme Court of Appeal

SCCU   Specialised Commercial Crimes Unit

SCOPA   Standing Committee on Public Accounts

SIU   Special Investigating Unit

SSA   State Security Agency

TRC   Truth and Reconciliation Commission

Cast of characters

1. Jacob Zuma
President of the ANC and
South Africa

2. Sizakele Khumalo
Zuma's first wife

3. Nompumelelo Ntuli Zuma
Zuma's fourth wife

4. Tobeka Madiba Zuma
Zuma's fifth wife

5. Gloria Ngema Zuma
Zuma's sixth wife

6. Sonono Khoza
Zuma's lover and mother of
his child

7. Duduzane Zuma
Zuma's son and businessman

8. Duduzile Zuma
Zuma's daugther and
businesswoman

9. Khulubuse Zuma
Zuma's nephew and
businessman

10. Schabir Shaik
Zuma's former financial
adviser and convicted
fraudster

11. Moe Shaik
Former head of the secret
service in the Zuma
administration

12. Jackie Selebi
Former police chief, convicted
of corruption

13. Michael Hulley
Zuma's private attorney and
presidential legal adviser

14. Ajay Gupta
Friend of Zuma family
and head of Gupta family's
business empire

15. Atul Gupta
Head of Gupta family's
Sahara computer business and
New Age newspaper

16. Rajesh Gupta
Youngest Gupta brother and
business partner of Duduzane
Zuma

17. Jagdish Parekh
Head of the Gupta family
business and shareholder in
Imperial Crown Trading

18. Richard Mdluli
Suspended head of crime
intelligence in Zuma's
administration, accused
of murder and corruption

19. Bheki Cele
Former chief of police who
was fired by Zuma

20. Menzi Simelane
Chief prosecutor in the Zuma
administration, declared unfit
for his job

21. Nomgcobo Jiba
Appointed by Zuma to act as
chief prosecutor

22. Lawrence Mrwebi
Head of Commercial Crime
Prosecutions, appointed by
Zuma

23. Willem Heath
Former head of the Special
Investigating Unit and adviser
to Zuma

24. Mokotedi Mpshe
Former acting prosecutions
head who withdrew Zuma's
corruption charges

25. Billy Downer
Zuma's corruption prosecutor

26. Julius Malema
Former president of the ANC
Youth League, axed by
Zuma's ANC

27. Blade Nzimande
General secretary of the South
African Communist Party and
member of Zuma's Cabinet

28. Gwede Mantashe
Secretary general of
Zuma's ANC

29. Jeff Radebe
Zuma's Justice Minister

30. Nathi Mthethwa
Zuma's Minister of Police

31. Siyabonga Cwele
Zuma's Minister of State
Security

32. Mac Maharaj
Zuma's spokesperson and
former Minister of Transport

33. Kgalema Motlanthe
Deputy president of the ANC
and South Africa

34. Tokyo Sexwale
Zuma's Minister of Housing
and businessman

35. Brett Murray
Artist and creator of *The Spear*

36. Moss Phakoe
Assassinated former ANC
councillor and union leader

Preface

Unlike his predecessors, Jacob Zuma didn't rise to power with a Big Idea. Nelson Mandela had the Rainbow Nation and Thabo Mbeki had the African Renaissance. Zuma had nothing but a corruption trial.

Yes, he was a jovial man of the people with an intuitive common touch, and of course his legacy in the ANC goes much deeper than what happened after the arrest of Schabir Shaik, but Zuma didn't become president of the ANC and of South Africa because of his clear vision or fine policies.

He became president because enough ANC branch members believed he was the victim of a conspiracy concocted by Mbeki, the first generation of BEE millionaires and the Scorpions. Mbeki's so-called 1996 Class Project was also rejected by the left, who saw him as a cold-blooded capitalist with scant regard for the plight of workers and communists. Although Zuma had no track record in the union movement, he became a Trojan horse for desperate interest groups with bleak futures. And so they pushed a compromised man to the front because he had nothing to lose and was the only ANC leader brave enough to put Mbeki, who was seeking a third term as ANC leader, in his place.

With the support of grassroots party leaders, the trade unions, the communists and the party's youth league, Zuma toppled Mbeki in Polokwane in a turning-point moment for Africa's oldest liberation movement.

Five years later, Zuma is at risk of being toppled himself by the same people – except for the communists – who put him into power. How did this happen so fast? Why are the same people who pledged to lay down their own lives for him now vying for his blood? Perhaps the answer can be found in a letter Nkululeko Mfecane, an Eastern Cape teacher, wrote to my newspaper, *City Press*, in July 2012:

> I am writing this letter seeking help. I am also writing as one of the disgruntled Eastern Cape educators who has been work-ing since January, and has not been paid a cent to date … The challenge we are facing in Eastern Cape has been going on since 2010. Basic Education Minister Angie Motshekga was dispatched to deal with these issues.
>
> Motshekga visited the province, established a task team to resolve everything that wasn't working well and also to restore the province to where it belongs in terms of the standard of delivery the ANC said it expected.
>
> The challenges were later elevated to President Jacob Zuma's office after it was established they were too comprehensive for the minister's liking and understanding. They needed, appar-ently, someone who could be more decisive.
>
> The president came, set up his task team, listened to our challenges and promised to deal with them.
>
> The province was later put under administration, mean-ing that all its functions would now be under the national government.
>
> The embattled Eastern Cape education superintendent-general, Modidima Mannya, was fired amid SA Democratic Teachers Union (Sadtu) protests that saw the province obtain-ing a mere 54% matric pass rate last year.
>
> In came Cosatu general secretary Zwelinzima Vavi to try and resolve the challenges.

A deal was struck where we were told all 'temporal' educators had to report back for duty and that financial issues would be addressed.

He left and we were all relieved that finally the nightmare was a thing of the past – only for it to resurface just a few days later.

This is the reason why I do not trust the marriage between Cosatu, Sadtu and the ANC.

Nothing concrete ever seems to come of this. As an educator, I love this nation, I am a taxpayer and I voted ANC. But then again, I have a family to take care of.

I am on my knees asking you, City Press, to help us, not only as 'temporal' educators, but as South Africans. Also, please help the ANC to come to its senses and do the right thing for the learners.

They are facing a bleak future because of the incompetent cadres occupying top offices and because of our president, who doesn't seem to know when to stand up and stamp his authority.

Instead he will say: 'Let's debate it.' What is to be debated when the provincial administration is crumbling? How many people are leaving this province for better opportunities because of this incompetence?

Is it not one of the reasons why Western Cape Premier Helen Zille call us 'refugees'?

With all this in mind, I don't see myself voting ANC ever again.

I would rather suffer than give my vote to a populist politician who will emerge and promise us the world while being interested only in family and close friends.

Parents must also come to the party as this affects their children.

I am a young professional who is wise enough to know that crime does not pay – but do we need to go and steal to survive, despite having decent qualifications?

This reminds me of a newspaper headline after Zuma's

3

acquittal, which read 'Living in Zumania'.

I never thought 'living in Zumania' was going to bring such low morale to public servants, let alone South Africans at large. It's like a dark cloud is hanging over us.

We have indeed made a mistake voting in Zuma as president.

There are three things about Mfecane's letter that struck me: firstly, that Zuma actually took the trouble to listen to the teachers' complaints and promised to do something about them. Secondly, that despite 'promising us the world', Zuma did nothing about their situation besides encouraging debate. And thirdly, that Zuma was 'interested only in family and close friends'.

Before and since his election as president, Zuma has been embroiled in a number of scandals – from bribery allegations to nepotism to sex scandals to protecting dirty policemen. His lack of a clear vision, his ineptitude at implementing policies and at leading in times of crisis are probably the closest we will get to reasons for his declining support.

Zuma's struggle credentials and peacemaking efforts in KwaZulu-Natal are well documented and acknowledged. What I was interested in were those things that wouldn't make his official biography or hagiography. This is a book about Zuma's dark side: the things he has done that make people like Nkululeko Mfecane pick up their pens and state openly that voting for Zuma was a mistake.

Introduction

'Number one is desperate now. He will do anything to stay in power,' says the man opposite me, sipping on his second cup of black coffee. He is an ANC man, a hard man, born and raised in the struggle. He is worried. Speaking about the decline of the movement he believes in with his whole heart doesn't come easily. He is scared. I need to take out my cellphone battery when we meet. 'Paranoia has set in at the highest levels. The amount of tapping going on is fucking crazy. All comrades now have two or three cellphones,' he says in a hushed voice, frowning.

I don't know if he's telling the truth. I've seen the two, three cellphones when I meet sources in bars, restaurants or parking lots. There's the official number, the unofficial off-the-record number and the deep-off-the-record number. I often make the joke that if all the people who believe they are being bugged are really being listened to, that leaves half of the rest of the population to do the tapping. It doesn't matter if the paranoia is based on real evidence or perception. Perception is truth, and in the months leading up to the governing ANC's 53rd national elective conference in Mangaung, paranoia has set in at an unprecedented level.

Comrades are scared about whom they speak to, where they eat or who they are seen with in public.

'Try to come with a different car next time. Park on the other side of the building. And don't call me on my official phone, ever,' says the hard man. He's just explained to me why, despite his flaws, Zuma should be re-elected at Mangaung. 'This one-term shit will cause instability, not only in the ANC but in the whole country. If we start kicking people out after one term we will end up with a civil war, like the rest of Africa.'

Wow, what a reason to re-elect a party president, I think: to prevent civil war.

Hard man says that the ANC is acutely aware of Zuma's flaws and will put a 'ring of steel' around him in his second term, which means he won't be allowed to make important decisions unilaterally.

Another comrade, an ANC woman who has given most of her adult life to the party, says she's advising her kids to go study abroad and get residency overseas. 'Look what this man is doing,' she says, with disdain for Zuma in her voice. 'He only cares about himself and his family. This is banana republic stuff.'

It is a few months before Mangaung and President Jacob Gedleyihlekisa Zuma is fighting the political battle of his life to stay in power. Although he had told journalist Moshoeshoe Monare in 2008 that he would 'prefer to leave after one term', Zuma later denied this, saying he would never say such a thing because it was up to the ANC to decide if he would serve one or two terms as president.

Five years after defeating Thabo Mbeki convincingly at Polokwane, Zuma was on the ropes, fighting fire after fire over his handling of the multiple crises in his administration. The party of Oliver Tambo and Nelson Mandela was, again, searching for its soul, which, according to loyal comrades and opponents of the ANC, had become corrupted.

Something was rotten in the state of Zuma.

While I was writing this book, the ANC in the Northern Cape elected a provincial executive. Four of the five members elected to lead the party in this province for the next five years were implicated in corruption or fraud scandals. The story did not make headlines, nor were there mass protests or national outrage over the election of four accused persons to lead the governing party in one of the poorest provinces it governs.

At about the same time my newspaper, *City Press*, was at the centre of a perfect storm following the publication of an artwork, by artist Brett Murray, titled *The Spear*. The painting, a parody of a famous poster of Lenin, showed Zuma with his genitals hanging out. The ANC and Zuma took us to court, organised mass protests against the Goodman Gallery (where the painting was being exhibited) and asked its members to boycott *City Press* – the first such call since the party came to power in 1994. Blade Nzimande, the Minister of Higher Education and Zuma's strongest ally, called for the artwork to be destroyed.

Whenever I found myself drowning in confusion over the state of affairs in South Africa, I remembered the hard man's words: 'He will do anything to stay in power.'

In spite of all the scandals plaguing Zuma's term in office, analysts predicted that, against all odds, he was set to secure a second term in office. Perhaps this had something to do with the ANC's culture of not speaking out against power in public, with the party's almost covert style of campaigning behind the scenes. Or perhaps it came down to one thing, the only thing Zuma's foes and friends agree on – that he is a masterful strategist.

I am often reminded of the fact that Zuma ran ANC intelligence from the mid-1980s. 'He knows everything about the party. He knows everybody's dirt. A lot of people cannot afford for Zuma to start speaking,' another ANC veteran tells me. This became a popular refrain during the time that Zuma, who is also affectionately called 'Msholozi' (from his clan name), was facing corruption charges relating to the R70 billion Arms Deal. Zuma's suited strategists and grassroots supporters agreed: if this man starts to talk, he could take the party down. Such speculation was fuelled by Zuma himself, who told his supporters outside court that 'one day' he would reveal the identities of his persecutors.

Of course, Zuma's power and grip over the ANC cannot be explained only by his knowing, metaphorically, where the bodies are buried. As president, Zuma made a number of telling appointments to crucial Cabinet positions, especially in the criminal justice cluster. In most of these cases, the appointees were Zuma loyalists. A significant number had, like Zuma, chequered pasts. I realised over time that Zuma surrounded himself with people who depended on his goodwill to stay in power and enjoy the fruits of the governing elite. They also depended on him turning a blind eye to the accusations, allegations, charges or rulings against them. Logically, these people weren't always the best candidates for the job. Zuma's appointments of people to lead state institutions like the police, the prosecuting authority and the intelligence services also created the inescapable impression that, ultimately, he was protecting himself.

It would be fair to say that, during the four years in which corruption charges were preferred against him, Zuma developed a paranoia about being prosecuted, convicted and jailed for taking money in return for political favours. A court had already found that he was part of a corrupt relationship with his former financial adviser, Schabir Shaik. Another court was to decide whether Zuma had accepted the money and benefits with a guilty mind. When the charges against him were dropped on the most dubious of legal grounds, Zuma had reason to be fearful.

He kept his friends close. Through Jeff Radebe (Minister of Justice), Nathi Mthethwa (Minister of Police) and Siyabonga Cwele (Minister of State Security), Zuma kept a tight grip on the criminal justice system. The three ministers, all from Zuma's home province of KwaZulu-Natal, are some of his closest allies in Cabinet and the ANC, and are viewed as crucial to his chances of securing a second ANC victory. Zuma protected them, even when Cwele's wife was convicted of drug smuggling and Mthethwa was exposed as a beneficiary of a dodgy crime intelligence slush fund.

Six months before the Mangaung conference and three years into the Zuma presidency, the South African Police Service (SAPS), the police crime intelligence division, the National Prosecuting Authority (NPA), the Special Investigating Unit (SIU) and the State Security Agency (SSA; both the domestic and foreign intelligence agencies) were all headed by acting appointees. These institutions, crucial to the government's fight against crime and corruption, were rudderless, in disarray and barely surviving in an environment of fear and loathing.

It is impossible to divorce this sorry state of affairs from the ANC's current power battles. Zuma knew that to win in Mangaung, he needed the support of his police and intelligence chiefs; all the better if he also had a sympathetic ear at the NPA. It was, after all, a former head of the NPA who almost spoiled the Polokwane party, in December 2007, when he announced during the conference that Zuma would face corruption charges in the new year. Despite a looming corruption case, Zuma went on to be elected as ANC leader. He never saw the inside of a courtroom to defend his innocence. The rest is history.

It is five years later, and Zuma is again running for the office of ANC president.

This book is not an objective analysis of everything Zuma has done since becoming president in May 2009. It is also not a biography. I am an investigative journalist, interested only in the truth. Naturally, when a person is elected president of my country, I follow his every move and his money and interrogate every decision he makes in order to navigate through the bullshit and spin that South African journalists are increasingly being fed. The book is a critical and probing look at how an affable, man-of-the-people leader became a bad president; how, in five years, bad decisions, bad judgement and bad leadership moved some of Zuma's staunchest supporters from 'Kill for Zuma' to 'Anyone But Zuma', from passionately singing *'Awuleth Umshini Wam'* (bring me my machine gun) to angrily chanting *'Dubul' uZuma'* (shoot Zuma). It is an attempt to explain why loyal cadres carry three cellphones and advise their children to leave the country they fought for.

Part 1

Bad decisions

Julius

'We are prepared to die for Zuma. The future belongs to us. We do not want a situation where the state prosecutes its own president. This issue is dividing the country. We are prepared to take up arms and kill for Zuma.'

1

On a rainy afternoon in May 2009, one month and three days after corruption charges against him were dropped, Jacob Gedleyihlekisa Zuma was inaugurated as the fourth president of a democratic South Africa.

While I watched the inauguration from my home, blankets and umbrellas were dished out to guests at the Union Buildings to keep them dry and warm. The *Mail & Guardian* reported that 'in Africa it is considered a blessing when it pours during a ceremony'.[1]

The inauguration was attended by the great, the bad and the ugly, including former president Nelson Mandela, his successor (and Zuma's foe) Thabo Mbeki, Zimbabwean president Robert Mugabe, Libya's brother leader Muammar Gaddafi and Swaziland's King Mswati III.

During his inauguration speech, Zuma made these commitments 'before the eyes of the world':

> For as long as there are South Africans who die from preventable disease;
>
> For as long as there are workers who struggle to feed their families;

For as long as there are communities without clean water, decent shelter or proper sanitation;

For as long as there are rural dwellers unable to make a decent living from the land on which they live;

For as long as there are women who are subjected to discrimination, exploitation or abuse;

For as long as there are children who do not have the means nor the opportunity to receive a decent education;

For as long as there are people who are unable to find work, we shall not rest, and we dare not falter.

Zuma is good at saying the right things. The speech also highlighted the importance of diverse views, freedom of expression and strong democratic institutions, insulated from abuse:

We seek a vibrant, dynamic partnership that is enriched by democratic debate that values diverse views and accommodates dissent.

Therefore, we need to make real the fundamental right of all South Africans to freely express themselves, to protest, to organise, and to practise their faith.

We must defend the freedom of the media, as we seek to promote within it a greater diversity of voices and perspectives.

We must deepen the practice of participatory democracy in all spheres of public life.

We must strengthen the democratic institutions of state, and continually enhance their capacity to serve the people.

We must safeguard the independence and integrity of those institutions tasked with the defence of democracy, and that must act as a check on the abuse of power.

Just over three years into his presidential tenure, Zuma should be a worried man. Hardly a day goes by without news reports about communities lacking decent housing or water; about unemployed youngsters taking to the streets over lack of jobs and poor service delivery; about schools holding classes under trees without the necessary learning materials.

An extreme example of the prevailing hardship endured by South Africa's overwhelmingly black poor class (government and researchers refer to them as 'the poorest of the poor') was the shocking death of four children from Verdwaal in North West in November 2011. The four Mmupele children, aged two, six, seven and nine, died of hunger in the veld after they got lost searching for a young woman – mother to two of the children – who had gone out looking for food. The last they had eaten was borrowed mealie meal, which they had finished two nights before.[2]

Thandi Modise, the North West premier and deputy secretary-general of the ANC – elected on the Zuma slate – responded on behalf of the government, saying that the Mmupele children's death had left her 'shocked and bewildered'. She shifted the focus to the police investigation, saying a case of child neglect against the two mothers of the children was being investigated. Modise further revealed that three government agencies were 'on the ground' and thanked the NGO Gift of the Givers for distributing 300 food parcels to families in Verdwaal.

What Modise didn't address in her elaborate statement was the real issue why Elizabeth Mmupele, mother of two of the children, left them behind, an act the premier claimed could be a criminal offence of 'neglect'. Elizabeth, five months pregnant, told the *Sowetan*: 'I went to my mother's work to look for something to eat, I was hungry and my children and younger siblings were also hungry because we had not eaten the previous night. We did not have any food in the house.'[3] I suppose it was much easier for Modise to make a statement about a police investigation than to try to explain why children in her province were dying of hunger 17 years after the ANC came to power. Zuma himself was silent on the matter.

Abbey Makoe, political editor at the SABC, wrote a scathing column in the *Daily News* about the Mmupele children's death. 'How can a filthy-rich country like South Africa, that likes to beat its own drum about prosperity and modern economic planning, still have children dying of hunger?' he asked. In their darkest hour, the Mmupele kids did not turn to their fellow South Africans for help, Makoe said, adding that their births weren't even recorded by the Department of Home Affairs. This meant they were so 'unimportant in life' that they couldn't have accessed basic government services. 'It also means that 17 years into our much-hailed democracy, such people, whose only sin is poverty, cannot vote in the elections. They have no money, no hope, no voice.'[4]

The tragic story of the Mmupele children stands in stark contrast to the lofty undertakings Zuma made 'before the eyes of the world' on 9 May 2009. His commitment to promote diverse views, a free press and strong democratic institutions would also later be seriously challenged by the ANC's attempts to push through Parliament a highly problematic bill that would muzzle investigative journalism, the appointment of tainted individuals to head crucial state institutions and a burning debate about a painting of Zuma by artist Brett Murray.

2

The day after his inauguration, Zuma announced his Cabinet. It was a mixed bunch, with several Mbeki supporters surviving the cut. Zuma brought in a number of unknown candidates and appointed trusted allies, mostly from KwaZulu-Natal. Zuma also rewarded the loyal cheerleaders who had got him elected at Polokwane: SACP general secretary Blade Nzimande, former ANC Youth League firebrand Fikile Mbalula and ANC Women's League president Angie Motshekga. For their undying support during his legal battles, Zuma rewarded Cosatu by appointing unionists Ebrahim Patel and Noluthando Mayende-Sibiya to his Cabinet.

Over the next three years, Zuma would reshuffle his Cabinet three times, resulting in only 33 (53%) of the original appointees remaining in their positions by the end of 2012. Eleven members of the executive (18%) either resigned or were fired; 16 (26%) were moved to other positions in the executive during the three years; and two, Minister of Public Service and Administration Roy Padayachie and Deputy Minister of Health Molefi Sefularo, passed away during their terms.

Shortly after their appointments, I did an investigation for the *Mail & Guardian* on the business interests of Zuma's Cabinet members. Most of the big post-apartheid scandals that have hit the ruling party have emanated from conflicts of interest – politicians and civil servants who wanted their bread buttered by both the private sector and government. The results were telling: 27 members (42%) of Zuma's new executive, including himself, were registered as directors or members of private companies. Most of the new ministers said they would resign from their companies, while others said there was no conflict of interest between the nature of their business and their portfolios.

Tokyo Sexwale, Zuma's Housing minister, had by far the most companies registered under his name. He was also the richest member of the executive, having been ranked in 2008 as South Africa's 20th richest person – worth R1,3 billion – by the *Sunday Times* Rich List. Sexwale's appointment was an interesting one, since he had initially challenged Zuma and Mbeki for the party's top job at Polokwane. When he saw the writing on the wall, he threw in his lot with the Zuma camp.

His appointment as Minister of Human Settlements by Zuma was viewed as a masterful move on the part of the president. After building up his Mvelaphanda business empire (and making his debut as a TV star in the South African version of *The Apprentice*), Sexwale was ready to return to politics. But Zuma gave him a poisoned chalice: a portfolio almost impossible to succeed in. The former Robben Islander had much greater ambitions than housing, which remains one of South Africa's biggest socio-economic challenges. In July 2011, Sexwale admitted that 12,5 million poor people were still in need of shelter. The government had built three million houses since 1994, but still had to construct more than two million.[1]

Five years on from Polokwane, and Sexwale was again unofficially campaigning for the ANC presidency. Seen as the 'leader' of the 'Anyone But Zuma' campaign, the minister toured ANC regions, especially in the Eastern Cape, to gain votes. He became Zuma's strongest critic from within the Cabinet in the run-up to Mangaung, using every public platform to take a swipe at the president and his policies.

Other Cabinet ministers with business interests included Siphiwe

Nyanda, Sicelo Shiceka and Gwen Mahlangu-Nkabinde, who were all fired by Zuma during one of his three Cabinet reshuffles.

* * *

On 3 June 2009, Zuma delivered his first state of the nation address to Parliament – almost exactly four years after he was sacked as deputy president by Thabo Mbeki. South Africa was in a number of ways a different country, not least because of the global economic crisis that had slowed down economic growth and job creation. So it was not a surprise when Zuma focused on issues of employment, national pride and crime. He said he would 'intensify the fight against crime and corruption'. He explained the name-change of the Safety and Security ministry (to Police) to 'emphasise that we want real operational energy in police work' and set the target for reducing serious and violent crimes at between 7% and 10% per year – the same target his predecessor couldn't achieve.

Zuma also pledged his support for the 'continued transformation of the judiciary. The transformation should address key issues such as the enhancement of judicial independence, entrenching internal systems of judicial accountability as well as ensuring full access to justice by all.' Then he turned to the three pillars of government. 'The success of the democratic system as a whole depends on good relations of mutual respect and a spirit of partnership among the Executive, the Legislature and the Judiciary. This is very important for our constitutional democracy,' the president said. The tension between these three branches would intensify in years to come.

Zuma's statement was significant, as it came a few months after ANC secretary-general Gwede Mantashe caused a furore over his comments that some judges were 'counter-revolutionary forces'. In an interview with the *Mail & Guardian*, Mantashe had lashed out at judges of the Constitutional Court after they lodged a complaint with the Judicial Service Commission (JSC) over Western Cape Judge President John Hlophe's alleged interference in Zuma's corruption case.[2] Mantashe had accused the judges of indirectly attacking Zuma and the ANC. 'You hit the head, you kill the snake. When there is that attack on him [Zuma], it is a concerted attack on the head of the ANC. Everybody says it is an innocent attack on him. We will know that it is an attack on the ANC,' Mantashe said. His attack on the judiciary would be followed by numerous others from senior party leaders.

In his first state of the nation speech, Zuma committed himself and his administration to the fight against corruption in the public service. 'We will pay particular attention to combating corruption and fraud in procurement and tender processes, application for drivers' licences, social grants, IDs, and theft of police case dockets,' he said, and asked the citizens of South Africa to assist the police in fighting crime.

Whatever you may think of Zuma, you have to admire his comeback abilities: from corruption accused in 2008 to corruption fighter in 2009. How did he do this?

3

They say a man is known by the friends he keeps. So who were the men and women the ANC elected to lead the party, and the country, with Jacob Zuma?

By the time the Polokwane conference got under way in December 2007, the ANC was split firmly between the Mbeki and Zuma camps. Lobbyists for each camp distributed lists containing the names of preferred candidates, to be voted in at the conference. Some names appeared on both lists, while ANC stalwarts such as Pallo Jordan, Cyril Ramaphosa and Zola Skweyiya made the cut despite not aligning themselves firmly with either camp.

The 80-member National Executive Committee (NEC) elected by the ANC at Polokwane did not only include a president implicated in corruption, but a number of convicted criminals, suspects in criminal investigations or individuals who had been censured as a result of disciplinary hearings. This made me wonder what effect Zuma's rejection of the corruption charges against him as a political conspiracy had had on other dodgy comrades. Did it open the door for them also to claim they were the victims of political conspiracy the moment they were arrested or charged? It would be naive to think that the criminal justice system is not open to manipulation or selective prosecution. But it would be equally naive to think that every crime or corruption case against a political bigwig is part of a conspiracy to promote or sink a political agenda.

But let's get back to the NEC. After the names were announced, I decided to do a quantitative measurement of the tainted comrades in the newly elected ANC leadership. (The list that follows appeared in the *Mail & Guardian*[1] in January 2008.) I discovered that 16% of the NEC were either post-apartheid convicted criminals or suspects in criminal investigations. If you added those who had been disciplined or had unanswered questions hanging over their heads, the figure increased to 29%. I heard afterwards that a number of people, including ANC supporters, cut out and kept the list as a reminder of what happened at Polokwane.

The criminals

Winnie Madikizela-Mandela (fraud and kidnapping)
A kidnapper and fraudster, Madikizela-Mandela has escaped jail twice. She was charged in 1991 with the kidnapping and murder of 14-year-old Stompie Seipei.

She was convicted of kidnapping and sentenced to six years' imprisonment. The sentence was reduced to a fine of R15 000 on appeal.

Madikizela-Mandela's next run-in with the law was in 2001 when she was charged with obtaining loans for non-existent ANC Women's League employees. She was found guilty on 43 counts of fraud and 25 of theft.

Madikizela-Mandela was sentenced to five years' imprisonment. The theft charges were overturned on appeal and her sentence reduced by 18 months and suspended for five years.

Tony Yengeni (fraud)
The ANC's former chief whip pleaded guilty in February 2003 to a charge of fraud after failing to declare to Parliament a

47% discount on his Mercedes-Benz 4x4. Michael Woerfel, former South African head of the European Aeronautic Defence and Space Company (EADS), approved the discount. EADS tendered for lucrative Arms Deal contracts.

Yengeni served 20 weeks of his four-year sentence.

Bathabile Dlamini (fraud)

The secretary-general of the ANC Women's League is a Travelgate fraudster who pleaded guilty in October 2006.

As an ANC MP, Dlamini abused her parliamentary travel vouchers (which amounted to R254 000). She used them to pay for hotel accommodation, car rentals and other benefits.

Dlamini was given a five-year suspended sentence and fined R120 000 payable over 24 months.

Enoch Godongwana (drunk driving)

The court had tough words for this former Eastern Cape finance MEC after he was convicted of drunk driving in 2003. Godongwana was twice over the legal limit and refused to undergo a breathalyser test after he was caught in East London.

He was fined R8 000 or 200 days in jail, and received a suspended three-year sentence for drunk driving.

Ruth Bhengu (fraud)

Also a Travelgate fraudster, Bhengu resigned as an MP after pleading guilty to defrauding the parliamentary travel scheme of R43 000.

She was sentenced to two years' imprisonment or a R45 000 fine, and given a three-year suspended sentence. Bhengu was subsequently appointed deputy mayor of the Ugu District Municipality in KwaZulu-Natal.

Jackson Mthembu (contempt of court)

The former Mpumalanga chief whip has been embroiled in numerous scandals, but has only been convicted once – on a

contempt of court charge, after pleading guilty to ignoring a
R500 traffic fine in 2002.

As MEC for transport and public works in Mpumalanga,
Mthembu admitted to spending government money on ANC
trips, not following protocol with the purchase of 10 BMWs for
his colleagues on the executive committee and crashing a state
car without a driver's licence.

Mthembu was acquitted of fraud in 2001 after he was accused of falsifying a state contract for a building company that
employed him.

Ndleleni Duma (fraud)

Another Travelgate convict, North West MEC for sports,
arts and culture Duma pleaded guilty to a charge of theft of
R51 000 from Parliament when he was an MP. He was fined
R30 000 or imprisonment of three years.

The suspects

Jacob Zuma (racketeering, corruption, money laundering and fraud)

Zuma was charged in 2005 after his former financial adviser,
Schabir Shaik, was convicted of having a generally corrupt relationship with the ANC deputy president.

His trial was scheduled to start in September 2006, but was
struck off the roll by Judge Herbert Msimang after the state
unsuccessfully applied for a postponement.

Zuma faced 16 charges relating to his relationship with
Shaik, an alleged Arms Deal bribe from French firm Thales
and not declaring his benefits from Shaik to the South African
Revenue Service.

Blade Nzimande (fraud)

Nzimande was the subject of a South African Police Service

investigation into claims by controversial businessman Charles Modise that he handed the general secretary of the SACP R500 000 in cash that subsequently went astray.

Ngoako Ramatlhodi (corruption)
The former Limpopo premier has been in the news since corruption allegations were levelled against him in 2003.

The Scorpions were investigating claims that Ramatlhodi and former Limpopo minister Thaba Mufamadi were secret shareholders of Northern Corporate Investment Holdings, which owns 30% of Cash Paymaster Services (CPS). CPS was awarded a multimillion-rand tender for the disbursement of social grants.

Billy Masetlha (fraud)
Former spy boss Masetlha was charged in the Pretoria Commercial Crimes Court of paying information technology expert Muzi Kunene R152 000 to manufacture false emails that attempted to show a political conspiracy against Zuma.

Nyami Booi (fraud)
An experienced ANC MP, Booi too is a Travelgate accused who declined to enter into plea agreement with the state. He appointed his own legal team and was yet to face fraud charges.

Thaba Mufamadi (corruption)
Like Ramatlhodi, Mufamadi was being investigated by the Scorpions for receiving bribes in a social grants tender award. He resigned as Limpopo MEC for public works in 2006, but Premier Sello Moloto denied that his resignation was related to the investigation.

Playfair Morule (culpable homicide)
This former Free State safety and security MEC was accused of being responsible for the death of a Bloemfontein pedestrian

in September 2006. The state alleged that Morule's negligence led to the man's death.

Moved, resigned or disciplined

Jessie Duarte (resigned)

Duarte was forced to quit as Gauteng's MEC for safety and security after a commission of inquiry found there was a 'strong suspicion' she had covered up a car accident while driving without a licence.

Angie Motshekga (disciplined)

Gauteng's education MEC was reprimanded in 2004 for having a 'close relationship' with a company that had benefited from government's grants payout system and of which her husband and former premier, Mathole, was a director.

Sibongile Manana (moved)

The former Mpumalanga health MEC was moved to another portfolio after the Scorpions started their investigation into fraud and corruption in her department. Manana has never been formally charged.

Under a cloud

Baleka Mbete (dodgy driver's licence)

To avoid the long queues, Speaker Mbete in 1996 requested former Mpumalanga safety MEC Steve Mabona to organise a driver's licence for her. The Moldenhauer Commission of Inquiry established that her licence was false, but could not find evidence of a guilty mind on her part.

Malusi Gigaba (under departmental investigation)
The deputy home affairs minister was exposed in 2007 for running a 'leadership academy' from his office and buying expensive flowers for his wife with state money.

He has repaid the flowers money.

Siphiwe Nyanda (Arms Deal discount)
The former army chief admitted in 2001 that he had received a discount of R150 000 on a new Mercedes-Benz S320 from EADS.

Ncumisa Kondlo (corruption)
An ANC MP and SACP deputy chairperson, Kondlo is the widow of Nelson Mandela's former bodyguard, Thobile Mtwazi, who was the empowerment partner of Parliament's security firm, Africa Strategic Asset Protection (Asap). The company was exposed for allegedly paying bribes to win state contracts. Kondlo had received two payments from Asap.

Mathole Motshekga (corruption, fraud and nepotism)
Although an internal ANC commission in 1998 cleared the former Gauteng premier of allegations of squandering donor funds, questions remain about the finances of the National Institute for Public Interest Law and Research that he headed.

David Mabuza (corruption allegations)
Mpumalanga's transport MEC was implicated in a school stationery corruption scandal in 2003, but was never charged.

Joyce Mashamba (nepotism)
The Limpopo sports, arts and culture MEC irregularly appointed her son to the human resources unit in her department.

Nosiviwe Mapisa-Nqakula (Travelgate repayments)
The Minister of Home Affairs and her Cabinet colleague

husband, Safety and Security Minister Charles Nqakula, have allegedly been allowed to repay thousands of rands to the liquidators of the travel agencies embroiled in Travelgate.

Cleared

Sankie Mthembi-Mahanyele (investigation into housing tender)
As Minister of Housing, Mthembi-Mahanyele was embroiled in a conflict of interest debacle involving the Mpumalanga Motheo housing scandal. A commission of inquiry cleared her.

Ayanda Dlodlo (fraud and theft)
Dlodlo is a former Scorpions director against whom charges of fraud and theft were withdrawn in the Pretoria Commercial Crimes Court.

Sicelo Shiceka (corruption)
Shiceka, a former Gauteng MEC for local government, was in 1999 accused of corruption by his head of department, but was cleared.

Madikizela-Mandela, the 'mother of the nation' who came first in the NEC election, has not played an active role in politics under the Zuma administration. Most notably she testified for ANC Youth League leader Julius Malema during the disciplinary hearing that saw him expelled from the governing party. After being kicked out, Malema and his allies found solace at Madikizela-Mandela's Soweto home. In 2011, Tokyo Sexwale, the Human Settlements minister, roped in Madikizela-Mandela to head up an investigation into the prevalence of open toilets in the country. This came after a number of exposés about rural communities still using bucket toilets in the Western Cape and Free State. Although she has not publicly expressed a view on who should lead the ANC after Mangaung, her association with Malema and Sexwale puts Madikizela-Mandela squarely in the 'Anyone But Zuma' camp.

Yengeni remained a staunch supporter of Zuma throughout his term. It was only towards the end of 2012 that he started falling out with Zuma's allies, most notably Blade Nzimande, whom he allegedly asked, 'Who the fuck do you think you are?' after the latter supposedly suppressed debate critical of Zuma at a June 2012 NEC meeting.

In 2010, the ANC appointed Yengeni as head of its political school for cadres. After a three-day political school for the ANC's leadership in 2012, Yengeni said the school would 'decrease unwanted tendencies' and ensure that 'all members are guided by the principles, values and objectives of the ANC'.[2]

Bathabile Dlamini was appointed Social Development minister in Zuma's Cabinet and became a ferocious driver of government's anti-drinking campaign.

Enoch Godongwana was appointed head of the ANC's economic transformation committee under Zuma and deputy minister of the newly established Department of Economic Development. He resigned in January 2012. The official reason given was that he was to pursue 'personal interests', but reports said that he and Economic Development minister Ebrahim Patel didn't get along. At the same time, Godongwana was embroiled in a scandal around the 'disappearance' of R100 million from the pension fund of the South African Clothing and Textile Workers' Union (Sactwu).[3] In August 2012, a commission of inquiry found that Godongwana and his wife, Thandiwe, were 'party to the carrying on of the business of the company, either fraudulently or at least recklessly'. The Hawks had begun an investigation into the alleged fraud.

Ruth Bhengu was appointed chairperson of Parliament's transport portfolio committee. In 2012, she was implicated in a conflict-of-interest debacle after her company, Riblore 22, entered into negotiations with the South African National Taxi Council (Santaco) to source and supply oil, which Santaco would sell to its members.[4]

If the deal went through, it would effectively mean that the chairperson of the committee exercising oversight over South Africa's transport industry would directly benefit from the industry by selling oil to taxi owners.

Jackson Mthembu became the ANC's public face after he was appointed as party spokesperson in 2009. In 2010, Mthembu was arrested in Cape Town for driving drunk at 7am in a bus lane. He pleaded guilty in the Wynberg Magistrate's Court and was slapped with a R12 000 fine. He apologised to all South Africans and said, 'It was a stupid mistake, it was poor judgment on my part. Fortunately no-one lost his life through my poor judgment.'[5]

Ndleleni Duma remained in Parliament and is active in the ANC's Western Cape structures.

As far as the list of suspects goes, the charges against Zuma were dropped in April 2009 – a month before the general elections that led to him becoming president. Zuma's fortunes changed as a result of intercepted recordings that were leaked to his attorney.

Blade Nzimande was never charged after Charles Modise, the whistleblower and alleged corruptor, changed his tune. In an affidavit that, strangely, appeared in Zuma's corruption case, Modise accused former Cosatu president Willie Madisha and SACP treasurer Phillip Dexter of pressurising him into making the bribery allegations against Nzimande. Madisha and Dexter, who both later joined the ANC breakaway party COPE, denied these claims. Madisha stuck to his story that he gave Nzimande R500 000 in two black rubbish bags, and Dexter (who rejoined the ANC in January 2012) maintained that the money never went through the SACP's books.[6]

Ngoako Ramatlhodi had a lucky escape from prosecution in November 2008. After an initial announcement by the NPA's spokesperson that the former Limpopo premier would be prosecuted for corruption, Ramatlhodi's lawyers made representations to acting NPA chief Mokotedi Mpshe, who subsequently decided 'it would not be in the interest of justice' to pursue the matter further.[7] Ramatlhodi became an important player in Zuma's team: he was appointed head of the ANC's election committee, chairperson of Parliament's justice portfolio committee and was appointed by the ANC to serve on the Judicial Service Commission (JSC), where he became a vocal opponent of judges who were deemed too independent. In November 2010, Ramatlhodi was promoted to the executive when Zuma appointed him Deputy Minister of Correctional Services.

Billy Masetlha was acquitted of fraud in January 2009 after the state couldn't prove that he had authorised payments to an IT expert to create the so-called hoax emails that purported to show a plot against Zuma. The saga around the hoax emails, which caused deep division within the ANC before the Polokwane conference, has never properly been explained – and neither has Masetlha's role in the saga. Deputy President Kgalema Motlanthe, who first received the documents and believed in their authenticity, never testified in Masetlha's trial to explain his side of events. In his 2012 book *Eight Days in September*, former Cabinet secretary Frank Chikane described the hoax emails as a 'bolt from the blue'. Chikane, together with Scorpions investigators, DA politicians and journalists, were falsely implicated in the hoax documents. They succeeded in driving a wedge between him and Motlanthe, Chikane wrote, and were successful in making Motlanthe choose sides in the battle between Zuma and Mbeki for the ANC's top job.

Masetlha declined a parliamentary seat in 2009 and said he had to sort out his personal affairs first. 'I owe the world R2 million for upkeep and so on. I lost just about everything (after losing my job and fighting off criminal cases). I have got to find money to pay those people as quickly as I can,' the former head of the National Intelligence Agency (NIA) was quoted as saying.[8] Masetlha continued working for the ANC.

Nyami Booi pleaded guilty to theft in September 2009 for using parliamentary travel vouchers worth R20 000 to cover travel expenses of R92 000. He was fined R50 000 and promised to repay Parliament. In November 2010, he was sacked as chairperson of Parliament's Defence portfolio committee after he fell out with former Defence minister Lindiwe Sisulu (who was redeployed by Zuma as Minister of Public Service and Administration in June 2012). Booi is still an ANC MP.

Thaba Mufamadi was appointed as chairperson of Parliament's standing committee on finance. His Scorpions case fell away with that of Ramatlhodi when Mpshe declined to prosecute the matter. In 2012, several newspaper articles revealed the extent of Mufamadi's business empire – a property company that leases urban buildings to state organs. In March 2012, Parliament's joint ethics committee cleared Mufamadi of wrongdoing, finding he had properly declared his business interests in Manaka Property Investments. But questions of conflicts of interest were again raised in April, when *City Press* revealed that Manaka, co-owned by Mufamadi and Limpopo premier Cassel Mathale, had benefited from government lease deals worth at least R520 million.[9] Some of these contracts were awarded without going to public tender.

In September 2008, the Bloemfontein Regional Court convicted Playfair Morule of culpable homicide and slapped him with a R36 000 fine. In 2009, Morule was deployed as executive mayor of Mangaung until he was removed in early 2011 because of internal ANC power battles.

Jessie Duarte was spokesperson for the ANC until she was promoted to the Presidency, where she had a short and turbulent stint as chief operating officer. She resigned in April 2010 to pursue 'other interests', but inside sources reported that she and Lakela Kaunda, Zuma's office head, didn't see eye to eye.[10]

Angie Motshekga, the ANC Women's League president, was appointed Basic Education minister. In mid-2012, she was in the firing line after Grades 1 to 3 and Grade 10 pupils in Limpopo had still not been given textbooks for the 2012 school year. It was only after Section27, an NGO, went to court that Motshekga was ordered to provide schooling materials to Limpopo's learners. She still missed the deadline and blamed the province's former education administrator, Dr Anis Karodia, for the textbook mess. Karodia, a former Education Department head in North West, was deployed to Limpopo by Motshekga in December 2011 after the provincial education department was placed under national administration. During a visit to Limpopo in June 2012, Motshekga blamed Karodia for the non-delivery of books and said she had fired him for bad performance. But she had lied. The following Sunday, *City Press* exposed the truth by publishing a letter Motshekga had written to Karodia a month earlier, thanking him for his 'sterling work' in Limpopo. Motshekga thus became the face of the poor state of education in South Africa. She refused to resign and Zuma did not take any steps against her, in spite of the fact that children in poor areas were yet to receive learning materials seven months into the school year. In September 2012, four months after schools in the Kuruman district of the Northern Cape were closed by angry residents protesting about poor service delivery, Motshekga visited the area. She only visited some of the hotspots because she feared for her safety. Justice minister Jeff Radebe said, during the ANC's policy conference in June 2012, that the Limpopo textbook scandal was a 'matter of shame'. As president of the ANC Women's League, Motshekga remained an important ally for Zuma on the road to Mangaung.

Sibongile Manana became an MEC in Mpumalanga – first for community safety and security, and later for culture, sport and recreation.

* * *

The careers of most NEC members with clouds over their heads also blossomed under Zuma's presidency. Baleka Mbete stayed on as party chairperson; Malusi Gigaba was deputy Home Affairs minister until his promotion to the powerful Ministry of Public Enterprises in November 2010 following a Cabinet reshuffle; Mathole Motshekga was appointed as the ANC's chief whip in Parliament; and David Mabuza became premier of Mpumalanga, remaining in his position despite a series of political assassinations, corruption scandals and service delivery protests in that province.

Joyce Mashamba was Limpopo's sports, arts and culture MEC until March 2012 when premier Cassel Mathale fired her. But she was soon reappointed as deputy speaker of the provincial legislature. Nosiviwe Mapisa-Nqakula became Zuma's Correctional Services minister (and later Defence minister). Sankie Mthembi-Mahanyele was appointed chairperson of the Central Energy Fund in February 2012, and Ayanda Dlodlo served as Deputy Minister of Public Service and Administration from November 2010.

During a Cabinet reshuffle in October 2010, Zuma fired Siphiwe Nyanda as Communications minister after he was implicated in a number of embarrassing episodes involving a security company, partly owned by his family trust, and his love of fine hotels and dining establishments. Abalozi Security Risk Advisory Services, in which Nyanda declared a 50% shareholding to Parliament, benefited from multimillion-rand government tenders, including a R55 million contract from Transnet Freight Rail. The *Mail & Guardian* exposed Nyanda's five-star hotel bills when he had to visit Cape Town on official business. The former minister stayed at the Mount Nelson and Twelve Apostles hotels because a bed had not been delivered to his government house.[11]

Sicelo Shiceka, who died in April 2012, gave Zuma no choice but to fire him in October 2011 after the Public Protector, Thuli Madonsela, issued a scathing report on Shiceka's free-spending habits. Not only did the late minister spend R640 000 of taxpayers' money on himself and his staff at the five-star One & Only hotel in Cape Town (Shiceka moved there after his official residence had an 'influx of mosquitoes') and check in under a false name at the Lesotho Sun, Shiceka also spent R550 000 on an 'official visit' to Switzerland, during which he visited a girlfriend imprisoned for drug smuggling. The trip was approved by Motlanthe after Shiceka lied to him about its purpose, saying he was traveling on 2010 FIFA World Cup business.

* * *

It is clear that the majority of rogues who were elected to serve on the ANC's NEC in December 2007 have prospered under Zuma's presidency. Despite lots of rhetoric by Zuma and his colleagues about fighting corruption and promoting clean governance, very little has been done in five years to rid the ruling elite of those individuals who choose self-interest and enrichment above serving the people of the country.

4

On 18 December 2007, at Polokwane, Jacob Zuma defeated Thabo Mbeki by 2 329 votes to 1 505 to become the twelfth president of the ANC. Zuma and his 'coalition of the wounded' claimed victory after a fierce battle that split the party between two of its most senior leaders and their supporters.

The events of the sixteen months that followed Zuma's Polokwane victory up to his inauguration as president in May 2009 are well documented. In short: the ANC disbanded the Scorpions; Judge Chris Nicholson ruled that there had been political interference in Zuma's corruption prosecution; Mbeki was recalled as president; Kgalema Motlanthe became caretaker president and fired Vusi Pikoli, the fearless head of the NPA; somebody leaked intercepted recordings of telephone conversations to Zuma's lawyer, Michael Hulley, and acting NPA boss Mokotedi Mpshe withdrew the corruption charges against Zuma based on these tapes.

These events cleared the way for Zuma to become president, without talk of a political solution to get rid of the criminal charges against him. But it is impossible to assess Zuma's presidency without going back to those turbulent times. The spy tapes, as they became popularly known, still continue to haunt Zuma, and the DNA of the NPA has been fundamentally influenced and changed by Mpshe's fateful decision to let Zuma off the hook. There is still the possibility that a court could reinstate the corruption charges against Zuma, which may explain a lot of the bad decisions he has made during his term in the West Wing.

Julius

'Zuma was the only leader in the ANC courageous enough to challenge Thabo Mbeki when he wanted a third term as party leader. But that courage was very personal. It was informed by personal fear of being arrested and going to prison ... Actually, we went to fetch him from a prison door. When you are in that situation, you fight because you have nothing to lose ... but if you win, you know that chances are that you will not be arrested.'

5

Why is Zuma so scared to go back to court? What are the charges he would have to face? Although the weightiness of the charges against him paled into insignificance when the spy tapes surfaced, it was always clear that the case was not withdrawn because it was weak. Quite to the contrary: a profusion of documents produced during the Shaik trial clearly showed how Zuma's lifestyle and that of his family was funded by Schabir Shaik. In return, Zuma assisted Shaik in promoting and growing his Nkobi business empire. This is not my opinion, but rather what Judge Hilary Squires and 15 judges after him in the Supreme Court of Appeal and the Constitutional Court found.

I am often asked what charges Zuma would have had to face if he had gone to court, and what evidence the Scorpions had found of a quid pro quo (counter-performance) on his part. What follows is the last indictment against Zuma – served on 28 December 2007, ten days after he was elected ANC president – before the charges against him were dropped.

IN THE HIGH COURT OF SOUTH AFRICA
(NATAL PROVINCIAL DIVISION)

In the matter of: –

THE STATE

versus

JACOB GEDLEYIHLEKISA ZUMA

THINT HOLDING (SOUTHERN AFRICA) (PTY) LTD
(formerly known as Thomson-CSF Holding (Southern Africa)
(Pty) Ltd)
(hereinafter also referred to as **Thomson Holdings**)
(as represented by **Pierre Jean-Marie Robert Moynot**)

THINT (PTY) LTD
(formerly known as Thomson-CSF (Pty) Ltd)
(hereinafter also referred to as **Thomson (Pty)**)
(as represented by **Pierre Jean-Marie Robert Moynot**)

(hereinafter also referred to as the accused)

INDICTMENT

The State alleges that the accused are guilty of the following crimes:

<u>COUNT 1:</u> **RACKETEERING** in contravention of Section 2(1)(e) read with Sections 1, 2(2) and 3 of the Prevention of Organised Crime Act, No. 121 of 1998, as amended:
Whilst employed by or associated with any enterprise, conducts or participates in the conduct, directly or

indirectly, of such enterprise's affairs through a pattern of racketeering activities.
(Accused 1 to 3)

COUNT 2: **CORRUPTION** in contravention of section 1(1)(b) read with section 1(2) and 3 of the Corruption Act, No. 94 of 1992.
(In terms of section 156 of Act 51 of 1977 only in respect of accused 1)

In the alternative (as separate counts)

SUBCOUNT 1: CORRUPTION in contravention of section 1(1) (b) read with section 1(2) and 3 of the Corruption Act, No. 94 of 1992. (In respect of the period 25 October 1995 to 26 April 2004)

SUBCOUNT 2: CORRUPTION in contravention of section 3(a) read with sections 1, 2, 21, 24, 25 and 26 of the Prevention and Combating of Corrupt Activities Act, No. 12 of 2004. (In respect of the period 27 April 2004 to 1 July 2005)

Alternatively to subcount 2:

RECEIVING AN UNAUTHORISED GRATIFICATION BY A PERSON WHO IS PARTY TO AN EMPLOYMENT RELATIONSHIP in contravention of section 10(a) read with sections 1, 2, 21, 25 and 26 of the Prevention and Combating of Corrupt Activities Act, No. 12 of 2004. (In respect of the period 27 April 2004 to 14 June 2005)

COUNT 3: **CORRUPTION** in contravention of section 1(1)(a) read with section 1(2) and 3 of the Corruption Act, No. 94 of 1992.
(In terms of section 156 of Act 51 of 1977 only in respect of accused 2 and 3)

In the alternative (as separate counts)

SUBCOUNT 1: CORRUPTION in contravention of section 1(1) (a) read with section 1(2) and 3 of the Corruption Act, No. 94 of 1992. (In respect of the period 25 October 1995 to 26 April 2004)

SUBCOUNT 2: CORRUPTION in contravention of section 3(b) read with sections 1, 2, 21, 24, 25 and 26 of the Prevention and Combating of Corrupt Activities Act, No. 12 of 2004. (In respect of the period 27 April 2004 to 1 July 2005)

Alternatively to subcount 2:

GIVING AN UNAUTHORISED GRATIFICATION TO A PERSON WHO IS PARTY TO AN EMPLOYMENT RELATIONSHIP in contravention of section 10(b) read with sections 1, 2, 21, 25 and 26 of the Prevention and Combating of Corrupt Activities Act, No. 12 of 2004. (In respect of the period 27 April 2004 to 14 June 2005)

COUNT 4: CORRUPTION in contravention of section 1(1)(b) read with section 1(2) and 3 of the Corruption Act, No. 94 of 1992.
(In terms of section 156 of Act No. 51 of 1977 only in respect of accused 1)

COUNT 5: CORRUPTION in contravention of section 1(1)(a) read with section 3 of the Corruption Act, No. 94 of 1992.
(In terms of section 156 of Act No. 51 of 1977 only in respect of accused 2 and 3)

COUNT 6: MONEY LAUNDERING in contravention of section 4, read with sections 1 and 8 of the Prevention of Organised Crime Act, No. 121 of 1998
(Accused 1 to 3)

In the alternative

ACQUISITION, POSSESSION OR USE OF PROCEEDS OF UNLAWFUL ACTIVITIES in contravention of section 6, read with sections 1 and 8 of the Prevention of Organised Crime Act, No. 121 of 1998

COUNT 7: FRAUD
(In terms of section 156 of Act No. 51 of 1977 only in respect of accused 1)

COUNT 8: FRAUD
(In terms of section 156 of Act No. 51 of 1977 only in respect of accused 1)

COUNT 9: FRAUD
(In terms of section 156 of Act No. 51 of 1977 only in respect of accused 1)

COUNTS 10–18: FRAUD (9 COUNTS)
(In terms of section 156 of Act No. 51 of 1977 only in respect of accused 1)

In the first alternative

MAKING FALSE STATEMENTS IN INCOME TAX RETURNS in contravention of section 104(1)(a), read with section 66 of the Income Tax Act, No. 58 of 1962,

In the second alternative

FAILING TO SHOW GROSS INCOME OR MATERIAL FACTS IN TAX RETURNS in contravention of section 75(1)(c) read with sections 1 and 66 of the Income Tax Act, No. 58 of 1962.

It was an exhaustive charge sheet, much broader than the two counts of corruption Zuma was originally charged with when his case was struck off the court roll by Judge Herbert Msimang in September 2006. During Shaik's trial, the Scorpions traced payments by Shaik to Zuma from 1995 to 2002 totalling R1,3 million. This time the Scorpions had analysed the bank statements of Shaik and Zuma up to 1 July 2005, and found that, in the ten-year period, the president had allegedly received 783 payments, totalling R4 072 499,85, from his corrupt financial adviser. A schedule of payments attached to the charge sheet showed that Shaik's payments to Zuma increased through the years, and even escalated after his own corruption trial had started. Even after Zuma had been charged by the NPA, Shaik's payments kept coming, climaxing in 2006 – after Zuma had been charged and Shaik convicted – at R764 371 for the year. The following table shows the number of transactions and value of payments made to Zuma annually over ten years:

Year	Number of payments	Total value of payments
1996	1	R3 500
1997	8	R44 500
1998	39	R262 476
1999	40	R174 014
2000	44	R181 648
2001	61	R549 475
2002	73	R590 694
2003	138	R470 304
2004	167	R502 889
2005	181	R528 624
2006	31	R764 371
Total	783	R4 072 499

Zuma's prosecutors also added the charges of racketeering, money laundering and fraud to his charge sheet.

Racketeering

A relatively new charge in South African jurisprudence, racketeering is seen as a 'super charge' that enables the state to convict everyone who is party to a corrupt enterprise. Introduced by the Prevention of Organised Crime Act, No 121 of 1998, racketeering may include individuals, partnerships, corporations or any other legal entity that engages in a 'pattern of racketeering activity'. In Zuma's case, the state identified Nkobi Investments as the corrupt enterprise. The enterprise 'operated as an ostensibly legitimate group of companies, whose main business was to form joint ventures with foreign and local businesses, more particularly as a "Black Economic Empowerment" ("BEE") partner, and so to bid for lucrative contracts, primarily in the public sphere.'

The enterprise had little to offer in terms of capital or expertise and relied on Shaik's 'much heralded "political connectivity" to attract partners with these resources,' the indictment stated. The objectives of the enterprise, according to the indictment, were to 'cultivate and maintain corrupt relationships with persons in positions of political power and high government office, including accused no 1 (Zuma) in order to cultivate "political connectivity"'. Zuma, the state argued, was 'employed by, alternatively associated with, the enterprise' and the payments to him 'amounted to a salary'.

This was ground-breaking stuff in terms of prosecuting politicians for allegedly engaging in corrupt behaviour. Not only did the state aim to prove that Zuma had been bribed by Shaik, but it went further by charging him with effectively being employed by a racketeering enterprise for his political connections.

The Zuma case would have been the first successful prosecution of a politician for racketeering in South Africa if the state had succeeded with this charge. So far, the only successful racketeering cases in the country have involved an abalone poaching ring, drug smuggling and a prostitution racket. Since the Zuma charges were dropped in 2009, the NPA has not charged a politician with racketeering.

45

Corruption

The state further charged Zuma with two counts of corruption. Very often, people mistakenly refer to Zuma's prosecution as an 'Arms Deal trial'. That is not true. The two corruption charges on which Shaik was convicted were separate: the one concerned the Arms Deal, the other did not. Zuma faced exactly the same scheme of charges.

The first charge of 'general corruption' referred to the series of 783 payments totalling R4,1 million made by Shaik to Zuma between 1995 and 2005. Attached to the indictment was a schedule of the 783 payments. The schedule revealed that the payments from Shaik and his companies to Zuma ranged between R10 for a car wash to R400 000 to Development Africa, an entity associated with the building of Zuma's homestead in Nkandla. Also included in the payments were school fees for Zuma's children, doctors' fees, cash payments to Zuma, hotel bookings, travel expenses, car bond payments, a trip to Cuba for the Zuma family, payments to the ANC and the settlement of legal bills.

These payments, according to the state, 'make no legitimate business sense, in that neither Shaik, the Nkobi group, nor the other relevant entities could afford the payments, being at all times in a cash-starved position (at least until August 2004), relying on and at times exceeding bank overdrafts and thus effectively borrowing money from banks at the prevailing interest rates to make the said payments interest free'. On the other hand, the state said, Nkobi's survival depended on obtaining new business with Zuma's assistance.

In effect, Shaik, as Zuma's special economic adviser, provided the following services free of charge: managing Zuma's financial affairs; corresponding with his creditors; negotiating with his creditors; corresponding and meeting with his bankers; providing legal advice and services through Shaik's lawyers; utilising the administrative resources of the Nkobi Group for managing Zuma's affairs; attending to the accommodation requirements of Zuma; attending to the financial and other affairs of Zuma's family; assisting Zuma to complete his tax returns; and assisting Zuma to complete his declarations of interest to Parliament and the Cabinet.

These, according to the state, constituted benefits to Zuma.

In return, Shaik 'advertised' his political connectivity to Zuma, relied on Zuma to meet or correspond with prospective business partners in order to advance Nkobi's interests, and threatened prospective business partners that he would resort to Zuma if they did not act in accordance with his wishes. Zuma, the state charged, allowed Shaik to act in this manner because he paid him.

According to the indictment, Shaik used Zuma's assistance and/or name in negotiations with the following businesspeople or projects:

- David Wilson of the Renong Group of Malaysia, concerning the Point development
- Peter Watt of Altron
- Deva Ponnoosami of Southern Crest Marketing Services and Professor John Lennon of Glasgow Caledonian University, concerning the Eco-Tourism School
- Thomson-CSF France
- Kuwaiti businessmen Ali and Fouad Al-Ghanim
- The establishment of an Nkobi Bank
- Kent and Jeffrey Crane of Crane (Africa)(Pty) Ltd, and James Roth of Roth International (USA)
- Hakim Belo-Osagie, Chairman of United Bank for Africa PLC (Nigeria)
- Grant Scriven of Venson PLC (UK)
- Jean-Marc Pizano of ATE
- The Indonesia–South Africa Business Club
- Haryono Eddyarto of PT Surveyor Indonesia
- The Cyprus Development Bank Limited
- Ron Coopersmith (USA)
- Bruce Allen Johnson of the Hudson Institute (USA)
- IGT (USA)
- Peter Shortt of the International Business and Development Group (UK)

- John S Kendall of Unisys Corporation (USA)
- John Chettle of Freedman, Kroll and Simonds (USA)
- Dr Khalid Abdullah Tarique Al-Mansour
- Queen City Properties (Pty) Limited
- PFI Briefing
- Wilberforce Institute
- An Aids project
- Her Majesty's Consul
- Procon Fischer (Pty) Limited
- Professor Ronald Green-Thompson

Zuma's intervention, on Shaik's behalf, in the Renong, Eco-Tourism School and Venson cases was accepted by Judge Squires as proof of his 'readiness' to assist Shaik and the Nkobi business. John Lennon testified in the Shaik trial and David Wilson's affidavits were admitted as evidence. Both were on the witness list to testify against Zuma. What would they have said?

6

Renong Berhad is a Malaysian construction company that tendered in 1995 to redevelop Durban's Point area. The area, close to the city's harbour, was neglected and the province had decided to invest in creating a waterfront-based project with residential and business properties. At the time, Zuma was KwaZulu-Natal's MEC for Economic Affairs and Tourism.

In two affidavits to the Scorpions, Renong's head of foreign operations, David Wilson, detailed his interactions with Shaik and Zuma at the time of the project. Renong tendered to be the main contractor and presented its bid to the Point Waterfront Company (Pty) Ltd, which was overseeing the tendering process. The company was headed by businessman Mzi Khumalo. As part of its presentation, Renong included a BEE component. Wilson said Khumalo had assured them that the BEE partners were approved by government.

Shaik was part of a different consortium that lost out to Renong. At some stage, Shaik suggested joining forces, but this was rejected by Wilson. By mid-1996, nothing had been done on the project because of Shaik's insistence on being part of it, according to Wilson. He reported this to his company chairman, Halim Saad, who suggested that Renong obtain government assurance that the chosen BEE partners were indeed 'politically acceptable'.

A letter presented to the court showed that Shaik himself had visited Saad in Malaysia in June 1996. An arrangement had been made that Saad would write to Zuma to confirm that Shaik would be included in the Point development. In his judgment, Judge Squires wrote: 'That suggests at least a proposal that Saad write to Zuma, opening the door to Nkobi participation, but on the basis that such accommodation would be a government decision and not something for which Renong could be blamed by the already selected BEE partners. Thereafter Shaik could use his influence to activate the stationary condition of the project.'

On 8 June 1996, Saad wrote to Zuma, seeking his advice on who Renong should appoint as its BEE partner. Zuma wrote back, saying that Saad or another senior Renong representative should meet with him in South Africa.

According to Wilson, he was tasked to meet Zuma, and arranged this through Shaik. The meeting took place in early February 1997 at Shaik's apartment. Wilson stated under oath in his affidavit:

> Mr Jacob Zuma was clearly uncomfortable during the meeting and I gained the clear impression ... he was there under sufferance ... He [Zuma] said that he was not happy with the persons nominated to represent the empowerment interests in the Point development, although he offered no explanation for this. He proposed that Mr Schabir Shaik should be involved in the project and stressed repeatedly that he would be a good partner for the job. During the course of the discussions, it became increasingly clear that Mr Jacob Zuma was acting as if Mr Schabir Shaik had some sort of hold over him. At one point, Mr Zuma made mention of the support and assistance he received from Mr Schabir Shaik. I gained the strong impression that this support and assistance was of a financial nature.

Despite Zuma's efforts, Shaik was not included in the consortium. In his evidence, Shaik denied having a meeting with Zuma and Wilson, but Squires found that he had lied:

The essential dispute is that Shaik said no such meeting took place. Wilson says one did and having regard to the repeated instances in Shaik's evidence when he resorted to falsehood to avoid a result that contradicted his case, we are eventually amply satisfied that Wilson's affidavit, supported as it is by the objective facts, can be accepted as the truth of the matter, namely that Zuma sought to persuade Wilson to accept Nkobi as one of the Black Economic Empowerment partners for the Point Development Project.

Professor John Lennon (no relation to The Beatles) is a Scottish academic from Glasgow Caledonian University, who came to South Africa in 1998 as part of a trade mission exchange. Lennon flew to Durban to give evidence in the Shaik trial after Squires rejected a request for him to testify via a satellite link. He testified that he had met Shaik at a presentation in Johannesburg about the possibility of opening eco-tourism schools in KwaZulu-Natal and Durban. After the meeting, Shaik gave him an Nkobi Holdings brochure. Zuma also attended the presentation, and that, according to Lennon, was a good sign, as he wanted buy-in from local politicians. Lennon subsequently met Zuma at his Durban office and requested from him a letter of support for the project. Lennon testified that, with such a letter, he could raise funding in the UK and from the Development Bank of Southern Africa. Although Zuma was excited and keen to provide him with a letter, Lennon didn't hear anything from him for a long time.

In January 1999, through Shaik's London agent, Lennon complained about the delay in getting a letter from Zuma. A few weeks later, a signed letter arrived from Zuma. Curiously, the letter was faxed from the fax machine of Nkobi Holdings. Zuma's letter read:

I have had discussions with one such company namely Nkobi Holdings, head-quartered in Durban. They are keen to participate in this venture as it fits well with their own leisure plans. I suggested to them to make contact with yourselves directly to

51

speed the process and hopefully together you will both enhance
the Kwazulu Natal tourism industry through raising the profile
and excellence of the personnel involved in this industry.

Lennon testified he found it strange that Zuma would suggest a local
partner at such an early stage, as they were still dealing with 'bread-
and-butter stuff'. The fact that the letter came from Shaik's office,
and that Zuma had to be helped to write a letter, 'did not fill me with
confidence'.

On the same day, Shaik's office faxed through a letter confirming
Nkobi's interest in being Lennon's partner. 'It was a busy day for the
fax machine. Faxes were coming through thick and fast,' Lennon
testified. Shaik was seeking a confirmation from Lennon that Nkobi
would be his partner on the project. When he referred Shaik to
environmental associates in South Africa he was already working
with, Lennon received an angry response. Shaik's colleague, Martyn
Surman, wrote to him: 'I have to advise you that he [Shaik] finds
your response insulting to say the least and that he considers that it
lacks the business ethics which it deserves. Mr Shaik has asked me to
advise you that he is prepared to give you three days in order to come
back to him, sketching out the issues referred to above, failing which
he will go back to Minister Zuma.'

In a subsequent letter to his UK business partner, Shaik wrote:
'Also inform me of your precise discussion with Professor John
Lennon with regards to my request from him, as he has not yet responded to my letter. I will regard this matter as being, somewhat
serious. I shall be meeting with Minister Zuma tomorrow and if I
do not receive the information as requested in my letter dated 15th
February 99, I shall move to inform Minister Zuma and seek to do
whatever is necessary to stop Professor Lennon's process.'

Lennon said he got the clear impression that only one person could
get Zuma's signature: Schabir Shaik. The project never took off. 'I
thought, naively, that they only wanted to get the project going. The
letter suggests that there was a degree of influence over Zuma. It
was unusual, unfortunate and tragically unforgivable, given that it

stopped a project that would have been worthwhile. I did not reply to their letter. I wanted nothing to do with them. Despite our best efforts we got nowhere with the project. We had to move on. It was very disappointing.'

No witnesses were called on the Venson matter, but the Scorpions presented to the court a letter written by Shaik to Zuma on 5 October 2000. In it, Shaik requested Zuma's assistance to arrange a meeting with then Minister of Safety and Security Steve Tshwete about a potential fleet outsourcing deal with the police. Businessman Grant Scriven, of British vehicle management company Venson, and Shaik wanted to discuss the deal with Tshwete. Zuma intervened, and the meeting happened. Squires remarked:

> The letter is plainly a request to invoke Zuma's help to gain direct access for this visitor to the top decision-maker in matters of administration of the country's police force. Moreover, it was a request to accommodate the convenience of this visitor who, it appears, would only be in the country in the following week. It is equally clearly not an access that any unconnected businessman could expect to achieve, merely for the asking and it was evidently so arranged. Scriven and Shaik had the meeting with Minister Tshwete, but nothing came of it.

These three episodes, together with Zuma's involvement in the Arms Deal, which I address in the following chapters, convinced Squires that Zuma 'did in fact intervene to try and assist Shaik's business interests'. Who knows what other worms could have come crawling out had the Zuma trial continued and all those businesspeople on the NPA's new indictment were asked to tell their tales?

7

Zuma's prosecutors built in a small bridge that linked the first 'general corruption' charge to the second charge of specific corruption – the Arms Deal charge. The bridge was an alleged continuation of the same pattern of Zuma's assistance to Shaik's business interests.

During 1998 accused 1 (Zuma) intervened and assisted Shaik, the Nkobi group and the Thomson-CSF group to resolve a dispute that had arisen regarding Nkobi's participation with accused 3 (Thint) in the acquisition of ADS.

From the point of view of Nkobi, this was an instance of obtaining the assistance of accused 1 to ensure the group's survival by obtaining profitable new business.

From the point of view of accused 1, this was an instance of him using his powers as MEC and/or Deputy President of the ANC to further the private business interests of Shaik and the Nkobi Group.

From the Thomson-CSF perspective, this was an instance of obtaining advance political support, approval or assurance from accused 1 for its choice of South African partners to gain an advantage over its bidding competitors for business relating to the Arms Deal described as follows.

Accused 1's assistance as described, and his anticipated assistance relating to the Arms Deal was informal and it did not form part of the official bidding/selection process.

The abovementioned dispute was resolved in principle with accused 1's assistance during 1998. The legalities pursuant to the agreement in principle regarding the restructuring that ensured Nkobi's participation in ADS with accused 3 (Thint), were completed in September 1999.

The major difference between this specific corruption charge and the general corruption charge was the presence of a clearly defined bribe. Whereas the bribe detailed in the first charge was Shaik's series of continued payments towards Zuma's living expenses, this charge involved the negotiation of a R500 000 per year bribe from French arms firm Thales (previously called Thomson-CSF).

Zuma was accused of soliciting a bribe, through Shaik, to protect Thomson-CSF against an Arms Deal probe. Through a series of complex transactions, the state claimed, the money was eventually paid from a Thomson-CSF account in Mauritius via a Shaik company to Development Africa, a trust belonging to Zuma's friend and benefactor, Vivian Reddy. Reddy assisted in paying for Zuma's Nkandla homestead.

The 'smoking gun' the state had against Zuma on this count was the so-called French fax that confirmed a bribe agreement between Thomson-CSF, Shaik and Zuma. The fax – a letter from Thomson-CSF employee Alain Thétard to his superiors in Paris – was sent on 17 March 2000. The Scorpions got hold of it through Sue Delique, a former secretary for Thomson-CSF who had angrily left the company, taking with her a batch of documents and computer disks.

A translated version of the fax reads as follows:

Following our interview held on 30/9/1999 with S.SHAIK in Durban and my conversation held on 10/11/1999 with Mr JP PERRIER in Paris, I have been able (at last) to meet JZ in Durban on 11th of this month, during a private interview, in the presence of S.S. I had asked S.S. to obtain from J.Z a clear confirmation or, or failing which an encoded declaration (the code has been defined by me), in order to validate the request by S.S at the end of September 1999. Which was done by JZ (in an encoded form). May I remind you that the two man objectives of the 'effort' requested of THOMSON are: Protection of THOMSON CSF during the current investigations (SITRON), Permanent support of JZ for future projects. Amount: 500 k ZAR per annum (until the first payment of dividends by ADS).

The Arms Deal, as we know it today, was a protracted process by which the newly elected ANC government aimed to build up South Africa's military capacity. (The process was initiated by the old National Party government, and former state president FW de Klerk ended up marrying the ex-wife of Tony Georgiades, a key Arms Deal middleman.) In a complex series of transactions, dogged by allegations of bribery and fraud, the government purchased new submarines, corvettes, fighter jets and helicopters for the South African National Defence Force (SANDF). At today's rates, including financing costs, the full transaction is estimated to have cost the country R70 billion. Schabir Shaik's brother, Shamin 'Chippy' Shaik, was at the time head of acquisitions at the SANDF, and was instrumental in choosing where to buy which weapons.

Schabir Shaik himself benefited from the Arms Deal through the government's purchase of four corvettes from the German Frigate Consortium. This specific project was named Sitron. In 1999, the government said the total cost of the corvettes was R7 billion. Thomson-CSF was keen to be involved in this tender and was anxious about choosing the right BEE partner.

Shaik first became involved with Thomson-CSF through his shareholding in Thomson-CSF Holdings (Southern Africa) (Pty) Ltd (later known as Thint Holdings) and Thomson-CSF (Pty) Ltd (later known as Thint). Both companies were incorporated in South Africa in 1996 by the French parent conglomerate in order to participate in joint ventures. In May 1996, Nkobi Investments acquired

10% shares in Thomson Holdings. In July 1999, Nkobi transferred its 10% shares to Thomson-CSF International in France. Nkobi owned 25% of Thomson-CSF at the time of the Arms Deal.

The company through which Shaik and the French benefited from the Arms Deal was called African Defence Systems (ADS), formerly owned by the Venter family's Altech. At the time of the Arms Deal, 80% of ADS was owned by Thomson-CSF (Thint) and 20% by a BEE company called Futuristic Business Solutions (FBS). FBS was partly owned by relatives of former Defence minister Joe Modise – Lambert Moloi, a retired Umkhonto we Sizwe (MK) commander and Modise's brother-in-law, and Tshepo Molai, Moloi's son-in-law.

Still, the French were unsure whether they had chosen the 'right' empowerment partner. Until that was established, Thomson removed Shaik as indirect shareholder in ADS. In his trial, Shaik testified that it was former presidents Nelson Mandela and Thabo Mbeki who had expressed reservations about his BEE status to the French. This, he testified, was embarrassing for him and his prospective business partners.

Shaik sprang into action. In March 1998, he told the French that Zuma wanted to meet them to resolve the BEE issue. This led to a meeting in London in July 1998 between Zuma, Shaik and Thomson's bosses, at which 'Zuma indicated that he approved of Nkobi as a suitable partner'. Zuma explained BEE to the French and told them it 'did not only include black people, but all Africans'. This directly led to Nkobi and Shaik's stake in ADS being reinstated.

ADS successfully tendered to install combat suites – the technical and mechanical stuff – on the corvettes, while the Germans built the ships. The value of the combat suite contract was estimated at R1,3 billion, with R450 million coming directly to ADS.

* * *

This was the one part of Zuma's involvement in the Arms Deal that the state aimed to prove – that he directly benefited his benefactor's business interests. The other part pertained to his 'protection' of Thomson-CSF in government's Arms Deal investigation.

On 3 November 2000, Parliament's Standing Committee on Public Accounts (Scopa), consisting of ANC and opposition MPs, recommended a joint investigation into the Arms Deal involving the Auditor General, Public Protector, the Scorpions and the Special Investigating Unit (SIU), led at the time by Judge Willem Heath. What distinguished the SIU from the other bodies was the fact that it had statutory powers to apply for corrupt tenders to be set aside by the courts. The logic behind this was to punish corrupt business-people where it hurt most – in their pockets.

On 19 January 2001, Zuma, as Deputy President and leader of government business, signed a letter to IFP MP Gavin Woods, the then chairperson of Scopa, attacking his committee's decision to include Heath's unit in the Arms Deal probe. The letter based this on a finding by the Constitutional Court that a judge was not allowed to head an investigating body.

Woods testified that he found the letter from Zuma 'unnecessarily personal and hostile'. This led to the resignation of ANC MP Andrew Feinstein, a vocal member of Scopa and a supporter of an in-depth Arms Deal probe. Judge Squires, in his ruling, found that the result of the letter was a 'clear indication' that there would be no SIU investigation of Scopa's concerns or PAC MP Patricia de Lille's allegations of corruption in the Arms Deal. Zuma gave his letter 'the widest publicity, including dispatch to the contracting parties involved in the arms acquisition process. If they were not concerned about the outcome of any inquiry into the exercise there would hardly be any need for that,' Squires ruled.

This, the state claimed, was proof of Zuma's attempt to protect Thomson-CSF against an investigation that could have seen its contract with the South African government being cancelled. In 2006, in a media interview, Mbeki admitted to authorising the letter Zuma signed.[1] Heath never forgave Mbeki for excluding him from the Arms Deal investigation, as would be evident when I interviewed him years later.

The charge of money laundering against Zuma related to the treatment of the R500 000 'bribe' from Thales, and that it was allegedly concealed through a number of transactions to pay for his Nkandla homestead. The fraud charges concerned Zuma's alleged failure to declare his benefits from Shaik to Parliament and the secretary of Cabinet; defrauding Parliament by lying in a Parliamentary answer to former DA MP Raenette Taljaard about meeting French Arms Dealer Alain Thétard in Durban; and defrauding the taxman by not declaring his income from Shaik for the years 1996 to 2004 (nine separate charges).

After many years of investigations and legal wrangles, the state was finally ready to prosecute Zuma in August 2008 – to give him his day in court.

8

Zuma and his legal team applied a so-called Stalingrad strategy to fight his legal battles. Although he always insisted on having his day in court, Zuma fought the state through a plethora of legal applications, which had the effect of delaying the start of his prosecution.

The year 2008 was going to be a make-or-break one for Zuma. He had just been elected ANC president and would face a national election in sixteen months' time. His corruption trial was scheduled to start in August, which meant that the chances of his prosecution starting and ending before the 2009 election were slim. Because whoever loses in a criminal trial may take the judgment on appeal, it looked almost impossible that Zuma would be able to assume the post of president of South Africa without corruption allegations hanging over his head.

On the day he received a new indictment against his client, Zuma's lawyer Michael Hulley released the following statement on his behalf:

> Today, 28 December 2007, the Directorate of Special Operations (Scorpions) served on Mr Jacob Zuma an indictment to stand trial in the High Court on various counts of racketeering, money laundering, corruption and fraud. According to the

indictment, which was served on Mr Zuma's Johannesburg residence in his absence, the trial is to proceed on 14 August 2008.

We find the timing of the service of the indictment most
peculiar. Of course this comes shortly after the choice of Mr
Zuma as president of the African National Congress (ANC) in
a highly contested election. In light of the NPA proposing a
trial date in August 2008, one cannot imagine the need for such
haste and the service of the indictment over this Christmas
period, when much of the world, commercial, legal and otherwise, is at rest.

The timing of the service of the indictment is calculated to
quickly redress the popular support and call to leadership of
the ANC which Mr Zuma's election so obviously demonstrates.
This lends credence to the long held view that the Scorpions
are influenced and their prosecution informed by political
considerations.

These charges will be vigorously defended, in the context of
the belief that the Scorpions have acted wrongly and with improper motive calculated to discredit Mr Zuma and ensure that
he play no leadership role in the political future of our country.

It was an extraordinary statement for a lawyer to make – effectively
accusing the Scorpions and the NPA of improperly (and illegally)
abusing their powers to knock Zuma out of South African politics.
It was, however, not a surprising statement. Because Zuma did not
come to power at Polokwane by propagating a specific policy or
ideology, he had to play the role of victim in order to drum up political support. This rhetoric, that he was a victim of Mbeki and his
'hit squad', the Scorpions, became truth for a lot of Zuma supporters. 'We didn't vote for Zuma, we voted against Mbeki' was said to
me numerous times by ANC delegates who attended the Polokwane
conference. Julius Malema's statement in July 2012 summed it up
nicely: we campaigned for Zuma because he was brave enough to
take on Mbeki. But, acknowledged Malema, 'that courage was very
personal. It was informed by personal fear of being arrested and

going to prison'.[1] Following Malema's logic, this meant that Zuma became president of the ANC, and later South Africa, because he had to defeat Mbeki at Polokwane in order to save himself from going to prison. 'If you win, you know that chances are that you will not be arrested,' the expelled youth leader said, perhaps prophetically.

*   *   *

On Monday 4 August 2008, Zuma launched a final attempt to prevent his prosecution from proceeding in the Pietermaritzburg High Court. Ten days before his trial was scheduled to start, his lawyers argued before Judge Chris Nicholson that the NPA should have invited him to make representations before a decision was taken to recharge him. Zuma argued that the last decision to charge him, taken by acting NPA head Mokotedi Mpshe, was a review of the August 2003 decision, by Mpshe's predecessor Bulelani Ngcuka, not to prosecute Zuma. Therefore, Zuma argued, he had a legitimate expectation to be asked to make representations to the NPA.

The Zuma case had become more than a normal court application. Thousands of ANC supporters were bussed in to attend a vigil the night before his case was due to be heard, and high-profile ANC leaders supported him at court. The atmosphere was captured by an ANC supporter who attended the night vigil: 'He's a very important man to us. He's not a fighter. He's a leader. Only God will judge him.'[2]

While Advocate Kemp J Kemp SC argued the technical point on Zuma's behalf, pro-Zuma chanting could be heard inside court. Kemp, on Zuma's behalf, added spice to his arguments by not only arguing the technicality about Zuma's right to make representations, but also linking this to so-called political interference in his case. In his affidavit before court, Zuma dragged Mbeki into the case by pointing out that they 'hotly contested' for the position of ANC president at Polokwane. 'This contest had attracted a great deal of general interest and media interest almost throughout the year of

2007,' Zuma said. He 'and those who wish me to occupy a leadership role in the ANC, were concerned about criminal charges being re-launched at all and moreover being launched at a critical time in the political process'. He accused the state of engineering a 'stratagem to cloak me in the guise of an accused at the critical moment in the political process and so to hamper the prospects of my election as ANC President (or whatever other position the delegates would see fit for me to occupy)'.

The NPA, Zuma said, had a 'grim determination to prosecute me at all costs, even at the cost of the state's Constitutional duties, in order to eliminate me as a political leader'. This was vehemently denied by the NPA.

*   *   *

Kemp's arguments found fertile ground in the mind of Judge Nicholson, who ruled on 12 September 2008 that the charges against Zuma were invalid. The NPA was supposed to invite his representations before recharging him, the judge ruled. He also gave credence to Zuma's claims of a political conspiracy: 'I am ... not convinced that the applicant was incorrect in averring political meddling in his prosecution,' said Nicholson. The judge continued to say he could not ignore the 'dark mutterings emanating from [Zuma] that if he goes down others will follow him. Like a blinded Samson he threatens to make sure the temple collapses with him. The impression created is that the applicant [Zuma] has knowledge he will disclose if he is faced with conviction and sentence.'

Nicholson took it upon himself to recommend the institution of a commission of inquiry to 'properly rid our land of this cancer [the Arms Deal] that is devouring the body politic and the reputation for integrity built up so assiduously after the fall of Apartheid'. If Mbeki could appoint a commission (the Hefer inquiry) to investigate claims that Ngcuka was an apartheid spy, it seemed 'so much more important to appoint a commission to thoroughly investigate whether there is truth in the allegations of widespread corruption and, if there is not, to clear the name of President Mbeki and those others unjustly accused', Nicholson said.

Eight days later, Mbeki resigned as president of the republic after being recalled by the ANC on the strength of Nicholson's judgment. Four months later, the Supreme Court of Appeal overturned Nicholson's judgment and castigated him for making findings about things he knew nothing about. Zuma had won the battle, but the war was back on.

9

In a fascinating and strangely under-reported address delivered at an international law conference a year later, Advocate Billy Downer, who headed the prosecutions of Shaik and Zuma, hit out at three consecutive heads of the NPA for the fact that Zuma's case never came to court.

Downer, a Deputy Director of Public Prosecutions in the Western Cape, was part of the original Arms Deal team assembled by Ngcuka. He was specifically responsible for the Thales/Zuma leg of the investigation and worked closely with Scorpions investigators as part of the unit's prosecutor-led investigation style. When Advocate Gerda Ferreira resigned from the Scorpions, Downer took charge of the entire Arms Deal probe.

In a speech to the Middle Temple conference in October 2010, Downer revealed that he and his team had been overruled three times, by Ngcuka, Pikoli and Mpshe.

* * *

In 2003, Ngcuka announced at a public press conference that, although there was a prima facie case against Zuma, he would not be prosecuted. The case was not winnable, Ngcuka controversially said. But he made this decision against the advice of Downer and Ferreira. 'Mr Ngcuka announced publicly that the investigating and prosecuting team, of which I was a part, had recommended that Mr Zuma should be prosecuted. The national director of public prosecutions [Ngcuka] therefore took an original decision not to prosecute, against the advice of the two line prosecutors and, indeed, the other members of the investigating team,' Downer said.

According to him, Ngcuka's decision not to prosecute Zuma was constitutionally significant for three reasons:

1. It was a decision taken by the national head of the NPA, not a Director of Public Prosecutions responsible for a specific province. Downer said: 'It is debatable whether the framers of the Constitution ever intended the NDPP to have any original powers of decision at all.'

2. Ngcuka disagreed with Downer and Ferreira's decision that Zuma should be prosecuted with Shaik: 'With hindsight, Mr Ngcuka might wish that he had followed our advice,' he said. Downer juxtaposed Ngcuka's decision with the independence afforded by the Italian prosecution authority to Milan regional prosecutor Fabio de Pasquale, who had 'waged a valiant campaign over years against Prime Minister of Italy Mr Silvio Berlusconi, with some remarkable successes. Mr de Pasquale has been able to implement his own decisions in the less hierarchical Italian system.'

3. Ngcuka's motives were criticised by the political and legal community for years. Zuma accused Ngcuka of taking a deliberate decision to smear him by announcing publicly there was a case against him, but not having the guts to take him to court. This, Downer said, 'fuelled the debate some years later about the succeeding NDPPs' motives for deciding to prosecute Mr Zuma after the Shaik trial. Mr Ngcuka and the NPA (including me), in all the court papers where this issue has been raised, have vigorously

and in depth denied any improper motive. Nevertheless, the negative public spin accorded to the Ngcuka decision not to prosecute, which was said to have poisoned the later decisions to prosecute Mr Zuma, tended to add some public force to the calls to drop the Zuma charges entirely, and even to abolish the Scorpions, which agency Mr Ngcuka famously founded and headed.'

A number of sources inside and outside the ANC told me over the years that Ngcuka's decision was abused by Zuma to garner sympathy for his cause – that he was the victim of a political conspiracy. Ngcuka, they said, honestly thought he was protecting the ANC and Zuma when he decided not to prosecute him but rather to go for Shaik. But Zuma needed a villain for his conspiracy to succeed, I was told, and Ngcuka was the perfect candidate: the man who told the world there was a prima facie case against him and briefed newspaper editors about the allegations against Zuma, although he might have saved him from imprisonment.

*   *   *

According to Downer, the prosecution of Zuma was a 'legal inevitability' after Judge Squires' judgment in the Shaik matter. 'One could not possibly, in the face of that judgment, do nothing. It was clear as daylight that a prosecution had to follow. It does not mean that Mr Zuma is guilty, but the judgment just made it clear that there was such a strong case against him, it would be quite improper not to prosecute.'

The Scorpions proceeded to search the properties of Zuma, his lawyer and his associates, and seized more evidence. In his address, Downer reveals that Pikoli, then the National Director of Public Prosecutions (NDPP), acted against Downer's advice that the legal challenges to the raids should be dealt with first before Zuma's prosecution started. A number of individuals raided by the Scorpions, including Zuma himself, his lawyers Michael Hulley and Julekha

Mahomed and businessman Jurgen Kögl, brought legal challenges against the raids in court. This meant that the state couldn't use the documents seized in the raids in its case against Zuma until the courts had declared the raids lawful.

Downer and his team argued that Zuma should not be recharged before these legal challenges had been dealt with, but was overruled by Pikoli. This meant that the state had to argue for a postponement of the trial when it came to the Pietermaritzburg High Court on 20 September 2006. Judge Msimang lashed the state for not being prepared to proceed and threw out the case.

'Yet again, the NDPP chose not to follow our advice, this time to delay Mr Zuma's prosecution until we had gathered all the new evidence that we had set about obtaining,' said Downer.

*   *   *

After the legal challenges to the raids were finally dealt with by the Supreme Court of Appeal (SCA) – in the state's favour – Downer and his team finalised the draft indictment against Zuma. The SCA delivered its judgment on 8 November 2007. Two months earlier, Mbeki had suspended Pikoli for an alleged 'breakdown of trust' between him and then Justice minister Brigitte Mabandla. In early December 2007, Downer and his team were ready to move against Zuma. They recommended to Advocate Mokotedi Mpshe, a deputy NDPP who was acting as head of the NPA, that they were ready to prosecute Zuma. But this time politics came into play.

It was a few days before the ANC's Polokwane conference was due to start, and Mpshe and his colleagues decided it was a bigger risk to charge Zuma before than after the Polokwane conference.

Said Downer: 'Our plea was, as usual, to leave politics out of it and make the correct prosecution decision. So, once again, the decision to delay the announcement of the decision until after the Polokwane conference was one taken against the advice of the line prosecutors.'

The timing of Zuma's charges became very significant a few

months later when Mpshe released transcripts of conversations between Ngcuka and former Scorpions boss Leonard McCarthy.

Downer ended his address by posing four questions, which he said
remained:

1. Is Zuma guilty?
2. Did the intelligence agencies act irregularly when they released
   confidential recordings to Zuma?
3. Did someone in Zuma's team illegally receive the recordings
   from the intelligence agencies?
4. What are the prospects of prosecuting someone in high office in
   future?

These are valid questions, which cannot stay unanswered forever.
The evidence I have gathered over the years may shed light on some
of Downer's questions. And more evidence will emerge in future,
especially as Zuma loses popular support. As the Maasai saying goes:
truth is like fire – it cannot be hidden under dry leaves.

Moe

'The prosecution of ANC president Jacob Zuma is wrong. It is being done neither in the public interest nor in the interest of justice.'

10

In the latter part of 2008, a strange new debate started to emerge in the public domain: should a special political deal be made to indefinitely postpone or abolish the corruption case against Jacob Zuma? Implicit in the debate were a number of assumptions and beliefs: that Zuma absolutely had to become president of South Africa; that he could not be president of the country if corruption clouds were still hanging over his head; that he would probably be convicted if the court case against him went ahead; and that continuing with the prosecution against him would cause some kind of instability in the country. Some could, of course, have interpreted this as a threat to those in power: continue with the Zuma prosecution and see what happens.

The debate came on the back of a concerted effort by the 'new' ANC, elected under Zuma's leadership in Polokwane, to save Zuma from prosecution. The campaign was spearheaded by then Housing minister Lindiwe Sisulu and involved a 'brains trust' of three outsiders to assist the ANC in putting together a strategy to get Zuma off the hook. They were Professor Sipho Seepe, former judge Willem Heath and the University of Cape Town's Deputy Registrar of Legal Services, Paul Ngobeni.

It was reported at the time that the 'brains trust' was considering a strategy of showing the public that Zuma was being prosecuted unfairly, of creating doubt about the objectivity of the courts and the ability of the Constitutional Court to hear the Zuma matter fairly, and of suggesting a Truth and Reconciliation Commission-type process for the Arms Deal, whereby amnesty would be granted to those who fully and honestly declared their complicity in the acquisition process.[1]

Those in support of a political solution for Zuma's legal problems included Cosatu, the SACP, the then Justice portfolio committee chairperson Yunus Carrim, Business Unity South Africa (BUSA) chief executive Jerry Vilakazi and diplomat-turned-spy Moe Shaik. 'If there is a political solution that is legally and constitutionally tenable, surely we should all, whatever political party we come from, encourage it in the national interest? After all, aren't there precedents for this in the established democracies in cases that are broadly similar?' Carrim was quoted as saying, citing examples of legislation in Italy, France and the United States to prohibit the charging of sitting presidents.[2] Vilakazi banged the stability drum: 'This matter [of Zuma] must be brought to closure so that the country can proceed with certainty of political leadership. If it requires a political solution, let a political solution be found.'[3]

Shaik, brother to Schabir and at that stage a foreign affairs adviser, made a passionate plea for the Zuma charges to be dropped. He wrote in the *Mail & Guardian* that Zuma's prosecution was 'wrong' and that a 'vast many South Africans' believed the 'origins of this prosecution are soiled with the secret shame of the effort to prevent Zuma from assuming high office'.[4] For Shaik, the Zuma matter had become a personal one. His family had historical ties with Zuma through ANC intelligence. Shaik had been a key player in Operation Vula, the secret ANC intelligence effort set up in the late 1980s to facilitate the return of exiled ANC leaders to South Africa. And now his brother's conviction was about to prevent Zuma from occupying the highest office in the land.

* * *

The SCA's smackdown of Judge Nicholson's ruling not only, in effect, reinstated the criminal charges against the president-to-be, but did further damage to his conspiracy claims by reaffirming an age-old legal principle: that a prosecution is not wrongful merely because it is brought for an improper purpose. 'It will only be wrongful if, in addition, reasonable and probable grounds for prosecuting are absent, something not alleged by Mr Zuma and which in any event can only be determined once criminal proceedings have been concluded,' ruled Judge Louis Harms, who wrote the majority ruling in the case.

This meant that, even if Zuma was correct to claim that he was the victim of a grand conspiracy by Mbeki and the Scorpions to dent his political ambitions, it didn't take away from the veracity of the charges he had to face. If he had a case of corruption to answer, he had to face the music.

Time was running out for Zuma and his supporters to make the charges against him disappear. The ANC could hardly afford to embark on an election campaign with a president on trial for corruption, especially in the light of a recent breakaway from the ANC by erstwhile stalwarts Mosiuoa Lekota and Mbhazima Shilowa, who had formed the Congress of the People (COPE). Desperate times called for desperate measures.

11

I have been investigating the origin of the Zuma spy tapes for the past three years. I think I can finally put together a fair account of what preceded that fateful announcement on 6 April 2009 that changed the course of South African history – that the case against Zuma was too contaminated to be taken to court. What follows is my account, based on facts, court documents, secret documents leaked to me and interviews with countless people who had direct knowledge of, or intimate insights into, how Zuma came into possession of intercepted recordings that saved his life and career.

*   *   *

In 1999, Mbeki and Bulelani Ngcuka, then the NDPP, established a new crack crime-fighting unit called the Directorate of Special Operations (DSO), or the Scorpions, in the NPA. The Scorpions was specifically tasked to fight organised crime, taxi violence, politically motivated violence in KwaZulu-Natal and drug-related crimes in the Western Cape. The formation of the Scorpions almost immediately led to incredible acrimony and turf wars between it and the South African Police Service (SAPS), which was still seen as largely untransformed. The Scorpions consisted of former, mostly white, police detectives and newly recruited, mostly black, university-trained lawyers and investigators. The unit was well branded and exquisitely equipped, which gave it an 'elite' status that contrasted strongly with the often poorly trained, badly equipped police detectives. The NPA took its new investigators to the FBI in the United States and Scotland Yard in the United Kingdom for training, something that would later be used against it by the unit's detractors.

The unit achieved tremendous success in the cases it pursued – mostly high-level, complex crime investigations that required intensive cooperation between intelligence gatherers, detectives and prosecutors. The Scorpions adopted this model, which made it one of the most highly regarded crime-fighting outfits in the world before it was shut down in 2008, following an ANC resolution adopted at the party's Polokwane conference.

The head of the Scorpions for the biggest part of its existence was Leonard McCarthy, a senior career prosecutor who strongly supported the prosecution-driven investigations method followed by the Scorpions. At the time of the Scorpions' formation, Jackie Selebi, an ANC politician and diplomat, was National Commissioner of the SAPS. Selebi's disdain for the Scorpions was no secret. Selebi and his fellow commissioners saw McCarthy and his unit as arrogant and elitist. The Scorpions, they said, cherry-picked only the best cases and so managed to maintain a high conviction rate. One has to feel some sympathy for this argument: the police were expected to solve crimes of a similar nature, but without the fancy cars, laptops and forensic equipment, and with a bigger workload. That said, the Scorpions created an environment for ambitious sleuths to strive to succeed, and numerous former police detectives ended up working for McCarthy's unit. Another hallmark of the DSO was that it had the appetite to go after dodgy politicians. The unit was more independent – McCarthy was a presidential appointment and thus did not have to consult or seek the NDPP's approval for decisions to investigate. Selebi, on the other hand, was seen as a staunch ANC cadre, and the police rarely touched any cases that involved politicians.

So bad was the relationship between the Scorpions and the police that the latter registered a formal intelligence investigation into 'nefarious activities' allegedly committed by people in and outside the NPA, called Operation Destroy Lucifer (Operation 796). It is unclear when exactly the probe began, but indications are that SAPS crime intelligence started investigating the Scorpions as early as 2003.

Destroy Lucifer was headed by former crime intelligence bosses, first Rayman Lalla and later Mulangi Mphego, who were both close allies of Selebi. According to a secret leaked crime intelligence report, the NPA's 'activities' were 'manifestly designed to firstly subvert institutions of democracy and secondly, to compromise the ability of our Government to deliver on its mandate, and ultimately to undermine Government's integrity and legitimacy and the overall political reputation of the State'. How was this done? Through 'a multitude of concealed and complex activities, including espionage, blackmailing, corruption and money laundering, sabotaging and/or undermining and/or abusing the criminal justice system, malicious leaking of classified government information to newspapers and other unauthorised persons, and the abuse of government office either for commercial or political gain'.

In short, the police's crime intelligence division, under Selebi, had become more interested in what the Scorpions were doing than they were in investigating crime and infiltrating criminal networks. This could partly be explained by the coming together of the paranoid legacies of both the old-order South African Police and the ANC's security structures. Selebi, I imagined, seethed at the idea that suddenly he was no longer the only sheriff in town and that another policing unit could investigate, arrest and prosecute criminals. Similarly, Billy Masetlha, who headed the National Intelligence Agency (NIA), fumed at the fact that the Scorpions were gathering intelligence without his control.

These tensions reached boiling point in 2005 when Judge Sisi Khampepe chaired public hearings into the work and placement of the Scorpions. At these hearings, Selebi and Masetlha effectively accused the Scorpions of sabotage by leaking intelligence to foreign intelligence agencies and private intelligence operatives. Masetlha's evidence was directly opposed by Ronnie Kasrils, the Intelligence minister at the time, who was broadly seen as a supporter of the Scorpions. Ironically, Masetlha was later charged (and acquitted) of being involved in creating the hoax emails that were leaked to Kgalema Motlanthe to make him choose sides in the battle for Polokwane. Kasrils, in the hoax emails trial, accused Masetlha of playing 'Cold War spy games'.

* * *

The police intelligence report, which outlines the objectives of Destroy Lucifer, uses similar Cold War language. 'The framework of this operation is by its nature, very broad, and seeks to uncover activities that are regarded injurious to national security, including suspected maneuvers and penetration by enemy formations,' it reads. According to the report, 45 people and seven private entities were identified as suspects. Seven of the 45 people were former or serving NPA employees. 'Various intelligence gathering techniques were employed, including telephone and direct interceptions, remote data mining, source cultivation and agent penetration,' the report reveals. The report fails to say if these interceptions were done legally.

According to the document, suspects in the NPA were being investigated for the following reasons:

- Senior NPA prosecutors wanted to manipulate the TRC prosecution process by ensuring ANC members who were denied amnesty were being prosecuted.
- An email was being circulated about a senior NPA employee who had allegedly fathered a child by an underage mother, and this could be used to blackmail the employee.
- Investigators working for mining magnate Brett Kebble and his family had deliberately planted false information with Ngcuka to the effect that Selebi was investigating him. This led to the 'initial

deterioration' of the relationship between Selebi and Ngcuka that almost led to a 'fist fight' between the two over the mandate of the Scorpions.

- Ngcuka's business interests with local and foreign partners were questioned.
- A senior prosecutor in charge of high-profile investigations was 'untouchable' and had 'dirt' on all his bosses in the NPA, including sex tapes, information about extramarital affairs and proof of criminal conduct.
- The Scorpions team investigating Selebi allegedly threatened and intimidated witnesses to fabricate evidence.
- The police investigated Advocate Gerrie Nel, the chief prosecutor against Selebi, and procured a witness statement from Scorpions advocate Nomgcobo Jiba, who was subsequently suspended for cooperating with a police investigation,
- Ivor Powell, a former journalist who worked for the Scorpions, was allegedly leaking information to journalists. Powell had to 'block' a story about the 'infiltration of the Scorpions by MI6' (Britain's Secret Intelligence Service).

In a section titled 'the McCarthy tapes', the report states that crime intelligence was investigating a drug-related case linking Powell, Americans gang boss Igshaan Davids, the late ANC spy Bheki Jacobs and a senior NPA prosecutor. (Interestingly, Lieutenant General Anwa Dramat, the current head of the Hawks, was head of crime intelligence in the Western Cape at the time and would have been aware of the operation.) In 2008, Powell had been arrested for drunken driving while in Davids' company after meeting Davids to gather intelligence about recent gang killings and smuggling activity.[1] Charges against him were later dropped. He was never arrested or charged for drug-related charges. But here's the nub: according to the report, intelligence 'pointed to the suspicious involvement of McCarthy, resulting in the ultimate interception of his mobile number' as part of the drugs investigation. McCarthy's 'involvement' is not explained in any detail. Again, no mention is made whether the interception was done legally, with the approval of a judge. Significantly, the report states that the 'sustained monitoring of McCarthy's mobile yielded little evidential material that would be relevant to the drugs investigation' but that it 'nonetheless revealed a mine of intelligence'. Ka-ching!

* * *

McCarthy was probably never really a suspect in a drugs investigation, but crime intelligence somehow justified feeding his mobile number into the interception systems through this probe. The *Mail & Guardian* reported that McCarthy's phone calls might have been intercepted from June 2006 – around the time Selebi was implicated in the Brett Kebble scandal through his links to drug boss Glenn Agliotti.[2] How convenient for the police to be tapping the phone of the man ultimately in charge of the corruption investigations against Selebi and Zuma! And what did crime intelligence find in this 'mine of intelligence'? That the Scorpions boss maintained a 'subordinate' relationship with Ngcuka. That Ngcuka 'directed and manipulated' high-profile Scorpions cases, including those of Selebi and Zuma. That McCarthy had received a freebie trip to the 2007 Rugby World Cup in France. That while in France McCarthy had met a 'certain Irish spy'. That McCarthy 'deferred his judgment' on occasion to former deputy Justice minister Johnny de Lange. And that the deputy head of the NPA, Willie Hofmeyr, 'wanted to improperly influence McCarthy'.

The intelligence report stated that these 'nefarious activities' posed a 'danger and damage' to the criminal justice system and to South Africa's democracy, and that crime intelligence had decided to embark on a 'prosecution-driven intelligence-conversion drive, whereby portions of intelligence already collected, would be converted and, where necessary, enhanced in order to satisfy the criminal law thresholds, in order to prosecute those responsible'.

* * *

Enter Commissioner Richard Naggie Mdluli, the deputy head of police in Gauteng and a career policeman who had started serving the apartheid-era police force on the volatile East Rand in the 1980s.

12

On 31 December 2007, Jackie Selebi attended a New Year's party with his wife Anne, at the invitation of Thabo and Zanele Mbeki, at the presidential residence in Pretoria. Selebi had reason to celebrate the end of a tough year. Were it not for the swift removal of Vusi Pikoli as head of the NPA, he would have been arrested by the Scorpions in September that year on charges of corruption, racketeering and money laundering.

Selebi, the Scorpions claimed, was taking bribes from underworld bosses. The police chief vehemently denied such allegations, famously claiming on live television that 'these hands are clean'. Mbeki stood by his friend and comrade. But he had just been voted out as ANC president at Polokwane and Selebi's protection could not be guaranteed for much longer. At 3am on 1 January 2008, after partying the night away to the beats of Brenda Fassie, Mbeki received a telephone call from Mpshe, the acting NPA boss, advising the president that he was ready to arrest his police chief for corruption.

* * *

Although Destroy Lucifer was claimed to have been a legitimate police intelligence operation into 'nefarious' activities inside the NPA, it became abundantly clear in 2008 that it was the police's, and by extension Selebi's, response to Operation Bad Guys – the Scorpions probe into Kebble and the crime network around him. Selebi was one of the few law enforcement bosses who had stood by Mbeki during his battle with Zuma at Polokwane. The police chief didn't have a particularly pleasant relationship with Zuma; I was told numerous times that Zuma blamed Selebi for leaking details of his rape charge to the media. Selebi knew his time was running out. After the police failed to solve Kebble's murder of September 2005, the Scorpions took over the investigation and the Kebble tapestry, involving Agliotti, Selebi and a horde of other underworld figures, started to unravel. The Gauteng head of the Scorpions and a seasoned state advocate, Gerrie Nel, spearheaded Operation Bad Guys and soon became Selebi's enemy number one. To save Selebi, Nel had to be neutralised.

*   *   *

On 8 January 2008 at 9pm, returning from holiday with his family, Nel was arrested by about 20 armed policemen waiting for him outside his Pretoria home. Heading the investigation into Nel was Commissioner Richard Mdluli. After being detained at a police station overnight, Nel was brought to the Pretoria Magistrate's Court the next day, where the chief prosecutor refused to charge him with fraud and defeating the ends of justice. The charges related to Nel's testimony in the case of Scorpions prosecutor Cornwell Tshavhungwa. On the same day Nel appeared in court, Selebi launched an urgent interdict application at the Pretoria High Court, asking the court to prevent the Scorpions from arresting and charging him. Destroy Lucifer had effectively become the 'Save Selebi' campaign, and the police chief's allies were doing everything to get him off the hook.

Nel's arrest was widely condemned. Mpshe released a statement, expressing his 'shock and concern' at the way the police had lied to him to obtain an arrest warrant for Nel. It was clear that the police were on a desperate frolic of their own. Soon after the charges against Nel were thrown out of court for being baseless, a senior Scorpions advocate was suspended for allegedly assisting Mdluli and his troops in effectively cooking up the charges against Nel and obtaining an arrest warrant. Her name was Nomgcobo Jiba.

*   *   *

On 11 January 2008, two days after Nel was released, the Scorpions were dealt a further blow when Selebi submitted to the Pretoria High Court an affidavit by Advocate Lawrence Mrwebi, head of the Scorpions in KwaZulu-Natal, in which he described a desperate meeting of the unit's bosses in July 2007, discussing ways to save the agency. This came after the ANC had resolved, at its June 2007 policy conference, to do away with the Scorpions. According to Mrwebi's notes of the meeting, the four cases that were causing all the trouble were the investigations into Zuma, Mac Maharaj, Ngoako Ramatlhodi and Selebi (Operation Bad Guys). Some of the suggestions that were debated included going back to a 'Hollywood style' operation, with suspects arrested in the full glare of television cameras; lobbying politicians and businesspeople sympathetic to the Scorpions' cause; and publicity exercises to 'sell' the unit to the public ahead of the Polokwane conference.

According to Mrwebi's statement, it was mentioned that the Bad Guys investigation meant the 'life and death' of the Scorpions. 'That was indeed very strange to us as we would not be told of the reason for the importance of this matter for it to even require such high level intervention. To us it was an ordinary, albeit complicated organised crime matter, involving drugs, murder, and serious economic crime related matters. And it was no different from other matters we used to handle. The question the answer to which we had not been provided was and is why is this matter of such importance as to even pose a threat to the existence of the DSO,' Mrwebi wrote, failing to mention that the country's police chief was implicated in this 'ordinary' case.

*   *   *

Mrwebi's affidavit was clearly meant to embarrass the Scorpions, and played into Selebi's conspiracy theory that he was the victim of the unit's campaign to save itself from closure. The statement also ended up with Zuma's legal team, who used it to further their own conspiracy theory. It was claimed at the time by an NPA colleague that Mrwebi had attended high-level meetings with senior police officers and had even been flown from Durban to Pretoria in a police helicopter to attend these meetings. Mrwebi denied this.

On Mrwebi's version of events, Commissioner Rayman Lalla, the former head of crime intelligence, and the deputy head of the NIA, Arthur Fraser, contacted him to be interviewed as part of their investigation into the so-called Browse Mole intelligence report produced by the Scorpions. The Browse Mole report claimed to have uncovered evidence that Zuma's campaign to become ANC president was funded by foreign governments, primarily Angola and Libya. A Scorpions investigator compiled it from intelligence he received from private intelligence operatives. The document was made public in 2007 after somebody faxed it to the offices of Cosatu. The trade union federation, which was sympathetic to Zuma at the time, distributed it to the media. At some stage, it was said that parts of the report emanated from the KwaZulu-Natal office of the Scorpions, and so Mrwebi agreed to be interviewed. He made an affidavit and 'gave it to Lalla and no one else', he told the *Mail & Guardian* in an interview.[1] Lalla, a former ANC underground operative from KwaZulu-Natal, was perceived to be close to Selebi and Zuma. Mrwebi maintains he doesn't know how his statement ended up with Selebi. But he did agree to testify for Selebi during his corruption trial in 2010.

Because of the statement, implicating his superiors in supposed underhanded discussions, Mrwebi was suspended from the NPA be-tween January 2008 and September 2009. In October 2011, he made a spectacular career leap when Zuma appointed him as head of the Specialised Commercial Crimes Unit in the NPA, effectively put-ting him in charge of all corruption and fraud prosecutions in South Africa.

13

Why is all of this relevant to the Zuma spy tapes? Because a dusty court file from January 2009 – three months before Zuma was let off the hook – neatly links all the players in the Save Selebi campaign to Zuma's fate.

*   *   *

On 27 January 2009, Gauteng's deputy police chief, Commissioner Richard Mdluli, submitted an angry affidavit to the Johannesburg Labour Court in support of Scorpions advocate Nomgcobo Jiba, who had been suspended in the aftermath of the failed Nel prosecution. Jiba and Mdluli had been the main drivers behind Nel's arrest. In her charge sheet, the NPA claimed that Jiba acted against Nel in cahoots with the police because of Nel's role in the conviction of her husband, Booker Nhantsi, a former member of the Scorpions. Nhantsi, who worked as an attorney before being appointed a deputy director in the Eastern Cape Scorpions, was convicted of theft in the Mthatha High Court in 2005. In 2003, he had stolen funds totalling R193 000 held in a trust for a client, and had been sentenced to five years' imprisonment, of which two years were suspended for a period of five years.

Jiba 'blamed Advocate Nel for the fate of her husband and vowed to get back at him', read the preamble to her charge sheet. She did this by allegedly obtaining a copy of a January 2007 judgment by the Pretoria Regional Court in the fraud case of former Scorpions advocate Cornwell Tshavhungwa, who reported to Nel. Nel had been in charge of the Scorpions' probe into the Mpumalanga Economic Empowerment Corporation (MEEC) when Tshavhungwa allegedly took money from the MEEC for 'consultancy services' while investigating the agency. Nel's evidence in the case was heavily criticised by Magistrate AA Lamprecht, who said he was 'not entirely objective in his approach during the MEEC investigation' and that 'his mindset was subjectively clouded as a result of the trust that he had in the accused (Tshavhungwa)'.[1]

The NPA claimed that, from June 2007 to December 2007 – coincidentally the same period during which the Scorpions intensified their investigation of Selebi and months after Lamprecht had criticised Nel in his judgment – Jiba had 'had several consulations with members of SAPS in an attempt to build a criminal case against Adv Nel in a biased manner and based on the above-mentioned court record'. Jiba 'assisted members of the SAPS in an attempt to obtain a warrant of arrest against Adv Nel' and 'put members of the SAPS in contact with a member of the DSO in an attempt to obtain a complainant statement'. She allegedly approached a senior public prosecutor and other NPA officials to persuade them to issue a warrant of arrest against Nel. These prosecutors all refused because there was insufficient evidence.

Jiba was charged with dishonesty, insubordination, unprofessional conduct and bringing the NPA into disrepute. She immediately launched an urgent Labour Court application to prevent the NPA from continuing with the disciplinary proceeding against her. This application was dismissed, but she continued to fight the NPA in court, counting on Mdluli to save her.

* * *

As deputy police chief in Gauteng, Mdluli oversaw detectives and crime intelligence in the province. He had previously headed up the detective unit in Potchefstroom, where he was posted after serving for many years in his hometown of Vosloorus, with a short stint in Oudtshoorn. It is unclear when exactly he was drawn into Destroy Lucifer, and if his participation involved anything more than gunning for Nel and, by implication, protecting Selebi.

In his affidavit, Mdluli accuses the NPA top management of behaving like a 'gang of criminals' in protecting Nel from prosecution. But, more significantly, Mdluli admitted under oath that the police had intercepted Leonard McCarthy's calls, supposedly as part of a 'drug dealing' investigation. Extraordinarily, Mdluli attached transcripts of an intercepted conversation between McCarthy and the Scorpions' head of investigations, Thanda Mngwengwe, to his affidavit, without clearly stating that the interception was done legally, sanctioned by a court order.

In South Africa it is illegal to tap anyone's phone without a court order issued by a judge authorising such interception. Doing so, or fraudulently adding telephone numbers to a different court order, is a criminal offence punishable by imprisonment. In August 2012, *Eyewitness News* reported that the NPA had commissioned a legal opinion at the time of Jiba's Labour Court matter that said it was illegal for Mdluli to have given the transcripts to Jiba, and for her to use them in a public court hearing. In her own affidavit before court, Jiba didn't even address the issue of legality and merely stated: 'On 29 October 2007 the police intercepted a telephonic conversation between senior officials of the (NPA), Thanda Mngwengwe and Leonard McCarthy. Both are my superiors. In their conversation they stated, inter alia, that I have given a statement to the police in their investigation against Nel and that I should be dealt with.'

Similarly, Mdluli doesn't touch on the issues of legality in his affidavit. 'Our suspicions concerning the derailing and sabotage of our investigations against (Nel) were confirmed when we received information from another police officer relating to a completely different investigation that was conducted against certain persons involved in drug dealing. One of the people allegedly linked to that investigation was Leonard McCarthy.' By 'information' Mdluli meant 'interceptions'. Until such time as evidence is produced that McCarthy was indeed involved in drug dealing, we must assume that Mdluli's assertion was a red herring to justify the (illegal) interception of McCarthy's calls.

Mdluli's version of events is curious. According to him, information about Nel's conduct in the Tshavhungwa case was brought to him in August 2007 by Captain Tsietsi Mano. He then delegated Mano and Director Jan Mabula to investigate the claims. Interestingly, both Mano and Mabula were based at the organised crime unit in Potchefstroom, North West, which Mdluli headed before being moved to Gauteng. So Mdluli wanted the court to believe that, seven months after Magistrate Lamprecht criticised Nel's evidence, someone decided to lay a complaint against Nel with the police in North West.

Mdluli further stated that he contacted Prince Mokotedi, head of internal investigations at the NPA (who, like Mrwebi, testified for Selebi in his corruption trial) and asked for a senior Scorpions prosecutor to assist his investigation into Nel. Mokotedi gave them Jiba, Mdluli claims. What followed was a series of events that frustrated their investigation until one day, miraculously, interceptions of phone calls fell in Mdluli's lap. 'In all these circumstances it is abundantly clear in light of what is stated above based on the intercepted telephone conversation between [McCarthy and Mngwengwe] that there existed a well orchestrated plan to frustrate our investigations in order to protect [Nel],' Mdluli stated.

In the intercepted conversation, McCarthy calls Mngwengwe, who he also addresses as 'Lume', to tell him about the investigation against Nel: 'I was just given the most mind-boggling account of a process that commenced three weeks ago. Whereby Nomgcobo Jiba and some [senior Scorpions investigator] went to the police with a copy of a transcript or part of a transcript what that magistrate said about Gerrie Nel's evidence and said no, no, he must be charged and arrested and the police then opened a file, they assigned Commissioner Mdluli and I don't know who else to deal with this matter ...' McCarthy explains why Jiba might be doing this: '[She] has [an] axe to grind with Nel because he was central to her husband being fired and to bring him to jail.'

McCarthy also tells Mngwengwe that he wasn't 'too happy' with Nel's defensiveness when it came to the Tshavhungwa matter and thought Nel didn't want to know what Tshavhungwa, his subordinate, really did. 'You trust the guy so much that you ... just don't want to believe what you've been told.' But, says McCarthy, 'we've been played here and this is all part of a strategy to unsettle the work that we do and to target certain people, I said I've heard recently that Nel is now also coincidently being investigated for something.' McCarthy then advises Mngwengwe to meet with Advocate Sibongile Mzinyathi, the Director of Public Prosecutions for Pretoria, and discuss the Nel matter with him 'face to face or heart to heart'. Somewhat presciently, McCarthy predicts that the police may be 'vuilgat enough' (dirty enough) to first arrest Nel on the little evidence they have and then do a proper investigation.

He ends the conversation: 'Look, there's a conspiracy of sorts here, Lume. In fact, everyone agrees with that. Everyone agrees that this thing comes out of the blue and it's clearly aimed at destabilising ...'

*   *   *

Mdluli reveals that he took the interception to Mokotedi Mpshe, who was then acting head of the NPA, in January 2008. 'I played the audio recording in his presence, to which he listened. He also read the transcript of the recording in my presence. He was very surprised when he heard and read about the conversation.' Mdluli says he requested Mpshe to 'outsource' the prosecution of Nel, but Mpshe declined.

Mdluli's support of Jiba in the rest of his affidavit is relentless: the disciplinary process against Jiba was designed to intimidate her; the false impression was created that she was the architect of the Nel investigation; the NPA is furthering an 'illegal conspiracy' against her to 'defeat the ends of justice through false disciplinary charges'; and the top management of the NPA were 'criminals themselves who have no respect for the constitutional principle of equality before the law or of prosecuting without fear, favour or prejudice of those in the inner circle of this big mafia'.

Jiba denied acting against Nel out of vengeance and said she had been brought into the case by Mokotedi. She further stated that, after losing her first attempt to halt the disciplinary hearing, she had made representations to the Minister of Justice, who was by then Jeff Radebe. The timing is significant; when Jiba first approached the Labour Court in January 2009 and submitted Mdluli's affidavit and the intercepts, Zuma had not yet been let off the hook and Enver Surty was the Minister of Justice. A few months later, when she made representations to Radebe, Zuma was not only off the hook, but also president of the country.

Radebe evidently passed the complaints by Jiba and Lawrence Mrwebi, who was still under suspension for giving an affidavit to the police, to his embattled director-general, Advocate Menzi Simelane. Simelane had been severely criticised by the Ginwala commission of inquiry into Vusi Pikoli's fitness as NPA head, and had been effectively accused of lying while giving evidence.

Included in the Jiba court file is a letter from Simelane, signed on 15 June 2009, in which he advises the acting CEO of the NPA, Khotso de Wee, to suspend the disciplinary action against Jiba and Mrwebi 'pending my discussion with you and the DSO management involved in this matter'. Simelane, who, as director-general of Justice, had no jurisdiction over internal NPA affairs, told De Wee it was not desirable for a disciplinary to continue against someone who 'assisted the police in a lawful investigation', thereby making it clear that he believed the version put forward by Jiba (and Mdluli).

Three months later, on 18 September 2009, Jiba withdrew her case against the NPA after a settlement was reached. She and Mrwebi were reinstated as prosecutors.

* * *

91

In January 2011, I interviewed Mpshe after Zuma had appointed Jiba as a Deputy National Director of Public Prosecutions. I asked him the following questions:

Why did you take Jiba back into the NPA after she was suspended?

Mpshe: This matter dragged on for years, more than two years. She and another guy (Mrwebi) who was suspended sat at home as deputy DPPs, earning a salary paid by the taxpayer. She launched application after application, first at High Court in Pretoria, then in Labour Court. At the time I told Parliament the NPA was almost like Hollywood – there was such a lot of senior people on suspension. This situation couldn't continue like that. I decided it was in the interest of the NPA, the image of the NPA, and it would save money to reinstate her, if she dropped all the legal actions against the NPA.

Why did she never face a disciplinary hearing? Would charges have stuck?

Mpshe: She brought court applications, first to the High Court in Pretoria, then the Labour Court. Oh yes, dependent on the evidence I was given, the charges would've stuck. I was persuaded (by the evidence).

Was there any political pressure on you to reinstate her?

Mpshe: No, none whatsoever. It was entirely my decision, based on the reasons I gave you. I may have informed the minister of my decision at the time, but if there's anyone who must take blame for the decision, it is me.

14

For Jackie Selebi and Jacob Zuma, the country's police chief and president of the governing ANC, respectively, 2009 was going to be a critical year. Both were preparing to go on trial for corruption – Zuma in August and Selebi in October. It was widely accepted that the state had a much better chance of convicting Zuma than it did Selebi.

In Zuma's case, as Judge Squires had found, there was a detailed paper trail showing how Schabir Shaik financed Zuma's life through a succession of bank deposits and cash payments. In return, the judge found, Zuma assisted Shaik's business endeavours through his willingness to meet businesspeople (such as Professor John Lennon, David Wilson and the bosses of Thomson-CSF) and promote the Nkobi Group.

Selebi's case was different; there was no paper trail of money being deposited into his account by Glenn Agliotti. The state had to rely on verbal and circumstantial evidence only. Selebi, as Judge Meyer Joffe later found, collected cash parcels from Agliotti and accepted expensive gifts from the drug dealer for himself, his wife and his children.

But the political winds had turned against Selebi. In September 2008, Mbeki was recalled as president of the ANC and South Africa, and Selebi, whose contract had been extended by Mbeki in July 2008 for 12 months, was out in the cold. Despite making representations to the NPA, Selebi did not succeed in having his charges withdrawn, and the NPA's Operation Bad Guys team, led by Advocate Gerrie Nel, proceeded to prosecute, and eventually convict, the police chief for taking kickbacks. Would Selebi have been prosecuted if Mbeki had won at Polokwane? Probably not. And would Zuma have escaped prosecution if he hadn't beaten Mbeki for the ANC crown? Probably not. It would be unfair to accuse the entire NPA and every prosecutor in the land of being influenced by politics, but this was the year in which it became clear that politics ruled the roost when it came to high-profile prosecutorial decisions, and that the NPA had lost its ability to prosecute without fear or favour.

*   *   *

The 'Save Selebi' campaign had been largely unsuccessful, but they had one final trump card to play: the McCarthy tapes. Although the initial aim of the police's bugging of McCarthy was probably to get information on what the Scorpions were doing, specifically on Selebi, the police now had in their possession tapes that could be of great value to Zuma, who was desperately looking for something to get off the hook before the national elections, scheduled for 22 April. Selebi and police crime intelligence had that something: recordings of Leonard McCarthy and Bulelani Ngcuka discussing the timing of Zuma's charges before the ANC's Polokwane conference. And so two desperate worlds collided, both in search of a get-out-of-jail-free card.

It is unclear when exactly Selebi became aware of the existence of taped discussions between McCarthy and Ngcuka in the possession of SAPS crime intelligence. But Mulangi Mphego, Rayman Lalla and Richard Mdluli would, in all probability, have kept him abreast of the contents of McCarthy's discussions since at least 2007. The secret crime intelligence report stated, after all, that McCarthy's recordings delivered a 'mine of intelligence'. In his efforts to close down the Scorpions and save his own skin, Selebi would have kept close notes on McCarthy's comings and goings. (The crime intelligence community also speculated that the tapes somehow made their way from the police to a prominent soccer boss, but I could not verify this independently.)

In the summer of 2008, the crime intelligence recordings made their way to the office of Michael Hulley, Zuma's attorney. Although nobody has taken responsibility for delivering the tapes to Hulley, the *Mail & Guardian* published a compelling version of what allegedly happened, in May 2010. It is still unclear if Selebi sanctioned the delivery of the tapes to Zuma, but it makes sense that he would have turned to the future president to save him from imminent prosecution. Mphego, who was implicated as the person who transported the recordings to Durban, denies that he is the spy who saved Zuma.

> The M&G's two sources say Mphego first showed Zuma the recordings at a friend's home in KwaZulu-Natal before arranging to have them handed over to his lawyer. This was at the time Zuma was preparing to appeal his corruption case at the Constitutional Court.
>
> The M&G was told that Mphego flew to KwaZulu-Natal and played some of the recordings to Zuma at a house apparently occupied by a long-time Zuma associate, Erwin Ullbricht. The recordings are encrypted and, to be played, require highly sophisticated and restricted software, which Mphego provided.
>
> It is understood that a car was arranged to pick up Mphego at the airport and he flew back to Johannesburg on the same day.
>
> Ullbricht likes to refer to himself as Zuma's adopted son and signed the lease to rent a house in Durban for one of Zuma's wives, MaNtuli.
>
> When the M&G asked Ullbricht about the events, he said he lived in Johannesburg. When asked whether he had any properties in Durban, he said: 'Don't you guys have anything better to do? You are really being petty.'

Ten minutes later he called back and denied that he was the person we spoke to, although he was calling from the same number. He introduced himself as 'the real Erwin Ullbricht' and said the matter in question was highly delicate, but added 'I do not know what you are talking about'.

He later sent an SMS saying: 'Madam, you are causing war which is not actually called for. Think about that —'

The M&G's sources say Mphego made arrangements to drop the recordings and software with Hulley during the meeting with Zuma and the M&G understands that this was done at Hulley's office a few days later, although Mphego was not present.

At the same time another person was hard at work to make sure the charges against Zuma were dropped: Foreign Affairs official and Zuma lobbyist Rieaz 'Moe' Shaik. A former senior diplomat in Germany and Algeria, brother of Zuma's financial advisor, Schabir, and an ANC intelligence operative, Moe Shaik became instrumental in fighting for the Zuma charges to be dropped. He wrote newspaper columns on why a political solution for Zuma's situation should be found. He also had in his possession a taped video recording of an interview that Lalla and Mphego had conducted with Brett Kebble in 2003. Kebble, assisted by his close associate John Stratton, believed that he and his father, Roger, were being treated unfairly by Bulelani Ngcuka, who was NDPP at the time. At the time they were facing two cases of corporate fraud. A number of things Kebble told crime intelligence about in the interview closely correlated to the information that emerged from the spy tapes. The *Mail & Guardian* reported on the Kebble recording in June 2010: 'The recording is understood to have found its way to Zuma at the height of his battle to have corruption charges against him dropped and was seen by his supporters as further evidence that there was a political plot against him. In fact, it appears to disclose competing conspiracies. In the meeting, Kebble repeats and fleshes out claims he had already made in private – that he was a victim of an abuse of office by former director of public prosecutions Bulelani Ngcuka and his Scorpions investigators. But the recording also indicates how deeply the police bosses were embedded in the battle against Ngcuka. It shows them actively soliciting information from Kebble about Ngcuka, such as the claim that he had secret bank accounts in Geneva,' the paper reported.[1]

Kebble believed that Ngcuka was part of a conspiracy to promote and protect Mbeki's political aspirations and to use the NPA to counter those of Zuma. He and Stratton told Lalla and Mphego about this, claiming that Ngcuka's conspiracy was supported by Mbeki-linked businessmen Mzi Khumalo, Saki Macozoma and Moss Ngoasheng. 'I knew from a fairly early stage – because he came to tell me – that Mzi [Khumalo] had a close relationship with Ngcuka,' Kebble told the SAPS officials. 'He came and said, "You know these claims you've got against me [Kebble's company, JCI, was seeking to enforce a R30-million debt against Khumalo] – I know Bulelani very well and maybe if we can settle this thing he won't be so hard on you." I then started to look very closely at who was around Ngcuka and found these guys had a pattern of operating. They would get together regularly – Mzi, Saki, Moss Ngoasheng [former president Thabo Mbeki's former economic adviser] – and Bulelani and friends – get together and drink heavily every Friday night – and hatch their plots.'[2]

After giving the Kebble recording to Zuma, Moe Shaik decided to show the video to powerful people in the NPA, the ANC and the media to convince them of the conspiracy against Zuma.

In deputy NPA head Willie Hofmeyr, the Zuma camp found someone who was willing to discuss the possibility of the existence of a conspiracy against Zuma by the NPA and private businesspeople sympathetic to Mbeki. Moe Shaik represented the 'Zuma camp' in these private meetings with Hofmeyr and told him about the interceptions and the Kebble recording.

Hulley officially alerted the NPA to the existence of the tapes. Advocate Mokotedi Mpshe, the acting NDPP, immediately sent two of his most senior colleagues, Hofmeyr and Pretoria DPP Sibongile Mzinyathi, to Durban to listen to what Hulley had to offer. The only version of what transpired in Durban and thereafter was given by

Hofmeyr during evidence before the Commission for Conciliation, Mediation and Arbitration (CCMA) in a case brought by Faiek Davids, Hofmeyr's former deputy at the SIU. Davids was suspended from the SIU as a result of what Hofmeyr allegedly heard on the tapes Hulley played to them.

Hofmeyr, a former ANC cadre who was detained without trial in the 1980s for his political activities, played a key role in ensuring Zuma's trial didn't go ahead. Although he initially backed the Scorpions' case against the ANC leader, he was 'outraged' when he heard the spy tapes, and insisted that the NPA could no longer go to court with clean hands. Hofmeyr, I was reliably told, threatened to resign on a number of occasions if the Zuma case went ahead. When it came to the crunch, he lobbied Mpshe the hardest to let go of the Zuma charges. Hofmeyr held two jobs for more than ten years – that of head of the SIU (a unit operating separately from the NPA) and deputy head of the NPA, responsible for the Asset Forfeiture Unit. In November 2011, Zuma unceremoniously fired him from the SIU, replacing him with his predecessor, Advocate Willem Heath.

Davids took Hofmeyr to the CCMA because he believed it was illegal to use the Zuma spy tapes against him in a disciplinary hearing. (Hofmeyr didn't want the media to attend the CCMA hearing, but CCMA commissioner Bart Ford ruled that it was a matter of national importance and that us hacks could stay.) It emerged at the hearing that Hofmeyr never actually had in his possession the tapes on which Davids and McCarthy allegedly discussed Mbeki's chances of winning at Polokwane, but heard the conversation on the tapes played by Michael Hulley. He made 'contemporaneous notes' of what he had heard on Hulley's tapes, Hofmeyr testified. He said that he heard a conversation between Davids and McCarthy during which they referred to a conversation that Davids, Hofmeyr and former NPA head Bulelani Ngcuka allegedly had at the East London airport. Hofmeyr testified that Ngcuka had said state institutions should be used to support Mbeki in the run-up to the ANC's Polokwane conference.

Davids denied being part of the airport conversation. On the tapes, Hofmeyr testified, Davids could be heard telling McCarthy that he agreed with Ngcuka's sentiments and that he didn't understand how a unit like the SIU could remain impartial in the ANC leadership battle.

Hofmeyr testified that, in early 2009, Hulley indicated that they would make formal representations to Mpshe. 'They were very extensive representations, in total over 100 pages. Parts of the representations concerned allegations about a political conspiracy around the prosecution of Mr Zuma,' Hofmeyr testified. Hulley also made oral representations to the NPA's executive committee in February 2009 – a month after the SCA effectively restored the Zuma charges by overturning Judge Nicholson's ruling. 'Hulley particularly mentioned the role of the then head of the DSO, Mr McCarthy, that he was part of this conspiracy ... there were a number of allegations made about his contact with a variety of other persons; there were general allegations and the point made in oral representations, that the legal team (of Zuma) had recordings of telephone conversations that could substantiate allegations.'

Mpshe, according to Hofmeyr, decided that he (Hofmeyr) and Mzinyathi should themselves listen to the recordings Hulley had. 'Initially arrangements were made for us to listen to the recordings at his [Hulley's] office in Durban. We travelled to Durban to do so ... the recordings were on a memory stick and he [Hulley] was not able to get it to play on his computer. We took six hours trying to get it to play; we downloaded software from the internet, spoke to IT people at the NPA and even went to visit some IT specialists in Durban to see if they could get the recordings to play. In the end we were unsuccessful.' Hofmeyr and Mzinyathi travelled back to Pretoria without having listened to the spy tapes.

Hulley approached them again, and arrangements were made for them to listen to the recordings at the NPA head office in Pretoria. 'It was only something I learned afterwards,' testified Hofmeyr, 'that recordings made by the secret services in South Africa are specially encrypted. It is not possible to play them without special software only in the possession of the security services.' Hulley, a private lawyer, curiously had access to this specialised software and was able to deliver on his promise. He used his laptop to play the spy tapes to Hofmeyr and Mzinyathi. Hofmeyr said they had listened to 'about ten or twelve recordings' of a 'variety of different people talking to each other, mostly involving McCarthy'. The two NPA officials reported back to their bosses what they had heard. 'They had a great level of discomfort about what we had reported.' Hofmeyr's bosses wanted to knew if the recordings were authentic. 'We reported we did find they sounded authentic.' He said he had known McCarthy since 2001 and lived next to him in a house on the NPA's grounds.

Asked at the CCMA hearing how the NPA planned to use these recordings, Hofmeyr said the NPA executive felt they were 'sufficiently authentic' to be relied upon, but that 'it would be better if we can attempt to get the tapes in a proper and formal legal way'. This prompted Mpshe to write to the police and the NIA, asking for legal copies of the tapes.

'We were aware that the SAPS had intercepted McCarthy's telephone,' said Hofmeyr, referring the CCMA to Jiba's Labour Court application, in which she had used the intercepted conversation between McCarthy and Mngwengwe, submitted by Mdluli, as evidence. 'It was substantiated by a police officer [Mdluli] that this was indeed the recording of McCarthy's phone, it was used in a court case already,' said Hofmeyr. Asked how the NPA knew that McCarthy's phone was being tapped by the police, Hofmeyr said: 'The origins of that interception, I can't say much more about. In the court case some explanation was given, how the police officer [Mdluli] obtained the interception. My assumption was that, because it was being used in a court case, it was lawfully obtained on a judge's order. That was what the officer said.'

Hofmeyr was referring to Mdluli's explanation in his affidavit that McCarthy had been bugged as part of a drug-dealing investigation, and that Mdluli had received the interceptions from 'another police officer'. Although Mdluli never stated that a judge had authorised the tapping of McCarthy's phone, Hofmeyr testified that he assumed this had been done.

It was 'of concern' to the NPA executive committee that senior managers' conversations were being intercepted by the police, Hofmeyr said. 'A decision was taken that Mpshe would write to the police to ask if they did have interceptions of McCarthy's phone over the period relevant to the recording we had listened to... we did not receive any response from the police to that request. We did receive a response from NIA, indicating they did indeed have such recordings of McCarthy's telephone.'

Hofmeyr and Mzinyathi obtained formal permission to listen to the NIA's set of recordings of McCarthy's phone and inquired whether they were lawfully obtained. 'They indicated that as part of an investigation they were conducting after the leaking of the Browse Mole report ... they had obtained an interception order over McCarthy and other people involved in the production of that report.' The NIA gave Hofmeyr and Mzinyathi access to very specific records of interceptions.

When asked how the NIA recordings differed from those Hulley had, Hofmeyr said: 'They had all the recordings we had listened to as well as additional recordings; large numbers we listened to. The one recording they did not have was the one between Mr Davids and Mr McCarthy. They only had recordings of Mr McCarthy's one cellphone and he had more than one cellphone.'

The SAPS never responded to the NPA's request for access to the recordings that were probably given by them to Zuma's team. 'It was in the context of the investigation of Mr Selebi at the time ... I and many exco members of the NPA were involved [in the Selebi investigation] and we did not expect to receive cooperation. The relationship was very strained between the NPA and the SAPS at top levels,' Hofmeyr testified. Hulley, too, was 'unwilling' to give the NPA an electronic copy of his tapes.

Hofmeyr faced a tough time during cross-examination by Davids' lawyer, Advocate Roland Sutherland SC:

> *Sutherland:* When Hulley, who is a private person representing
> a person with a certain agenda, presented you with recordings,
> didn't you subject any of those tapes to any kind of technical

analysis to make sure they themselves are not fabrications?

Hofmeyr: No, we didn't have the tapes in our possession. They told us the format of the tapes made it impossible to be tampered with. We inquired into some detail whether it would be possible to alter or manipulated. But we took it in good faith.

Sutherland: But fabricating material was fashionable at the time?

Hofmeyr: I referred to Browse Mole [as fabricated material], not the recordings.

Sutherland: So you had to take it on good faith how the recordings were made. And you were not sure if interception orders were ever granted?

Hofmeyr: In respect of the NIA tapes, we did see the signed [court] order that was granted. The contents of the tapes were formally declassified by the DG of the NIA. It gave some credence to my belief that it was formally obtained.

On 27 September 2011, Commissioner Ford found that Hofmeyr and the SIU had violated Davids' privacy, and that the recordings – the police tapes played by Hulley to Hofmeyr and Mzinyathi – had been obtained illegally. This was the first time a legal forum had ruled on the legality of the tapes that got Zuma off the hook. Ford threw out the evidence, and the SIU was challenging his ruling in the Labour Court at the time of writing. Davids reacted by questioning Hofmeyr's own political neutrality.[5] Included in the notes Hofmeyr allegedly made of the conversation between Davids and McCarthy was the following remark: 'WH [Hofmeyr] started out saying he hates JZ, now he has walked over to his camp.'

15

The thing about spy tapes is that they don't actually start on one day and end on another. I've accepted the fact that continuous illegal surveillance of telephone conversations is now a common practice in South Africa. We've truly become a spy nation, where rogue intelligence agents run amok, feeding false numbers into the government's interception systems and every second private intelligence operative has the necessary equipment, freely available over the internet, to bug your and my phone conversations. The fact that the government agencies responsible for intelligence gathering are not doing anything about this state of affairs can only mean they are part and parcel of the problem.

So, when Advocate Mokotedi Mpshe stood in front of the nation on 6 April 2009 to announce that a set of spy tapes had landed on his desk, he wasn't talking about a complete set of interceptions, but about a series of conversations that had been carefully selected by someone to influence the outcome of the Zuma case. It's safe to assume that McCarthy's phone was bugged for a much longer period than from 4 November 2007 to 7 April 2008 – the five-month period covered by the spy tapes released by Mpshe.

The two weeks preceding Mpshe's announcement were marked by intense debate inside the NPA about the impact the spy tapes would have on Zuma's case. It was clear that the contents of the tapes would be leaked if the NPA didn't manage the process itself. After months of intellectual debate about a political or legal solution to see Zuma ascend to the throne, the matter came down to this: a set of telephone recordings, possibly obtained illegally. The team of prosecutors and investigators on the Zuma case, led by Advocate Billy Downer, vehemently argued for the prosecution to continue and for a court of law to decide whether the spy tapes fatally infected the prosecution. They were supported by Advocate Wim Trengove SC, who had assisted the team in Zuma's numerous applications against the state. After Zuma was let off the hook, Trengove delivered a scathing speech on Mpshe's decision, saying it may have been the 'tipping point leading to a slippery slope to the erosion of the rule of law'.[1] He said Mpshe's decision was based on peripheral considerations such as 'eleventh-hour shenanigans relating to the timing of the prosecution'.

On the morning of 6 April 2009, Mpshe called a meeting of his deputies – Hofmeyr, Silas Ramaite and Mzinyathi, who was acting in Mpshe's place – and Downer and his team to announce his final decision to them first. Advocate Trish Matzke, a special director in Mpshe's office, also attended the meeting. Mpshe told them he would be withdrawing the charges against Zuma because of the damage that had been done to the case by the spy tapes. Hofmeyr, one of the two officials who had listened to the tapes, was the biggest supporter of Mpshe's decision. Ironically, Mzinyathi, the other prosecutor who had to listen to the recordings, differed strongly from the decision to let Zuma off the hook and supported the argument that it was not for the NPA to make this decision, but for a court.

* * *

The NPA's main auditorium was packed as television cameramen set up their equipment for a mid-morning live broadcast of Mpshe's announcement. Journalists filled the room and anxious prosecutors looked on as Mpshe, followed by his deputies and Downer and his team entered the room and stepped onto the small stage. Their faces were grim, the atmosphere funereal. Mpshe took the microphone:

> I stand before you today to announce the most difficult decision I ever made in my life. It was not an easy task at all. I had the privilege of having listened to inputs and comments of very eminent jurists of the NPA and I am thankful to them for their candid and frank arguments.
>
> It was then, and it still is, difficult for me to comprehend that which is set out below could have happened. The painful facts that I am about to put before you have serious implications for the integrity and independence of the NPA, especially regarding the prosecution of Mr Zuma.

He said that the NPA had to 'expose this conduct' and become more independent and stronger. 'We have come across information about collusion between the former heads of the Directorate of Special Operations [McCarthy] and NPA [Ngcuka] to manipulate the prosecutorial process before and after Polokwane elections. We regarded these allegations as extremely serious and set out to investigate them as fully as possible within the limited time at our disposal.'

Mpshe's mention of 'limited time' was curious. Although the NPA was under no obligation to make a hasty decision, it was two weeks before South Africa's general elections. Was the NPA threatened by Zuma's lieutenants that they would expose the tapes themselves if the NPA didn't do so in 'limited time'?

Mpshe carefully set out the legal grounds that were addressed by Zuma's lawyers in their representations to the NPA:

1. The substantive merits
2. The fair trial defences
3. The practical implications and considerations of continued prosecution
4. The policy aspects militating against prosecution.

He continued: 'I need to state up front that we could not find anything with regard to the first three grounds that militate against a continuation of the prosecution, and I therefore do not intend to deal in depth with those three grounds.' In other words: there were no problems with the merits, fairness or practical implications of Zuma's case. But NPA policy might have been broken, thus 'militating against prosecution'.

Mpshe explained how the tapes fitted into Zuma's representations. 'In the course of the representations, the defence made certain very serious allegations about alleged manipulation of the NPA and indicated that these were substantiated by recordings of certain telephone conversations which it intended handing into court during the intended application for a permanent stay of prosecution.

'The NPA decided that it would listen to these recordings because it felt that the allegations were serious enough to impact on the NPA's decision if they were true. It felt it should do so despite the fact that it was not clear whether the recordings had been intercepted legally or were legally in the possession of the defence.'

This was a significant admission for a lawyer to make: he didn't actually know whether the material he was about to rely on to drop Zuma's charges were the fruits of a poisoned tree or not.

'Although the recordings sounded authentic,' Mpshe said, the NPA approached the relevant authorities to find out if they had legally obtained the same recordings:

> The National Intelligence Agency confirmed to the NPA that
> it indeed had legally obtained recordings of many of the same
> conversations which were obtained during the course of its in-
> vestigation into the circumstances surrounding the production
> and leaking of the Browse Mole report. NIA indicated that it
> was able to share these legally with the NPA for the purposes
> of the investigation and for reaching a decision in this mat-
> ter. Thus the NPA was able to make transcripts of the relevant
> portions of the recordings for this purpose and NIA has declas-
> sified these transcripts as they are not directly relevant to its

own investigation. The NPA is thus confident that its decision is based on information that was intercepted legally and obtained legally by the NPA.

I found it significant that the NIA admitted it knew about McCarthy's conversations with Ngcuka, but didn't independently institute any action against the Scorpions boss. Was the NIA not convinced that McCarthy was abusing his office, or were they only interested in evidence pertaining to the Browse Mole report?

Mpshe revealed that he had been in contact with Ngcuka and McCarthy. Ngcuka was visited by members of the Zuma prosecuting team, and McCarthy declined to respond to questions. Mpshe further requested the Inspector-General of Intelligence to 'formally investigate any possible illegality surrounding the recordings that were presented to it'. The outcome of such a probe, if any, has never been communicated to the South African public.

Mpshe quoted a litany of legal precedent on the task of a prosecutor, including, 'like Caesar's wife, the prosecutor must be above any trace of suspicion'. Was Zuma's prosecution done for an 'ulterior purpose' asked Mpshe. On that day, the NPA also released transcripts of the recordings that informed its decision. Mpshe proceeded to read from them.

The transcripts came with small print: the NPA paraphrased some of the discussion; all parts that were 'relevant' were included; discussions that were 'not relevant as this often deals with personal or other details' were omitted, and the NPA added its own comments to explain issues. The people who featured in the released transcripts were identified as businessman Mzi Khumalo (MK), McCarthy (LM), Ngcuka (BN), Luciano (a private investigator), former Justice minister Brigitte Mabandla (Min), Mbeki (pres) and former deputy SIU head Faiek Davids.

1. Date: 4.11.2007 18h25 – M Khumalo

MK: Urgent need for him to meet LM

LM: Koki won't arrest someone before we meet, then its ok

Arrange to meet on Wednesday afternoon, or have a dinner at 19h00

2. Date: 7.11.2007 10h25 – BN

LM: To come back to the thing we discussed on Sat, this matter is now up in the courts tomorrow

BN: not Monday

LM: The second thing is, I, remembering what you said on Saturday, I read yesterday's Business Day editorial, you must just read it

BN: Just remind me

LM: Yes, it's in line with your thinking

BN: Laughs

LM: I am serious

LM: The third issue is, I met with the guy I mentioned, and you know his line is almost like that of Sam

BN: [laughs]

LM: But he said he will. He says he will speak to the man but he is back over the weekend, but he knew, he feels very strongly that I should not see the guy directly

LM: So that he has a shield, so that if this issue comes up then he can say 'I don't know what the fuck you are talking about'

BN: Have you read the Business Day today

LM: No I haven't

BN: It's on that line, it says, I said, it says he knew about my statement beforehand

LM: Is it?

Apparent reference to the enclosed *Business Day* editorial of 6.11.07. The editorial is of the view that it appears to benefit Mr Mbeki when Mr Zuma is not facing charges.

There is regular reference to the need to meet or discuss with 'the man', 'the other fellow' or 'guy' or 'he'. In calls 17, 21, 25, 26, 28 it is clear that it is the President. In most other cases it is not clear who is meant.

Apparent reference to the enclosed *Business Day* article of 7.11.07. It discusses the Gevisser book, which states that Mr Mbeki asked Mr Zuma to resign before the prima facie statement.

BN: I don't know where he got it from but certainly that fellow never spoke to me

...

BN: But it is still long way away (before you go)

LM: The thing is happening in January boss, we even discussed it

Possible reference to LM appointment to World Bank in Jan 08.

BN: Why do you wake me up in the morning for that:

LM: no, no, the main thing is really my meeting with the other guy and what came out of it and the fact that this judgement is on us much quicker than what I thought, and I really I need to make a call

Meet with other guy.

LM: because I am told our guy has slipped out in the media saying he wants nothing to do with it

Apparent reference to NDPP stating that it will be decision for the DSO to take.

BN: yes

LM: – your acting ...

BN: I know

BN: you know very interesting there is different points of view across the board

LM: You don't want to join this dinner with Mzi?

BN: No, you will see, his view is completely opposite – he agrees with you. He and Sam agree with you. We had dinner on Sunday, quite a number of people, mine was there, Dlamini? was there

Discussion of timing of charge of Mr Zuma. Khumalo appears to be only one who supports LM in view that it should happen before Polokwane.

I put a hypothetical question to them, let's assume the judgement comes out in next few weeks and it's in favour of those guys, what must happen by when?

Mzi was the only one on that table who said lets do it now, he was the only one

If he tells you the truth he and tells you that, everyone there disagreed with him

3. Date: 7.11.2007 13h23 – BN

LM: I was not sure what wicket we ended ...

LM: I am not sure, did we say

BN: I said when you are done with Mzi, where are you eating

LM: I don't know

BN: He did not tell you where you are eating, are you coming to Johannesburg ...

LM: The other things is, are you now not going to see me as you initially indicated because I remember you said you might want to speak to me

BN: I said I will wait until we hear what this other fellow is saying and then I'll also talk to him, as I said to you

BN: There is not a wrong or right question about this thing here

BN: Nobody actually knows what the presentation is likely to be

LM: Maybe one should look at the aftermath, after 3 days,

BN: Exactly, exactly, let's see what's going to be, but I can tell you know, you know, I can even see his people

I saw the article only now, the one that you referred to

LM: There is also an editorial that I haven't read, try and read last week's, I mean yesterday's

BN: I will try to get it

Continued discussion.

4. Date: 9.11.07 13h55 – BN

LM: do you have Mzi's company name, I offered him a book and bottle of wine, I need his address my guys can't find it

LM: to have it delivered

BN: So therefore …

LM: No, no, we, I am also now studying the judgement you see, like a good coloured

BN: But these guys have already said they are taking the matter up

LM: Ja, But this does not mean that one has to hang up on there, you know, that we,

BN: I agree with you

LM: But I want to just, I am seeing the guys … get a sense of their views, think things over it, this is a legal issue, we will get to the right decision

LM: But nothing will happen in a rush, it is not going to happen that will not be that we tell them on Wed come and appear on Thursday

Discussion of SCA judgement.

5. Date: 26.11.07 20h43 – M Khumalo

MK: Congratulations

LM: There is nothing on our database

MK: I will ask him for the names of the people who came to search here

LM: Try to find out whether it is DSO or police

Assisting Khumalo with information regarding a raid on his businesses premises.

6. Date: 26.11.07 20h43 – BN

LM: I just thought I would check how you are doing

BN: I am not doing very well at all, not very well at all. I am so shocked, trying to work

Following a discussion about ANC provincial nomination conferences.

on it, it's the shock. I need time to work on it, just been shocked, just been shocked, shocked ...

BN: All the other stuff went the way we talked about it, remember I said we probably get 5 – we got all the 4 we said we were going to get. And, but the way we lost in the provinces where we were going to lose – still even now I can't explain, I don't understand it, I can't find that there are only 9 people in the whole province of Natal ...

BN: [discusses results] ... It is not natural to have such huge majorities in a province ... that one is not normal ...

LM: There is something wrong there – and also, that is my first reaction, it is actually two fold. It is either that the one side deliberately is obfuscating the issue, no go and vote and the real picture will emerge at the conference or these guys cooked the books ...

BN: In Natal I mean the comrades did say to them look guys vote for this guy know on the first round, don't show your hand because these guys might basically disqualify you from attending the conference ...

BN: So you the only one who can just save this country from its madness

LM: hmm

BN: You know

BN: I just can't believe it, I really can't believe it, I don't know, so we also busy now

LM: Hmm

BN: And a

Following a discussion about ANC provincial nomination conferences, LM is the only one who can save the country.

LM: And what does the big man say, is he oraait,

BN: I don't know,

BN: I want to, I will try to call him later tonight, he is in a meeting the whole day, at Shell house of all places [laughs] …

BN: I am not doing well, I am now going to compete with you for that job at the WB …

LM: I did what you said I should do, I must say

BN: you did right, right thing

LM: up until Friday, I received a strong memorandum to say charge and charge now –

BN: Friday

LM: No this Friday, the team says we have been fucking around with this thing, we are allowing ulterior considerations to come in, it will become an impossibility later – we now must take action and deal with 'finish and klaar' as Jackie Selebi says, but we will talk when I see you

Appears as if BN requested that LM obtain the view of the team to bolster the argument that charges should be brought before Polokwane (in case it was needed).

7. Date: 6.12.07 11h07 – BN

BN: I am in Kimberley, do you have contacts here

LM: only [mentions 2 names]

BN: I am thinking which delegates I can go and see, who can take me to delegates

LM: I don't have sufficient contacts, the one guy who might be a contact we are on verge of charging

BN requests LM to identify potential ANC conference delegates in Kimberley to be lobbied.

8. Date: 12.12.07 Wednesday 10h15 – SMS exchange BN & LM

BN: When are you filing

LM: We're stretched. It has tripled in size now. Likely to file tomorrow afternoon or Friday afternoon only. What up!

BN: The sooner the better. Not later than tomorrow. It will assist a great deal

Refers to the NPA's reply to Mr Zuma's application for leave to appeal to the Con Court in the search warrant matter. It was due on 14 Dec.

9. Date: Wednesday 12.12.07 10h41 – BN

...

LM: We must have one of those Yengeni nights – remember we said we will not leave this fucking hotel until its done

BN: If this thing comes out the way we discussed it yesterday, those key issues, right it will be a devastating one for them, and it will cause people to wake up to know what they are actually doing without being dramatic, without you making arrests, it will say, this is what we have this is what we have, and we are forced to state it now and people will wake up think what are we doing

LM: Friday, by Friday people are packing bags, they won't even read the fucking newspapers

BN: That is the thing, that is the thing, that is why it will be good if it could come out today [ie Wednesday]

LM: Today is difficult, I will call a Yengeni night, we are not leaving here until we finalise this tomorrow morning, we file by lunch time and give it to the media,

BN: You made my day

The reference is to a meeting with Mr Yengeni's lawyers that lasted late into the night.

This is a discussion about the need to file the Con Court papers earlier so that it can be reported in the newspapers before the delegates leave for Polokwane.

10. Date: Thursday cell 13.12.07 12h20 – BN

LM: What is the mood like?

BN: Is it out?

LM: no no, I am just checking the pulse of securities

LM: You know, I thought I will give call you once a day, twice a day to hear whether the position has not changed. That thing will only be filed tomorrow ... I can only get so much out of these guys, we only worked to 10 past 11. The kid wants to go on leave, Trengove is on leave and wants to see it as he has to argue it in court. So we will probably only file tomorrow at about 12h50, we have a date for 10 to 1

BN: how does it look

LM: its ugly, you need someone who can nit-pick and read through all that shit of 212 pages, and look at para 79 ...

BN: Can you deliver a draft to my place?

BN: I will be in Johannesburg

LM: I will get, I will rather come myself, I don't want to take changes

BN: No I will be late tonight,

LM: I will wait for you, or see you first thing in morning. I don't want intermediaries here,

BN: ok, your right,

LM: Zuma will say we are conspiring against him

LM: can I ask, the script has not changed yet,

BN: Ya, no

LM: because [do/don't] feel like going to Polokwane and charging him there

Cont discussion about the need to file Con Court papers earlier.

The **position** or **script** are apparent references to whether Mr Zuma should be charged before or after Polokwane.

LM undertakes to deliver a draft of the Con Court papers to BN personally to avoid it becoming known.

It is unclear whether he says he 'do' or 'don't' want to do this.

LM: But listen, I think you guys must just keep your heads open about the 'when' factor because I mean we will file our docs tomorrow, we will, Mpshe is going on leave tomorrow and I am acting.

LM: We will have our section 2e order and our, our … we will have finalised the processing of the decision

BN: As long as you don't do it this weekend

LM: If we hold it back, it will be because the clever people like you and others are saying to us that the country needs cool heads but I would hate to have be seen to be wrong later

BN: just don't do it this weekend

LM: it might change

BN: I can't keep an open mind, you can't do it this weekend, our minds won't change

[The exchange is repeated several times]

BN: Just don't do it this weekend

LM: I won't move this weekend, if this change, just let us know

BN: it won't change

The when factor is an apparent reference to whether Mr Zuma should be charged before or after Polokwane.

The 's2(e) order' is a reference to the need for the NDPP to authorise all racketeering prosecutions.

BN makes it clear that they do not want Mr Zuma to be charged before Polokwane despite the fact that everything is in place to do so.

11. Date: 14 Dec 07 10h32 – Min of Justice

LM briefs the Minister of Justice regarding the filing of papers in the Constitutional Court

12. Date: Friday 14.12.07 10h53 – BN

LM: are you in position where I can drop something off or send someone to drop something off

BN: drop it at home, not there yet

LM: the one thing is a 8 pager, which you

LM prepares and sends a short summary of key issues that are newsworthy to BN for apparent distribution to the media.

should read because it deals with whatever is new. The rest is just same shit we have heard for the last 3 years ...

LM: I want to get this to you, I can't leave it in envelope with drivers and things it is too risky. My guy can drive to where you are and give it to you

BN: it's not possible, in East London

LM: Can also fax it to you,

BN: I will give you a fax no

LM: You must physically stand there and wait for it

13. Date: Friday 14.12.07 12h03 SMS – BN
BN: The fax number is 040 653 2223. Thanks

14. Date: Friday 14.12.07 12h32 SMS – BN
BN: I am standing next to the fax machine. Hope you won't forget me.

15. Date: Friday 14.12.07 12h43 SMS – BN to LM
BN at 12h43: Got it. Thank you very much
LM at 12h56: Hold onto it for a while, until ...

16. Date: Friday 14.12.07 13h08 – BN
LM: I just wanted to say its been filed, I am told you can show it even to the guy on the beachfront
LM: It is in court, anyone can access it – I just got an sms, it was filed 3 min ago

LM informs BN that papers have been filed and can be distributed.

117

17. Date: 16.12.07 15h13 – BN

BN: am back, I need to chat to you,

BN: we must chat, ne

LM: ja

BN: I had a chat with this fellow, he's going to call you immediately after conference. I met him yesterday, I need to chat to you about it ...

Apparent arrangement to meet the President .

18. Date: 16.12.07 – SMS exchange between Luciano and LM

LM: cats look defeated

LM: I have been advised to give Ouboet & Oujan a break in the interest of SA ... Tenous times. QV?

L: O Tempores a mores! Cui Bono? Primus Salus Pro Familia McCarthy et facimus novae vitae.

LM: Don't have a dictionary, Meaning ...?

L: Tell you when I see you next wk for delivery of Christmas presents

LM: Too Late

L: Who is asking you?

LM: High Power, can't disclose. Gov in power. Undertaking.

L: What did Jesus say? Give to the emperor what is due to him and to the church what is due to her. You serve at the pleasure of the emperor. Any other choice wld mean not serving at the pleasure of the emperor

LM: I hear you emperor sir. They're asking for a review. What

L: Primus salus amicus et familia. That's the motto

LM: Yea. Threatening to expose no. 1

As far as can be established, Luciano is a private intelligence operative.

Ouboet is Mr Selebi. Oujan is probably Mr Zuma.

The Christmas present appears to be information of some kind that is required.

Presumably a review of the cases.

118

L: Approach hold even if Lume looses [sic]

'Lume' is nickname for Mr Mngwengwe, the Investigating Director of the DSO.

19. Date: 17.12.07 – SMS exchange between Luciano and LM

L: Thought over night – 1. Recommend we help you find 2 sympathetic and credible international lawyers that can join each of the 2 reviews.

2. International component important for SA's reputation and your own. If carefully selected will support objective.

3. In ouboet's case need international component to deal decisively with o sullivan factor. Matter also high profile given K allegations, media interest and focus on crime in lead up to 2010.

4. Iro Oujan recommend a comprehensive review is done of ALL MLA and prosecution cases are done flowing from arms deal not just his by review panel with international lawyers as you originally recommended. cont

5. You can then deal with oujan in context of broader review.

6. If you are going to do this in interest of SA recommended you request

6.1 You submit review report to Special Committee of 4 ministers justice, intel, foreign affairs and safety and security. Do not take sole responsibility. Yr current line management structure will result in sole responsibility.

6.2 Recommend you come to clear agreement about SAG support for the next phase of yr career including a date.

Proposal for what appears to be a further review panel for the Selebi (and Zuma) matters.
The Selebi review panel had concluded its work at the end of November 2007.

K is probably Kebble.

SAG = SA Government?
The review panels appear to be linked to the future World Bank position.

119

6.3 You are going to need resources incl special budget because above all the media will have to be managed locally and globally. End.

20. Date: 17.12.07 – SMS exchange between Luciano and LM

Thank you Captain. I'll digest. Will see what happens tomorrow. We'll talk when you're here. Keep Well. Luciano

21. Date: 17.12.07 19h41 – BN

...

BN: We do need to chat, but this one is going to call you when he gets back before he leaves for Christmas

Appears to confirm meeting with the President.

22. Date: 18.12.07 22h10 – Mzi Khumalo

MK: Welcome back, this is a bad day for the whole country
LM: I am shocked ...
LM: I was given all these assurances, that scores are being made up, that the backlog is being worked away, that the guys are confident. ...
MK: Very early in the year, we must now sit and talk seriously about what we are going to do.
LM: Hmm ...
LM: Did you get wine and book I sent you
...
LM: Lets be merry, fest off and we will live to regroup another day, lets wipe the blood off our faces. Hey, I feel bad about it, my wife says to me you look like you lost your

Discussion with Khumalo, including the need to regroup after result of the election of the ANC president was announced.

mother, I don't feel good about it

23. Date: 19.12.07 12h26 – SMS BN to LM

BN: From now onwards you are on your own. It is imperative that you finalise your future plans pronto.

LM: sorry

Thanks, it's a sad day for our country

The morning after result of the election of the ANC president was announced.

24. Date 19.12.07 12h26 – BN

LM: how are things going, are things ok

BN: how can you ask that question, you know the agenda, you are a lawyer

BN: what can they do, I don't work for them, there are 2 things they can do to me

BN: Firstly, they can harass and detain me day in and day out – have been through those things with the previous regime ...

BN: No 2, I am not ashamed of the things I did, will stand my ground and fight them back ...

BN: and secondly, I don't think they want to do anything to me, they don't want to, they needed me, you know, they were campaigning on this ticket, of being a victim, that there was a conspiracy hatched by Mbeki and they used me to implement that. For which he compensated me by giving my wife Zuma's job ...

BN: What I meant about my message to you was, it is important that you sort out where you are going, immediately. And I think that the sooner you get out of that place, the better for you. Let them sort out their mess, this is not your responsibility, they want to sort

Discuss outcome of Polokwane and possible harassment of BN.

Refers to SMS above and to protect LM for the future.

out the mess, let them sort it out themselves

BN: There is nobody who will be covering your back, you are exposed completely, and I don't think you deserve that

LM: I am still shocked, I must say this …

BN: I am not worried about myself, they can try to harass me …

LM: you are saying I should leave this decision and let other people deal with it because

BN: I never said that, I never said that, I am just talking about you, knowing where you are going, and securing that immediately. I am just talking about you, not talking about your work. I am talking about you as a person, your work is your work, you deal with it, but your person, I don't think you must find … I can afford, am independent, I don't do business with government

LM: No orrait, we will see how things, I mean is the government going to do anything. Is the government going to hustle together or carry on with their lives over Christmas …

BN: won't see anything till mid January, people will rest now and see how things pan out

Made clear that LM must still continue to take the decision on Mr Zuma.

25. Date: Wednesday 19.12.07 16h06 – BN
BN: Hi

LM: I say we want to move on Friday

BN: ok

LM: We have become so accustomed to checking with everyone whether they think it is fine … and we have a minister who … is going on holiday

Probably Friday, 21 Dec.

LM: I don't know if that other call you referred to will ever come, these guys are still humiliated

LM: The longer we delay, the worse it becomes, we make it impossible for ourselves to proceed. If the guy wants us to meet and um … and just do it

BN: Ja

Possible reference to
meeting with President.

26. Date: 19.12.07 18h41 – Minister of Justice, President

Min: There is no any emergency or anything?

LM: there are things I need to discuss some things, including the Zuma case but it will be difficult to see you before 8th. But I need to see you, even if just for an hour

Discussion with Minister and
President regarding meeting.

Min: Under pressure here under Jackie's matter, how did it go to media now, that you have given the Minister a report, we have taken a decision

LM: Said to Tlali to try and keep this quiet … Don't know where Willie stands on this, but it is clear to me that this things have now shifted that we are not going to brief the Minister on anything. We have already taken decision

Min: Not thanks Leonard [phone is handed to President]

Pres: er, advocate, how are you?

LM: I am well, I am well, thank you

Pres: Do you know who is speaking?

LM: it sounds like the President?

Pres: Yes

LM: How are you President?

Pres: You have to choose Leonard now

whether you say former President or
President
LM: You will always be my president, you
will always be my president
Pres: Leonard, I wanted to just to say that
Minister told me some time back you had
asked to see me,
LM: yes
Pres: and indeed I had agreed, but then I,
you know, and I, you will have seen my busy-
ness, I get so busy up and down and so on
LM: ja
Pres: She reminded me about this, and I
said to her no, as soon as come back from
here, before I disappear on some short holi-
day, ok I will try and sort it out
Pres: I should be able to call you back on Fri
LM: I will be here
[phone is handed back to Minister]

27. Date: 20.12.07 – SMS LM and Luciano
L: what time would be good for me to bring
Christmas presents tomorrow morning?
LM: Court Classique [gives address]
L: I will be there. See you at 9. Thanks

Delivery of
'Christmas presents'.

28. Date: about 24.12.07 11h49 –
Voicemail to F Davids
LM: Davids, uh, McCarthy here, give me a
ring please, you send me 'n gevaarlike sms
here just before Christmas. I am Thabo man,
I mean we are still wiping the blood from
our faces, or egg, or egg and blood from our
faces. Saw the man on Friday evening, we
planning a comeback strategy. And once

Allegiance to Mr Mbeki,
confirm that they met,
and 'we' are planning a
comeback strategy.

we have achieved that, we will clean up all around us my friend. Bye

29. Date: 29.12.07 – Minister of Justice
LM: Since I spoke to you in Cape Town about my own intentions for the future, I met the President and wanted to give you feedback
Min: 2 things, the one: umm, the heat is on
Min: I did ask Mpshe, Because you know, you sit in the NEC, I said to Mpshe, there is no ways people will accept as fair if you guys go on to prosecute sooner, not like immediately, but sooner, otherwise they will read conspiracy, and really the situation is bad …
Min: And that is why they are pushing German thing, they are saying that here is dirty linen and there is other dirty linen in the cupboard– we must not think that these things will not come up later
Min: I said to Mpshe, Mpshe, why, he then said Billy and them are pressing for sooner, and said that they are angry about the slight delay
LM: No that was me
Min: I then said to him, why you objectively as prosecutors can't approach the JP and say this thing is going to take place and say this is a priority thing and what
Min: So No 1 phoned me this afternoon and say how do you charge now, appear in court starting in August?, because it is further on, you know what I mean.
LM: ya
Min: I said no, I did say to no … it is prudent

Internally, it appears that the decision was made on 21 Dec, the same date LM met with the President.

125

to go the route of you know should be no real big gap

LM: Let me explain to Min what happened, Firstly we took the decision on technically already on the 19th, there was a slight defect in the charge sheet which caused it to have it re-signed on the 24th.

We then could not hold of them, could not get sense of where they are and how we serve on them. We then looked at law, the law says we at the official address of the person, we could not do it on 27th and then did on 28th

Hulley would not answer the phone

The decision was taken on the 19th, but then there was a technical defect and the sheriff wanted more copies and then there were small mistakes that Tanda made and I got him to sign again on the 24th.

We tried to get Hulley on the day to arrange a date, but he would not pick up the phone.

We then we went to the JP's office, the registrar informed us that the first semester was already fully booked. That is why it was set down for August.

30. Date: 9.1.08

LM: Can we speak on this line, is it prudent to speak on the phone

In Feb 2008 LM receives a copy of an intercept of a call from his cell phone (recently published in a court case).

31. Date: 10.1.08

LM: Can we speak on this line

32. Date: 3.4.08

Discusses the fact that he had been ap-

World Bank position.

proached by World Bank and offered the
position

33. Date: 7.4.08

BN: They are going to release you, that's in
December, they have known that

Discuss that the President
and Minister will release
him for World Bank.

Mpshe said it was against the broad principle of 'abuse of process'
that McCarthy's conduct should be tested. 'The question for close
consideration is encapsulated in expressions such as "so gravely
wrong", "gross neglect of the elementary principles of fairness", "so
unfair and wrong", "misusing or manipulating the process of the
court". If the conduct can be so categorised, it would be unconscionable for the trial to continue.'

The following was clear from the released transcripts:

- That McCarthy was discussing the timing of recharging Zuma in
  relation to the ANC's Polokwane conference with outsiders like
  Ngcuka, Khumalo and a private investigator known as 'Luciano';
- That McCarthy was an Mbeki loyalist and was distraught about his
  defeat at Polokwane;
- That a private investigator had discussions with McCarthy about
  possible legal decisions he had to make in the future;
- That McCarthy was in direct contact with his political head,
  Brigitte Mabandla, about certain prosecutorial decisions; and
- The so-called conspirators had vastly different views about when
  Zuma should be recharged.

Said Mpshe: 'Using one's sense of justice and propriety as a yard-
stick by which McCarthy's abuse of the process is measured, an in-
tolerable abuse has occurred which compels a discontinuation of the
prosecution.' According to him, discussing the timing of bringing

charges against Zuma that were not linked to a 'legitimate purpose' amounted to an abuse of process. 'Mr McCarthy used the legal process for a purpose outside and extraneous to the prosecution itself. Even if the prosecution itself as conducted by the prosecution team is not tainted, the fact that Mr McCarthy, who was head of the DSO, and was in charge of the matter at all times and managed it almost on a daily basis, manipulated the legal process for purposes outside and extraneous to the prosecution itself. It is not so much the prosecution itself that is tainted, but the legal process itself.'

Mpshe repeated this point a number of times: although the prosecution of Zuma was not tainted, McCarthy's use thereof for other (political) purposes was a 'serious abuse of process and offends one's sense of justice'. Therefore, Mpshe said, it would be 'unfair as well as unjust' to continue with the prosecution. 'I have come to the difficult conclusion that it is neither possible nor desirable for the NPA to continue with the prosecution of Mr Zuma.'

Mpshe praised Billy Downer and his team for their professionalism and said they were not implicated in McCarthy's misconduct. He also indicated that they had recommended that the prosecution should continue 'even if the allegations are true, and that it should be left to a court of law to decide whether to stop the prosecution'. But he (and Hofmeyr) overruled this view because the NPA's conduct should at all times be beyond reproach. Mpshe said that he felt 'personally wronged and betrayed that on a number of occasions I have given evidence under oath that there has not been any meddling or manipulation of the process in this matter. It is with a great regret that I have to say today that in relation to this case I can not see my way clear to go to court in future and give the nation this assurance.'

During question time, I asked Mpshe whether he, as the person who ultimately had decided that Zuma should be recharged after the Polokwane conference, was affected or influenced by McCarthy's 'abuse of process'; in other words, whether their 'meddling or manipulation' had any effect on Zuma's case or prejudiced him in any way. Absolutely not, Mpshe said.

Mpshe ended by saying that a 'full and proper investigation' must be conducted by a judge or independent person into abuse at the NPA to make recommendations about any further actions to be taken, 'whether of disciplinary or criminal nature ... to ensure that such abuses never occur again'. More than three years later, such an investigation has still to be instituted.

And so Zuma was off the hook to fight the April 2009 elections as a free man, not because the case against him fell flat, but because McCarthy thought he could also use the timing of charges to score Brownie points with his political masters. And although, on Mpshe's own version, the Scorpions boss's discussions with Ngcuka, Khumalo, Luciano and Mabandla did not prejudice Zuma or have any real effect on the timing of his charges, it was enough to enable him to withdraw the charges. 'Remember that Zuma's people were telling the NPA there would be war if the case continued,' officials with close knowledge of Mpshe's decision told me afterwards. 'This [the spy tapes] was manna from heaven for him.'

With the dropping of the charges against Zuma, many of the key players moved off the stage. The careers of others blossomed under the Zuma presidency:

- McCarthy joined the World Bank as Vice-President for Integrity in June 2008. He has never returned to South Africa.
- In July 2009, Mdluli became head of crime intelligence after being interviewed by four of Zuma's Cabinet ministers. In June 2012, he was suspended from the police for alleged fraud and corruption.
- In October 2009, Zuma appointed Moe Shaik as head of the South African Secret Service. Shaik resigned in 2012 after falling out with State Security minister Siyabonga Cwele and became head of the Development Bank of South Africa's international division in August 2012.
- In November 2009, Zuma replaced Mpshe with Advocate Menzi Simelane, who in December 2011 was found to be unfit for his position.
- In February 2010, Jeff Radebe, the Justice minister, appointed

Mpshe as an acting judge in the North West. After that he was moved to the land claims court in Randburg.

- Zuma appointed Jiba as a Deputy National Director of Public Prosecutions in January 2010 and as acting head of the NPA in December 2011.
- In November 2011, Zuma appointed Hulley as his second legal adviser in the Presidency.
- Zuma fired Hofmeyr as head of the SIU in November 2011, leaving him with responsibility for the AFU only.
- In December 2011, Zuma appointed Heath as head of the SIU. After 17 days, Heath resigned from the position.
- By the end of 2012, the Democratic Alliance was still waiting for more transcripts of all the spy tapes the NPA received from the NIA. The DA had won a court case to take Mpshe's decision on review.

On 2 July 2010, the South Gauteng High Court convicted Jackie Selebi of corruption. Zuma issued no response. The ANC commented: 'The conclusion of the case today ... clearly indicates that South Africa as a country is governed by laws that are applied without any fear or favour to anyone, regardless of their standing. The ANC is of the view that the law has taken its course and again as part of the South African community, we reiterate our confidence in our judicial system. As we celebrate the successful, memorable and the first hosting of the FIFA World Cup in our country, we can indeed also be proud that our judicial system can stand amongst the best in the world.'

Part 2

Bad judgement

Julius

'This democracy is not a democracy of families. This is a democracy of the people of this country. We cannot sit back while families enrich themselves in the name of freedom.'

16

The harshest criticism that has been levelled against Jacob Zuma
came down to one thing: bad judgement. Whether it was his decision
to have unprotected sex (again) with another woman much younger
than him; his homophobic statements in September 2006 that when
he was growing up he would 'knock out' an '*unqingili*' (gay person)
who stood in front of him (Zuma had to apologise for this); his ill-
fated appointment of Advocate Menzi Simelane as head of the NPA
or his protection of Lieutenant General Richard Mdluli against
serious criminal charges, Zuma's bad judgement has unfortunately
clouded the good things he has done.

'We always knew JZ had fundamental weaknesses,' says one of
the president's former allies, who no longer trusts him to lead the
ANC or South Africa. Zuma's bad judgement will be his undoing,
the person says. 'Did Zuma know it was wrong to take a bribe from
Schabir? He doesn't understand corruption. Up to now he will justify
taking money from Schabir. Also with the women; he doesn't think
it was wrong to make all those babies.'

This is a startling thought: that the president of our country does
not understand corruption; that he thinks there was nothing wrong
with letting Schabir Shaik fund his lifestyle while he promoted
Shaik's business interests on the side; and that Zuma, once the head

of the National Aids Council, thought it was okay to continue to have
unprotected sex, even after his public apology to the nation for doing
so following his infamous 2006 rape trial.

*   *   *

The appointment of tainted, compromised or controversial people
into key positions marked Zuma's first term in office: Menzi Simelane,
Bheki Cele, Richard Mdluli, Willem Heath and Nomgcobo Jiba to
name a few. And his unwillingness to act swiftly against allies implicated in wrongdoing or mismanagement showed that he valued
loyalty above good governance. Take Basic Education minister Angie
Motshekga and Free State premier Ace Magashule; both are examples of Zuma supporters who have been spared the president's wrath
because of their strategic importance to him.

*   *   *

By the third quarter of 2012, thousands of schoolchildren in
Limpopo, one of South Africa's poorest provinces, had not yet
received their textbooks for the year. A sad story of corruption,
mismanagement and incompetence started to emerge. What did
Zuma do? He appointed task team after task team to investigate
the situation in the province. Motshekga's hand was eventually
forced by an NGO, Section27, which successfully brought a court
application against her that ordered the minister to do her job and
supply textbooks to the learners. Still, Motshekga's department,
which had taken over the administration of education in Limpopo
in December 2011, didn't comply with the rule and letter of the order, and by October 2012 not all children in Limpopo had received
their textbooks.

Was this enough to justify firing Motshekga? No. As president
of the ANC Women's League and an influential power broker in

the Gauteng ANC, she was too valuable to Zuma in the run-up to Mangaung. So the children continued to suffer.

* * *

In June 2009, Ace Magashule was implicated in a bribery scandal, involving a gambling licence, Zuma's friend Vivian Reddy and R3 million. At the time I was working for the *Mail & Guardian*, and we revealed that businessman Bongani Biyela was taking Magashule to court for blocking a business transaction worth about R1 billion. All provincial gambling boards are authorised to approve or decline changes of ownership of casinos located in their respective provinces. So, when Biyela and his partners wanted to sell their stake in Gold Reef Resorts, which owns the Goldfields Casino in Welkom, Magashule prevented his provincial gambling board from approving the transaction. His motivation became clear: proxies claiming to represent Magashule wanted a bribe. Reddy stepped in because of his 'closeness' to Magashule, and a series of events involving chartered jets, meetings at the Shell Ultra City in Kroonstad and tense negotiations in a luxury car parked in front of Magashule's office culminated in Biyela being asked for a R3 million bribe. Biyela refused to pay the bribe and turned to the courts, which ordered Magashule to approve the casino transaction.

Magashule and Reddy denied they had acted corruptly, but only Biyela's version was made under oath. Nothing happened: no investigation, prosecution or even query whether a premier and the president's friend were soliciting a bribe.

Magashule, with Zuma's support, has ruled the Free State with an iron fist. During his term, he controversially invented something called Operation Hlasela, which he used to dish out houses, food and other basic services to residents when he addressed rallies. Although it was also funded with government money, Magashule said Hlasela was like an NGO. Opposition parties complained that Operation Hlasela was not properly audited, and in November 2011 Public

Protector Thuli Madonsela registered an official investigation into Magashule's bizarre project.

Did he get into trouble for any of this? No. Magashule has remained one of Zuma's staunchest allies, and the Free State is clear on its support for a second term for the president.

17

When Jacob Zuma became president of the ANC in December 2007, he was not a rich man. It was clear from the forensic analysis submitted in the Shaik trial that Zuma effectively relied on Shaik to sponsor large parts of his lifestyle, including holidays, education and leisure expenses for his ever-expanding family. With Shaik in prison (for a little while, at least), Zuma had to find new ways of supporting himself and his family.

Over the next five years, Zuma's extended family would become much more active in business, their profiles boosted by their proximity to power. And so the term Zuma Economic Empowerment, or ZEE, was born, penned for the first time by David Masondo, a leader of the Young Communist League (YCL).

ZEE had two faces: the president's young son, Duduzane, who almost became a multi-millionaire overnight, and Khulubuse Zuma, the son of the president's brother, Michael. Because of his great bulk, Khulubuse Zuma became the proverbial 'fat cat' of ZEE, scooping up one business deal after another and showing off his flashy Mercedes-Benzes and motorbikes at VIP functions, while his mineworkers at Aurora's mines languished in poverty. Duduzane, on the other hand, remained a shy, almost naive figure with stars in his eyes. But both shot to prominence for the same reason, their meteoric rise in business following the election of their father and uncle as president of the ANC and later South Africa.

* * *

In March 2010, while I was working on the *Mail & Guardian*'s investigations team, we decided to do a thorough audit of Zuma Incorporated – the business interests of the president and his family. A clear picture emerged: following his victory at Polokwane, there had been a massive increase in the number of companies and business interests registered by Zuma spouses and kinfolk. It was a good time to be a Zuma:

> In the week that the presidency confirmed that Jacob Zuma's women and children are costing the taxpayer more than R15 million a year, an investigation by the *Mail & Guardian* suggests they are also bidding for private benefit from their presidential connections ... It gives a disturbing picture of the Zuma family's push into business, especially in the period since Zuma's ascension to the ANC presidency at Polokwane in December 2007. Of the 16 adults – wives, lovers and children – who can be linked to Zuma, 15 are in business, accounting, with Zuma, for 134 company directorships or memberships of close corporations. Only four of these appear to be Section 21 'not for profit' companies. At least 83 companies (62%) have been registered in the post-Polokwane period when Zuma's political future was secured.[1]

Nompumelelo Ntuli, then 33 years old, became Zuma's fourth wife on 8 January 2008, less than a month after he was elected as ANC president at Polokwane. This was the first time Zuma had tied the knot since the suicide of his third wife, Kate Mantsho, in 2000. Mantsho had had five children with Zuma, including Duduzane and his twin sister, Duduzile. In a suicide note left for Reverend Frank

Chikane, Mantsho described her 24-year marriage to Zuma as 'bitter' and 'painful'.[2] Ntuli, or MaNtuli as she became known, was described as a 'housewife' when she married Zuma, but soon started accumulating business interests. In the months following her wedding to Zuma, Ntuli joined seven private companies with interests in logistics, construction and trade. By 2012, MaNtuli had active business interests in ten companies and had established the MaNtuli Zuma J Foundation – a non-profit company. In one of her companies, her fellow directors include gospel star Deborah Fraser, Noluthando Vavi (wife of Cosatu general secretary Zwelinzima Vavi) and Ukhozi FM DJ Dudu Khoza. The company's registered address was a house in Sandton, owned by Zuma benefactor Vivian Reddy.[3]

In January 2010, Zuma married Tobeka Madiba, a 37-year-old cellphone company executive from Durban. At the time, Madiba had interests in five privately registered companies. In March 2012, she acquired four more business interests: three were in private companies co-owned by Dr Mandisa Mokwena, a former SARS deputy commissioner on trial for fraud, money laundering and racketeering. Mokwena and 12 other people, including SARS and Unisa employees, were arrested between 2009 and 2010 for alleged tender fraud at the taxman, where she was head of risk management. The state claims that Mokwena and her co-accused colluded in defrauding SARS of R11 million through dishing out 45 tenders for training and research to pals.[4] One of Mokwena's co-accused was her husband Barnard Mokwena, the executive vice-president for human capital and external affairs at Lonmin, who was also the mining house's spokesperson during the violent strikes of August 2012. The charges against him were dropped. In September 2012, I reported on Madiba's business links to an alleged fraudster. The first lady responded promptly, saying she was unaware of the fraud case when she joined the businesses and was introduced to Mokwena by a third party. She agreed it would 'not be appropriate' for her to be in business with Mokwena, and said Mokwena had proposed to resign from her directorships. At the time of writing, the fraud trial was continuing.

Although Madiba was not implicated in the scam, she became a business partner of Mokwena *after* the latter had been arrested and charged with fraud. They share directorships in Lavender Sky Investments 25 (Pty) Ltd, Vautrade (Pty) Ltd and Glenlyn Investments (Pty) Ltd.

In April 2012, Zuma took his sixth wife when he married Gloria Ngema, who he had been dating for years.

The members of Zuma's family who were affected most by his ascent to power were Edward Zuma, his son with Minah Shongwe; the twins Duduzane and Duduzile; their brother Saady Zuma; and Zuma's nephew, Khulubuse. Between the five of them, they accumulated 89 new business interests since Zuma's Polokwane victory.

Although Edward, Zuma's eldest son, added 27 directorships to his business portfolio, it didn't resolve all his money troubles. In June 2012, the sheriff in Durban seized his BMW X5 and furniture, a fridge, entertainment system and TVs from his home after he failed to settle a R1,5 million bill for the company that arranged his lavish October 2011 game reserve wedding. After his lawyer stepped in and 'arrangements' were made, Edward's belongings were returned.[5]

Khulubuse Zuma added 20 companies to his name after his uncle became leader of the governing party. By far the most controversial of these was Aurora Empowerment System, a mining company that has become synonymous with the words 'looting', 'inhumane' and 'disaster'.

ABOVE Zuma leaves the Pietermaritzburg High Court in September 2006 after appearing on corruption charges.
PHOTO: Felix Dlangamandla / Foto24

LEFT A visitor to the Goodman Gallery in Johannesburg walks past Brett Murray's painting of Zuma, titled *The Spear*.
PHOTO: Leon Sadiki / *City Press*

ANNUAL SALARY
MEDICAL AID
PENSION

SPOUSAL SUPPORT

PRIVATE VEHICLE

FLIGHTS – VIP SQUADRON

FLIGHTS – ADDITIONAL

THE COST OF ZUMA

In August 2012 Gareth van Onselen, a senior analyst with the DA, released a comprehensive study on the cost of President Jacob Zuma and his family to the state for his five years in office.

Because of a lack of transparency and financial statements from the Presidency, Van Onselen was not able to do an exact study. Therefore he took an 'extremely conservative' approach, and the cost in every category represents the 'absolute minimum', Van Onselen said. 'Most likely, the final and ultimately unknowable total will be far, far higher.'

APPROXIMATE **FIVE YEAR TOTAL**

R753 912

1. **Annual Salary**
   [R2 275 802.00 to R2 753 689.00]
   Approx. Five Year Total: R12 315 706.00

2. **Medical Aid**
   [At least R1 300 000 per year]
   Approx. Five Year Total: R6 500 000.00

3. **Pension Payout on Retirement**
   [Approx. R2 753 689.00]
   Approx. Five Year Total: R2 753 689.00

4. **Spousal Support**
   [At least R15 517 500.00 per year]
   Approx. Five Year Total: R77 585 000.00

5. **Private Vehicle**
   [70% of salary – R1 835 792.00, for two vehicles]
   Approx. Five Year Total: R3 671 584.00

6. **Flights – VIP Squadron**
   [An approximate average of:
   R46 838 476.00 per year]
   Approx. Five Year Total: R234 192 383.00

7. **Flights – Additional**
   [R6 331 174.67 plus additional cost of two planes]
   Approx. Five Year Total: R10 000 000.00

8. **Flights – VIP Protection Services**
   [Unknown]

FLIGHTS – HELICOPTERS
FLIGHTS – FERRY FLIGHTS
OVERSEAS ALLOWANCES
HOTELS
OFFICIAL RESIDENCES

PRIVATE RESIDENCES

VIP PROTECTION

EVERY **SECOND** COUNTS

One Year:	R150 782 406.00
One Month:	R12 565 200.00
One Week:	R2 899 622.00
One Day:	R413 102.00
One Hour:	R17 212.00
One Minute:	R287.00

Source: Gareth van Onselen. For the full research visit www.inside-politics.org
* In September 2012, it was revealed that the Department of Public Works had paid R238 million towards security upgrades at Zuma's Nkandla homestead. Van Onselen's total has been adjusted accordingly.

029.0000

9. **Flights – Helicopters**
[At least R14 400 000.00 per year]
Approx. Five Year Total: R72 000 000.00

10. Flights – Ferry Flights
[At R1 333 334.00 per year]
Approx. Five Year Total: R8 166 667.00

11. **Overseas Allowances – President**
[An average of R25 400.00 per year]
Approx. Five year Total: R127 000.00

12. **Overseas Allowances – First Ladies**
[Unknown]

13. **Accommodation – Hotels**
[An average of R420 000.00 per year]
Approx. Five Year Total: R2 100 000.00

14. **Accommodation – Official Residences**
[An average of R5 300 000.00 per year]
Approx. Five Year Total: R26 500 000.00

15. **Accommodation – Private Residences***
[R238 000 000.00] Five Year Total: R238 000 000.00

16. VIP Protection
[An average of at least R12 000 000.00 per year]
Approx. Five Year Total: R60 000 000.00

17. **Legal Costs:** [Unknown]

Wife 1:
Sizakele Khumalo
(no children)

Wife 2:
Nkosazana Dlamini-Zuma (divorced)

Children: 4
1. Msholozi
2. Gugu
3. Thuli
4. Thuthukile

Wife 3:
Kate Mantsho
(died)

Children: 5
5. Mxolisi (Saady)
6. Duduzile
7. Duduzane
8. Phumzile
9. Vusi

Wife 4:
Nompumelelo
Ntuli Zuma

Children: 3
10. Thandisiwe
11. Sinqobile
12. Baby (born 2010)

WIVES

Wife 5:
Tobeka Madiba
Zuma

Children: 1
13. Unknown

Wife 6:
Gloria Ngema
Zuma

Children: 1
14. Sinqumo

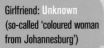

Girlfriend: **Minah Shongwe**

Children: 1
15. Edward

Girlfriend:
**Nonkululeko
Mhlongo**

Children: 2
16. Unknown
17. Unknown

Girlfriend: Unknown
(so-called 'coloured woman
from Johannesburg')

Children: 3
18. Unknown girl (lives
with Madiba Zuma)
19. Unknown
20. Unknown

THE ZUMA FAMILY
GIRLFRIENDS

A **BUSY** HUSBAND, BOYFRIEND AND FATHER

Wives:	6
Girlfriends:	4
Children:	21

Sources: *Mail & Guardian, City Press*
** These are Zuma's only known children, but
sources close to him say there may be many more.

Girlfriend:
Sonono Khoza

Children: 1
21. Unknown

1. Michigan Investments
(sole director)

2. Masibambisane Rural Development Initiative (chairperson)

5. Nompumelelo Ntuli Zuma (wife)

Wamuhle Construction

Vuna Imbewu

Intsika Yembokodo Development Projects

Unompumelelo Trading and Projects

Heavenly Promise 85

Bhekisisa Abantu

Mantuli Zuma J Foundation

Mantuli Foundation

6. Tobeka Madiba Zuma (wife)

Cherry Moss Trade and Invest 176

Lavender Sky Investments 25

Vautrade

Glenlyn Investments

Tobeka Madiba Zuma Foundation

RED: Joined company after Zuma was elected ANC president in December 2007

9. Edward Zuma (son)

Silvex 556

Isthebe Construction & Engineering

Southeast Network Construction SA

SA Guiding Star Trading

Nippon Import Export SA

Isthebe Petroleum

Isthebe Oil and Gas

Isthebe Foods

Dumaka Alternative Technology

Ocean Crest Trading 51

Khumusi Trading Enterprise

Izichwe Investment Holdings

Masikhuza

10. Gugulethu Zuma (daughter)

Born Free Investments 660

Nyenyedzi Productions

Vukani Africa Events and Training

14. Duduzile Zuma-Sambudla (daughter)

Alkara 350

Attractive Move Invest

DUZI Investment Holdings

13. Mxolisi (Saady) Zuma (son)

Myriad Brokers

Unogwaja Investments

Quandolor Investments

Tekwini Inkunzi Investment

Corpclo 2790

National Pride Trading 259

ZUMA INCORPORATED

THESE BUSINESS ENTITIES ARE **LINKED DIRECTLY** TO ZUMA OR INDIRECTLY THROUGH HIS WIVES, CHILDREN AND FAMILY.

Source: Company and Intellectual Property Commission (as at 26 September 2012)

3. Jacob Zuma Foundation

4. Jacob G Zuma RDP Education Trust

GREEN: Joined company after Zuma was elected president of South Africa in May 2009

7. Nonkululeko Mhlongo
(girlfriend)

Bambanani Micro Business Network

Imvusa Trading 582

Bucebo General Trading

Owabantu Logistics and Construction

Black Target Investments

Dobson Investments

Leading Role Trading and Projects

Mthunzy Holdings

8. Sonono Khoza
(girlfriend)

Amahle Management Services

Tes Projects Management

Flysawise

Imifula Development Corporation

Iningi Investments 190

Mayisane Investments

The Zodwa Khoza Foundation

Fire Raiders

11. Nokuthula Zuma
(daughter)

Born Free Investments 660

Nyenyedzi Productions

Aspigon 98

Spectacular Real Productions

12. Thuthukile Zuma
(daughter)

Born Free Investments 660

16. Khulubuse Zuma
(nephew)

Unigame

Impinda Transport

Dartingo Trading 191

Royal HTM Group

Aurora Empowerment System

Cyndara 92

Elatirex

Izichwe Investment Holdings

Labat Africa

Meziblox

Relibex

Sanchopath

Sanchophase

15. Duduzane Zuma
(son)

Mabengela Investments

Westdawn Investments

Gemini Moon Trading 254

Karibu Hospitality

Afripalm Horizons

CRCC Afripalm Construction

Dunrose Investments 180

Islandsite Investments 255

Sahara Holdings

Shiva Uranium

ABOVE Zuma and Julius Malema share a joke during an ANC Youth League rally in Stellenbosch in October 2010. PHOTO: Felix Dlangamandla / Foto24

ABOVE On 16 August 2012, the police shot dead 34 striking miners at Marikana in North West, the bloodiest day in post-apartheid South African history. Malema blamed Zuma for the shooting. PHOTO: Leon Sadiki / *City Press*

18

Aurora brought together two of South Africa's political dynasties: the Mandelas and the Zumas. Khulubuse Clive Zuma's fellow directors in the company were Zondwa Zoyisile Gadaffi Mandela, grandson of former president Nelson Mandela, Thulani Ngubane and Jacob Zuma's lawyer, Michael Hulley.

Before his uncle became president of South Africa in 2009, Khulubuse was a stranger to people outside Durban. In the coastal city he was known as a young newspaper seller, taxi owner and, well, nephew of Jacob Zuma. As *Sunday Times* political editor S'Thembiso Msomi wrote in *The Times*: 'Perhaps – as a childhood friend of mine charged the other day – I just can't bring myself to accept that the guy who used to man the newspaper stand from which I often bought my grandfather's copy of *Ilanga* is now swimming in money, while I toil away for a living wage. But, honestly, I have nothing against Khula – as we grew up calling him – and his wealth. It is just that the lightning speed at which he has been snapping up lucrative business deals, especially since his uncle Jacob Zuma became president, suggests that he is benefiting mainly from his proximity to the highest office in the land.'[1]

This has been a common refrain whenever the young Zuma's sudden wealth is discussed: why so fast?

* * *

Zuma grew up in KwaMashu with his businessman father, who sold 'everything from paraffin to coal and newspapers, and owned a laundry besides'.[2] He couldn't afford to study after school, and became his uncle's driver after Zuma returned from exile in 1990, Khulubuse told the *Sunday Times*' Chris Barron in August 2009. 'Watching JZ wheeling and dealing whetted his appetite to go into business himself.'

First Khulubuse tried security guarding, then taxis. This provided him with enough money to 'explore Africa', he told Barron. Zuma toured Nigeria, the Democratic Republic of Congo, Uganda, Tanzania and Mozambique, where he 'developed serious networks'.[3] In 2010, two of Khulubuse's companies, Caprikat and Foxwhelp, were awarded access by the DRC government to search for oil in two mining blocks that were held by British oil group Tullow.[4] Despite the company's objections, Zuma kept his exploration rights and started drilling for oil in 2012.

In 2009, Khulubuse Zuma and Zondwa Mandela started an investment firm, Aurora Empowerment System, that chased after the recently liquidated Pamodzi gold mines. After they bought Pamodzi's Orkney gold mine for R215 million, they went after the mine's Grootvlei operations on the East Rand, for an estimated R390 million.[5] Mandela was managing director and Zuma chairperson.

Aurora was going to be the young Zuma and Mandela's big entry into the competitive South African minerals market. But it only took a few months for the deal to unravel: by early 2010, it was clear they didn't have enough money to turn the Pamodzi mines around, and they began shopping madly for international investors to save the deals. Over the next two years, Aurora turned on the spin: first it was going to be Malaysian investors who would bail them out, then the British, then the Americans and then the Chinese.

In the meanwhile, a humanitarian crisis was unfolding at the two mines. Along with the money, the water dried up, toilets stopped working and miners went to bed hungry. At the entrance to Aurora's Grootvlei mine in Springs, workers spay-painted 'WHY ZUMA?' in big red letters over the official signage.

Beeld's Elise Tempelhoff visited the Grootvlei operation in April 2010 and interviewed the two men who were managing the canteen, before it was closed down: 'Every day Manie and Willem now watch the people from their car and see how they stone doves to death and cook them on open fires. "We also had 17 cats that lived between the workers and were fed from the kitchen. The workers also fed them. Only two are left. The people must get meat, they are desperate",' they told her.

At the time, Khulubuse was flaunting his wealth at parties, including showing off a new R2,5 million gullwing Mercedes-Benz SLS 63 AMG, as well as other additions to his collection of almost 20 luxury cars.

In July 2010, it was reported that Khulubuse had signed a memorandum of understanding with South Korean industrial giant Daewoo to buy 49% of the transport arm of Khulubuse Zuma's Impinda Group.[6] The *Mail & Guardian* revealed that President Jacob Zuma had met Daewoo Shipbuilding and Marine Engineering CEO Nam Sang-Tae on the same day that his nephew's company signed a deal with the company. A Daewoo spokesperson told the company that its deal with Impinda replicated a shipping joint venture Daewoo had with the Nigerian state oil company. 'Asked whether President Zuma had introduced his nephew's company to them, he initially said: "Yes, that's right," but later said he was not sure,' the newspaper reported.

When Khulubuse was asked about a potential conflict of interest, he responded: 'Who am I accountable to? I am accountable to my own future and the future of my children. You are confusing the issue of the meeting with the issue of the deal: they are not connected.'[7]

* * *

Amid reports of asset-stripping, suicide by unpaid workers and underground shootings of illegal miners, the extent of Aurora's plundering of the Pamodzi mines was laid bare by the trade unions in 2011. Solidarity and the National Union of Mineworkers (NUM) cooperated in exposing Aurora's rule. They revealed that, since Aurora had taken over the mines in 2009, 5 300 jobs had been lost, 42 000 people had been impoverished and fragile wetlands had been polluted.[8] After Khulubuse Zuma pledged R1 million to the ANC at a fundraising dinner, NUM spokesperson Lesiba Seshoka was quoted as saying: 'Over 2 000 workers remain unpaid for a period of over two years while the fat cat moves around with expensive, luxurious vehicles. He has the nerve to donate some of his excesses while poor workers starve.'[9]

In October 2011, Aurora was liquidated by the North Gauteng High Court after the company had failed to pay its service providers, and, in 2012, when liquidators started opening Aurora's dirty closets, the skeletons came tumbling out. It turned out that Aurora had a mere R2 000 in the bank at the beginning of 2012.[10] One of Aurora's liquidators told *City Press* that the company 'was bankrupt from the start ... it is almost a Ponzi scheme'.[11] While the company claimed it couldn't pay its workers' salaries, R260 million was paid to itself and creditors. The master of the High Court also instituted an investigation into the role of Pamodzi liquidator Enver Motala in selling off the assets to Aurora. 'It appears that what commended Aurora to Motala was the fact that a nephew of President (Jacob) Zuma and a grandson of former president Mandela were among its directors, and that it was in effect run by two friends of Motala, Messrs Faizel and Solly Bhana,' the deputy master of the North Gauteng High Court Christene Roussouw stated in court papers.[12] In April 2012, Khulubuse Zuma's assets were seized to repay Protea Coin Security the R10 million they were owed for providing security at Grootvlei. Among the items auctioned off were 7-, 5- and 3-series BMWs, a leather lounge suite and a microwave.[13]

In March 2012, Jacob Zuma distanced himself from his nephew's controversial business dealings, telling a breakfast meeting: 'I don't know whether I should just be getting into the business of a person simply because he's a nephew. I don't discuss business easily with my nephew.'[14]

As Msomi correctly reminded his readers in July 2010, the Zuma victory at Polokwane was partly driven by a strong feeling that only a small business elite had benefited from Mbeki's rule. 'The Polokwane victors vowed to put an end to this practice and promised measures to ensure BEE deals did not only benefit the same group of well-connected individuals. But if the Khula example is anything to go by, very little has changed over the past three years.'[15]

19

Probably the most controversial and high-profile business deal involving Zuma Incorporated during President Jacob Zuma's first term in office was a multibillion-rand iron ore mining transaction in the Northern Cape, involving Zuma's NBFs (new best friends), the Guptas.

Although they have been doing business in South Africa since the mid-1990s, the Gupta family shot to prominence in the Zuma era because of their close links to the president and his family. Six months after Zuma was elected ANC president at Polokwane in December 2007, the twins, Duduzile and Duduzane Zuma, had been coopted into the Guptas' network of businesses. Duduzile was appointed as a director of Sahara Computers, the family's main business, in June 2008. A month later, Duduzane became a director of Mabengela Investments (Pty) Ltd alongside Rajesh 'Tony' Gupta, the youngest of the three Gupta brothers, and in September Duduzane was appointed as a non-executive director, alongside Rajesh Gupta, of mining labour broking firm JIC Mining Services.

* * *

'The Guptas are the new Shaiks,' I was told on numerous occasions by people with knowledge of how the Zumas roll. Of course, there is no proof that, like Schabir Shaik, they actually paid money to Zuma and his family or that they were involved in corrupt dealings. But that the Guptas had cosied up to the president and his family was abundantly clear, and they weren't shy about it either. The Guptas' compound in Saxonwold, Johannesburg, became the new hangout for the Zumas, who previously would have counted on the Durban-based Shaiks for assistance.

After Schabir Shaik was controversially released from prison on medical parole in March 2009 due to a 'terminal illness', there was an expectation that he would receive a presidential pardon from Zuma for 'taking the fall'. But this never happened, and in March 2011 Zuma's then spokesperson Zizi Kodwa confirmed that there was no relationship between them at all.[1] The view that Zuma and the Shaiks had fallen out was further supported by Moe Shaik's departure as head of the secret service in early 2012. Shaik, I was reliably told, didn't see eye to eye with State Security minister Siyabonga Cwele, and Zuma chose Cwele's side in the battle. Moe left his position within the State Security department as part of a complete breakdown of leadership at the institution, which also saw the resignations of director-general Jeff Maqetuka and the head of domestic intelligence, Gibson Njenje.

* * *

In early 2011, *Sunday Times* journalist Prega Govender travelled to Saharanpur, a 'dusty, fly-infested' city in northern India, about 200km from Delhi, to trace the footsteps of the enigmatic Gupta family. The locals were full of praises for the 'hard-working' family and their late father, Shiv Kumar Gupta, Govender reported. It was Shiv Kumar, a distributor of soapstone powder, importer of spices from Madagascar and Zanzibar and owner of five 'co-operatives', who sent Atul, the middle brother, to South Africa in 1993 after a failed venture in China. The Gupta patriarch believed that 'Africa would become the America of the world'.[2]

Atul had a background in computer building, and in 1994 he registered Correct Marketing, a company that imported and sold computers. By 1997, the company had a turnover of R97 million and the name was changed to Sahara Computers. In the same year, Rajesh Gupta, the youngest brother, joined Atul in Johannesburg and both obtained South African citizenship. Ajay, the oldest brother and a chartered accountant who engineered the Gupta business empire in South Africa with their father, came to the country permanently in 2003.

'I am very proud of Ajay. He's the king of Saharanpur and he's our God. He's like a Bollywood celebrity here,' a family member in India told Govender. He contrasted their humble beginnings in Saharanpur with their opulent Johannesburg life:

> Their home in India contrasts with the brothers' lifestyle in South Africa, where they shuttle between a R52 million compound in Johannesburg (the Saxonwold property has four mansions) and Mark Thatcher's former house in Cape Town, which was advertised for sale for R24,5 million. Family members are escorted by bodyguards; use a helicopter and three fixed-wing aircraft; have nine pilots at their beck and call and enjoy the services of five personal chefs ... The contrast between the brothers' childhoods and their lives now are startling. Their children in Johannesburg are chauffeured to top private schools; their fathers were taken to primary school in a rickshaw.[3]

Sahara Holdings, the parent company of the computer business, had an annual turnover of R2 billion in 2011 and employed over 10 000 people.[4] The company claims an 11% market share in the South African computer business.[5] Sahara also began to invest heavily in cricket, and became the main sponsor for cricket players like Proteas captain Graeme Smith and major cricket stadiums in South Africa.

But it is the family's political connections that have attracted the most attention. Essop Pahad, a minister in Thabo Mbeki's Cabinet and close confidant of the former president, was appointed to Sahara's board after he (Pahad) resigned from the Cabinet. Pahad has been a family friend for years, and the Guptas also sponsored Pahad's venture into publishing when he launched *The Thinker*, a magazine that publishes long political articles, in 2009. Atul Gupta has been at pains to emphasise that he and his family were not only on friendly terms with the Zuma administration, but also with that of Thabo Mbeki. Gupta accompanied Mbeki on foreign trips to promote investment opportunities in South Africa.[6] The difference, in Zuma's case, was the haste with which the Guptas employed the president's children after he came to power.

The family may very well have had a close relationship with Pahad during the Mbeki years, and that would have made business sense. Pahad was Mbeki's chief bulldog and gatekeeper and would have been a useful contact for insights into government policy. But without offending her intellectual capabilities or seemingly friendly personality, what skills or capacity did the 26-year-old Duduzile Zuma bring to the board of Sahara Computers, in the 15 months she served as a director, apart from political connectivity? In an interview with Duduzane Zuma in March 2011, he called himself a 'politically exposed person'.[7] He disputed the claim that he only got involved with the Guptas after his father's election as ANC president. 'I was introduced to the Gupta family by my father in late 2001, just like I met many people. At that time, my father said, I've got an interest in taking an IT-direction in my life, and at that point they were doing the Sahara thing. It just made sense. Part of my first work experience was at Sahara, I didn't come onto the books recently. They showed me the ropes.'[8]

And so Duduzane went from a rookie computer trainee for the Guptas to probably their most crucial partner in a multibillion-rand mining deal that would hit the headlines in April 2010.

* * *

In November 2009, the Department of Mineral Resources awarded a 21,4% prospecting right for iron ore at Sishen in the Northern Cape to an unknown shelf company without any mining operations, Imperial Crown Trading 289 (Pty) Ltd (ICT). The award came as a surprise to the mining industry, mostly because the 21,4% 'prospecting right' was not really a prospecting right, but a stake in an operational mine where iron ore was mined.

To understand what caused the biggest minerals brawl in South Africa since 1994, we need to go back to 2001, when the South African government decided to privatise Iscor, as the South African Iron and Steel Industrial Corporation was generally known. Iscor had been established by the Union of South Africa in 1928 to enable the country to produce its own steel. The first steel works was opened in Pretoria, followed by plants in Vereeniging and Newcastle. Iscor's biggest plant, however, was in a new town called Vanderbijlpark, which was developed around the plant after the end of the Second World War.

To produce steel you need iron ore, and Iscor also owned the biggest iron ore mine in South Africa, at Sishen in the Northern Cape. So, when the government decided to privatise Iscor in 2001, it had two parts to sell off: a steel manufacturer and an iron ore mine. The steel plants were sold to Indian billionaire Lakshmi Mittal's ArcelorMittal South Africa (AMSA) and the mine to the Anglo American-owned Kumba Resources. As part of the deal, AMSA kept 21,4% of the mining rights at Sishen, in order to ensure a constant supply of iron ore.

Under new mining legislation, introduced in 2004, holders of mining rights had to reapply for their rights. In 2009, AMSA's stake in the Sishen mine expired, but, curiously, the company didn't reapply for the right. Instead, Kumba applied for the right (which would give it 100% mining rights at the Sishen mine) and so did the unknown ICT. AMSA later argued in court that the reason it didn't reapply for the right was that it was impossible for a 'fraction' of a mining right to be converted. AMSA accepted that Kumba held 100% of the mining right after the old-order right expired on

30 April 2009 and relied on its favourable supply agreement with Kumba (of cost price plus 3%) to secure its iron ore supply.

At the time ICT was awarded the mining right, in November 2009, the company had two directors: Gugu Mtshali, a former personal assistant to ANC treasurer-general Mathews Phosa and the romantic partner of Deputy President Kgalema Motlanthe, and Archie Luhlabo, former director of the Mineworkers' Investment Company (the investment arm of the NUM).

In March 2010, Jagdish Parekh joined the board of ICT. Parekh headed up Oakbay Investments, the main investment company of the Gupta family. Although sources claimed that Parekh in fact represented a company owned by the Guptas and Duduzane Zuma, he insisted that he only represented himself on the ICT board.[9]

Kumba went to court to challenge the award to ICT, claiming that ICT had been awarded the Sishen mining right fraudulently. In December 2011, Judge Raymond Zondo set aside the award to ICT, finding that, when Kumba converted its 78,6% stake in the mine to a new-order mining right, it had been entitled to 100% of the iron ore deposit 'because mining rights could not be subdivided under existing mining law'.[10] At the time of writing, ICT was appealing the judgment in the Supreme Court of Appeal.

In August 2010, AMSA CEO Nonkululeka Nyembezi-Heita announced that the company would enter into a major BEE transaction with the Ayigobi Consortium, led by businessman Sandile Zungu, a staunch Zuma supporter. AMSA also announced it would buy out ICT for R800 million in cash if the Sishen mining rights application was endorsed by the courts. The biggest beneficiary of the BEE deal would have been Mabengela Investments, the company of Duduzane Zuma and Rajesh Gupta. Mabengela owned 12,5% of Ayigobi and Duduzane Zuma apparently 50% of Mabengela. This effectively meant that, at the stroke of a pen, the president's son would have benefited to the tune of between R46 million and R104 million.[11] Other beneficiaries of Ayigobi included Gugu Mtshali, Motlanthe's lover (4,2%), Zungu (6,25%), the Guptas' Oakbay Investments (6,25%) and Parekh (25%).

Asked why the Guptas had been cut in on the deal, Nyembezi-Heita said: 'The Gupta family is not really participating as a BEE participant so much as they were a major facilitator in the transaction between ICT and ArcelorMittal South Africa. And this really just becomes a way to compensate them for that. Now this is a tried and tested method where facilitators get to participate in the equity deal as a recompense for their efforts'.[12]

Responding to a question why Duduzane Zuma would benefit so handsomely from the deal, an unidentified spokesperson for the Ayigobi group said: 'I can see what you're saying: was there a greater contribution from Mabengela to warrant it? Or was it purely based on the fact that he's the president's son that he qualifies for that additional percentage?"[13]

The pressure on AMSA increased as shareholders wanted to know from Nyembezi-Heita why a small group of Zuma's family and friends were to become multimillionaires overnight if the deal went through. AMSA shareholders like Sanlam and Rand Merchant Bank publicly opposed the transaction. Sanlam's Shoaib Vajey said the transaction was not being done in a transparent way.[14] 'They [ArcelorMittal] say this is unrelated to the ICT acquisition, yet all the parties in ICT are sort of reflected in the [new] deal as beneficiaries and key individuals and groups,' Vajey was quoted as saying. In February 2011, Nyembezi-Heita admitted that the announcement of a BEE deal may have been 'premature'.

* * *

In March 2011, *City Press* editor Ferial Haffajee and I sat down with the Guptas for almost three hours to discuss the controversy surrounding their relationship with Zuma and his children, their recently launched newspaper, *The New Age*, and their inclusion in the AMSA BEE transaction in spite of the fact that they were not born in South Africa. Ajay Gupta, the eldest brother and czar of the family's business empire, then predicted, correctly, that the Ayigobi deal would not fly. It was months since the deal had been announced by AMSA, but it was yet to be presented to shareholders. Somewhere, someone in AMSA had had a change of heart.

During the interview, Ajay Gupta revealed his role in the transaction. 'He [ArcelorMittal chairperson Lakshmi Mittal] asks me, when he does these BEE deals, as a friend, it's nothing official to do with ArcelorMittal South Africa. I've never even met the company's CEO or anyone in the company.'[15] He said he knew Mittal 'very well' and Mittal had told him 'many times' that he wanted to do a deal. According to Gupta, Mittal asked for a 'new entrant'. He recommended Duduzane Zuma, whom he calls 'Dudu'. In exchange for the $50 million funding he (Ajay) provided, he asked for a stake in the consortium, Ajay said.

In September 2011, AMSA announced that its empowerment transaction with the Ayigobi group was off. It was reported that due diligence processes had scuppered the deal.[16] Perhaps Kumba's allegations in court that ICT's application for the Sishen mining right was nothing more than a badly forged copy of their own played a significant role in the collapse of a deal that would have made Duduzane Zuma an instant millionaire.

Although the AMSA deal didn't work out, stories of the cosy relationship between the Guptas and the Zumas won't die down. Some in the ANC believe for a fact that Zuma consults the Guptas on all his Cabinet reshuffles and appointments. The family is not shy about their friendship with citizen number one and his offspring. But they insist they have not benefited financially from this, or that the relationship is corrupt.

Haffajee and I also pushed the Guptas on their relationships with politicians (DA leader Helen Zille had also visited the family compound) and when such relationships become conflicts of interest:

> Asked whether their Saxonwold compound has become a centre of political discussion and socialising for ministers and senior government officials, Ajay says: 'The two things, we don't mix them.' He denies that government policies or tenders are

discussed at their home, but easily admits that they have lots of politician friends who spend time at their estate. This includes Zuma; Human Settlements minister Tokyo Sexwale, who visited the family last Saturday to deliver 'gogo atchar' to the Gupta matriarch and share a 'Zulu meal' with them; and Mining minister Susan Shabangu, who he says could not be benefiting them because they receive many critical queries from her department about their mines.

As an example, the Guptas say they host a big function at their home yearly to celebrate Diwali, to which ministers 'and a few hundred people' are invited. Ajay denies that their access to top ANC politicians is extraordinary. Asked why other top businesspeople don't have this kind of access, Ajay says: 'Because they want the access for some benefit. I'm not using this thing for any commercial benefit or advantage. So that's why people are more comfortable with me.'

Asked to explain how these relationships with politicians start, Atul says the question shows a lack of understanding of cultural differences. Ajay says: 'Come with me to my hometown of Saharanpur (in India), and maybe a few hundred people will come to meet with me. Across the border, the politicians feel comfortable because I have no conflict of interest with them. If I have a conflict of interest, they will never come to me.'

Ajay Gupta says he meets politicians in 'any way … it can be someone who feels this is a good guy, let's meet with him, and yes, sometimes I also invite people to my functions. Most of them are long-term relations.' Prompted to explain further, Ajay says: 'For you he's a minister, for me he's a friend. Please understand that. If I ask a minister about his budget, he won't even say hello to me'.[17]

I left the interview with absolutely no doubt in my mind that the Guptas were aware of the high-stakes game they were in, and that they were walking a very tight rope between befriending powerful politicians, employing their children (we also later revealed that

Free State premier Ace Magashule's son Tshepiso was employed by Mabengela Investments and drove a BMW Z4 belonging to the Guptas) and doing business with government or in industries that are regulated by the government (the ICT deal and government advertising, including by the Free State, in *The New Age*).

* * *

In August 2012, Zuma Incorporated was in the news again. This time, the *Mail & Guardian* revealed that a new town, the first since 1994, would be built 3,2km from Zuma's homestead in Nkandla, KwaZulu-Natal. An opaque trust called the Masibambisane Rural Development Initiative, chaired by Zuma and primarily funded by government departments, was spearheading the development. It was reported that the development would cost R2 billion, of which R1 billion was expected to come from government departments.[18] Deebo Mzobe is a distant relative of Zuma (the president's mother is also Mzobe) and the deputy chair of Masibambisane: 'We lobby hard, yes. What is wrong with making sure somebody keeps their promise? We lobby business [Patrice Motsepe and Old Mutual are among Masibambisane's benefactors] as well. That is what we do,' he told *City Press*.[19]

Zumaville, as the proposed town became known, was the latest example of Zuma benefiting those close to him, his critics said. This was the second big government-led investment in Nkandla after it was announced in 2009 that the president's homestead would be upgraded at a cost of R65 million.[20] The upgrade would include a helicopter pad, police stations, military clinic and a visitors' centre. In September 2012, *City Press* revealed that the Department of Public Works had budgeted R203 million for security upgrades to Zuma's Nkandla homestead. The state had already spent R44 million on security upgrades, and Zuma's personal contribution was capped at R10 million. This led to a public outcry and saw the DA's parliamentary leader, Lindiwe Mazibuko, laying a complaint with the Public

Protector. Social commentator Songezo Zibi wrote: 'Unless one is astoundingly naive, it is clear that this is a case of looting. Why are these security arrangements so many times more than the apparent cost of building the structure to begin with? Does that not render the entire project unsustainable? It is clear that we are dealing with a kleptocratic system that allows this kind of thing to happen. We have to take a stand as citizens and say, "not in my name, not with my money, and this far and no further".'[21]

Public Works refused to disclose how much had been spent on the Nkandla project, but it was reported that the figure was close to R238 million.

Commenting on the facelift Nkandla has undergone since Zuma came to power in December 2007, expelled ANC Youth League leader Julius Malema told a crowd in Rustenburg in July 2012: 'We don't want a president who steals rural development money to develop our villages around here to build his KZN New York City in Nkandla. Instead of cutting ribbons of service delivery every week he is marrying every week and that is not good for the image of the ANC.'

20

On 30 January 2010, South Africa woke up to this *Sunday Times* headline: 'Zuma fathers baby with Irvin Khoza's daughter'.

'Holy shit!' was probably the thought that crossed most South Africans' minds when they learned that not only had their president had unprotected sex with another woman many years younger than him, but that she was also the Iron Duke's daughter. Irvin Khoza, owner of Orlando Pirates football club and chairperson of the Premier Soccer League, is a man feared by many. He has a long history in the ANC, and those who know say his contacts in the underworld stretch deep.

Nobody messes with Irvin Khoza. Except if your name is Jacob Zuma.

* * *

'President Jacob Zuma has fathered a child with the daughter of powerful soccer administrator and long-time friend, Irvin Khoza. Sonono Khoza, a 39-year-old divorcée, was pregnant when her father, Orlando Pirates boss and chairman of the Soccer World Cup local organising committee, was invited to share the stage with the newly elected president during a post-election bash at Nkandla, KwaZulu-Natal, in June last year [2009]. It is unclear whether the "Iron Duke", as he is known, knew then who was the father of his unborn grandchild,' the *Sunday Times* reported.

Zuma was in trouble and he knew it. Since his acquittal on charges of rape in May 2006, Zuma had managed to keep his bedroom antics off the front pages. Apart from two new wives – he got married to Tobeka Madiba three weeks before the Sonono scandal broke – Zuma had not reneged, publicly at least, on his promise after the rape acquittal that he would practise safe sex in future. Remember his apology after Judge Willem van der Merwe asked him to 'control your body and your sexual urges'?

A day after Van der Merwe found him not guilty of rape, Zuma said: 'I wish to state categorically and place on record that I erred in having unprotected sex. I should have known better. And I should have acted with greater caution and responsibility. For this I unconditionally apologise to all the people of this country.'

And here it was, in black and white – Zuma had erred again. The *Sunday Times* reported that the baby was born in October 2009, bringing to 20 the number of 'official' Zuma children. For impregnating Sonono out of wedlock, Zuma had to pay customary damages to the Khoza family, known as '*inhlawulo*' in Zulu. Neither the Iron Duke nor his wife Matina was impressed. 'Asked how she felt about her new grandchild and the fact that Zuma was the father, Matina responded: "No, we are not excited." Pressed to elaborate, she said: "I can't talk about [that]. Bye".'[1] Irvin Khoza, the *Sunday Times* reported, did not attend either of the family meetings held between Zuma and the Khozas. He 'felt betrayed and humiliated by the president's relationship with his daughter, particularly as he considered Zuma – who is six years older than him – a friend.'

Zuma's spin doctors went into overdrive. 'This is the thing he is most scared of,' we were told. Not the corruption charges that could still be reinstated, or the constant negative publicity about poor service delivery or about his family's proximity to one business family. No, another sex scandal was the thing most likely to sink him, the president believed. Zuma's libido became a popular dinner-table topic and his critics flayed him. 'President Zuma's behaviour directly contradicts the government's campaign against multiple sexual partners, and the inherent Aids risk in having unprotected sex,' said DA leader Helen Zille. Independent Democrats leader Patricia de Lille accused Zuma of hypocrisy. 'He is the one who is always preaching responsible sexual behaviour, but it seems he is sending a message which says, "Don't do as I do, do as I say".' ACDP leader Kenneth Meshoe suggested Zuma should 'like Tiger Woods' get treatment for his 'sex addiction'.[2] The international media pointed out that, with South Africa having the highest number of HIV infections in the world, Zuma was not leading by example.

Four days after the story broke, Zuma released this statement:

Statement by President Jacob Zuma on media reports about his child

3 February 2010

I have noted recent media reports about aspects of my personal life.

I have noted too that these reports have been the subject of much discussion in the public arena by various organisations and people from all walks of life.

I have therefore decided, after some careful deliberation, to make public comment on a matter that is otherwise intensely personal. I had been out of the country when this matter arose.

I confirm that I have a relationship and a baby with Ms Sonono Khoza. I said during World Aids Day that we must all take personal responsibility for our actions. I have done so. I have done the necessary cultural imperatives in a situation of this nature, for example the formal acknowledgement of paternity and responsibility, including the payment of *inhlawulo* to the family. The matter is now between the two of us, and culturally, between the Zuma and Khoza families.

It is unfortunate that the individuals concerned have been unfairly subjected to harsh media exposure merely because of the position that I occupy. Our Constitution and our laws require us to protect children from harmful public exposure. The Constitution states that it is inappropriate to place at risk, the child's well-being, physical or mental health, spiritual, moral or social development.

Both the Child Care Act and the new Children's Act also provides for the protection of children from exploitation. The naming of the child's parents has essentially exposed her to the public, which has serious implications in the long-term for her, and amounts to the exploitation referred to in the Act, because the media is making money out of the matter.

The media is also in essence questioning the right of the child to exist and fundamentally, her right to life. It is unfortunate that the matter has been handled in this way. I sincerely hope that the media will protect the rights of children.

Much has been made of the government's policy on HIV and Aids and this relationship. It is mischievous to argue that I have changed or undermined government's stance on the HIV and Aids campaign. I will not compromise on the campaign. Rather we will intensify our efforts to promote prevention, treatment, research and the fight against the stigma, attached to the epidemic. We will also continue with our campaign to ensure that every South African knows their HIV status, and that all those who need it have access to appropriate treatment.

We respect and uphold the freedom of the media. It is one of the freedoms we fought for, and which we will always defend. However, the President of the Republic, the mother and the baby are also entitled to the rights afforded to all South Africans in the Constitution. These rights cannot be waived just because of a position one occupies.

I would request that the dignity and privacy of the affected individuals in this matter be respected.

Zuma was criticised for attempting to divert the attention from his sexual behaviour to the rights of the child. The next day, his office released a terse statement, saying the president would take two days off 'following a hectic schedule'.

On 6 February, after his short leave, Zuma released another statement on the matter:

President Jacob Zuma's statement on the impact of events of the past week

6 February 2010

I have over the past week taken time to consider and reflect on the issues relating to a relationship I had outside of wedlock.

The matter, though private, has been a subject of much public discussion and debate. It has put a lot of pressure on my family and my organisation, the African National Congress. I also acknowledge and understand the reaction of many South Africans.

I deeply regret the pain that I have caused to my family, the ANC, the Alliance and South Africans in general.

I reiterate that I took responsibility for my actions towards the family concerned and the child.

I reaffirm my commitment and that of my movement to the importance of the family as an institution. I also reaffirm my commitment and that of my movement to the values of personal responsibility, respect and dignity.

I recognise the responsibility of leaders to uphold and promote these values at all times.

The statement came after immense pressure on Zuma from inside and outside the ANC. It was damage control 101, and apologising was the only option left for him. In meetings with ANC sources, I've heard the same refrain time and again: 'Everybody in the struggle knew that thing would be his downfall. It's his Achilles' heel. The man is out of control.'

In April 2010, Zuma's second wife, MaNtuli, was fined a goat after she expressed unhappiness about him taking another wife (Tobeka Madiba).[3] The *Mail & Guardian* reported that Nompumelelo Ntuli 'went berserk' when Zuma told her he was taking another wife. '[She] broke the security gates and demanded a taxi. When the security guards came after her, she allegedly went to another gate, gate four [of the Presidential guesthouse in Pretoria]. The house manager had given instructions to the gatekeeper not to open it, but she fought him. After hitting the police [who guard Zuma], MaNtuli's personal bodyguard was called. He later managed to get her into the car and drove her to the airport to catch a plane to Durban and her Morningside home.'[4]

In June 2010, the Zuma household was hit by another scandal, when a secret letter, allegedly written by aggrieved family members about MaNtuli's behaviour, was leaked to the media. The letter claimed that it was not clear if Zuma was the father of the child she was expecting at the time or whether she had been impregnated by her former bodyguard, who had committed suicide earlier in 2010. MaNtuli rejected these claims, saying: 'How a bodyguard could make a move on the president's wife who is also a mother to him? I have never slept with a bodyguard ... My child resembles the president. That is why I do not concern myself a lot about all these things that are said about me because I know where they come from.'[5] The baby was reported to be Zuma's child number 21.

To add to MaNtuli's salacious dramas, veteran actor Joe Mafela revealed that he had had an affair with her before she met Zuma and that they had a child together.[6]

* * *

Zuma's conservative gender views often land him in hot water, especially in a country with a secular Constitution like South Africa's. During an interview with talk show host Dali Tambo in August 2012, Zuma expressed his happiness over his daughter Duduzile's decision to get married: 'I was also happy because I wouldn't want to stay with daughters who are not getting married, because that in itself is a problem in society. I know that people today think being single is nice. It's actually not right. That's a distortion,' Zuma said. 'You've got to have kids. Kids are important to a woman because they actually give an extra training to a woman, to be a mother.' These comments led to outrage from gender groups and an official complaint against Zuma being lodged with the Commission for Gender Equality.

While Zuma was preaching conservative family values, newsrooms around the country remained on 'baby watch' as rumours reached us about more Zuma babies. Naturally, we had to be careful as this had become Zuma's weak spot and could easily be abused by his opponents. We published none of the rumours, as we could find no corroborating evidence that they were indeed true. Without at least one of the parents confirming a pregnancy story, it is almost impossible to go to print. But what became abundantly clear was that Zuma's libido, having been identified as his weak point, would certainly be used against him again, especially in the context of a battle for power. Watch this space.

21

As the ANC's former head of intelligence, it was hardly surprising that Zuma took control of appointments in Cabinet's justice and security cluster after he became president. 'He told the left [Cosatu and the SACP] that he will choose the security ministers, but he took some advice on the economic portfolios,' a former adviser told me. 'And he managed to mess it up in less than two years.'

Zuma appointed three of his staunchest allies from KwaZulu-Natal to head up the cluster: Jeff Radebe (Justice), Nathi Mthethwa (Police) and Siyabonga Cwele (State Security). The other member of the cluster was Lindiwe Sisulu, who occupied the Defence portfolio from 2009 to 2012.

The portfolios of Justice, Police and State Security experienced tremendous turbulence during Zuma's first three years in office and were constantly under fire for alleged political interference in the processes of state. By the end of 2012, none of the crucial appointees chosen by Zuma and his ministers to head the NPA, the SAPS and the State Security Agency (SSA) remained in their jobs. Advocate Menzi Simelane, the NDPP, was out of a job after the Constitutional Court found that Zuma didn't apply his mind when he decided Simelane was a 'fit and proper' candidate for the job; General Bheki Cele was fired as police chief by Zuma in June 2012 after a board of inquiry found he too was unfit for his job, and the director-general of the SSA, Jeff Maqetuka, took early retirement in November 2011 after he butted heads with Cwele. Maqetuka's deputies, domestic intelligence chief Gibson Njenje and foreign intelligence boss Moe Shaik, followed suit after they also fell out with Cwele.

Radebe (who oversaw the deterioration of the NPA), Mthethwa (who lied about receiving upgrades at his private residence from a crime intelligence fund) and Cwele (whose wife, Sheryl, was convicted of drug-trafficking and allegedly received official protection by Cwele's department during her trial) survived three Cabinet reshuffles, and all stayed in their positions. 'Zuma cannot afford to go to Mangaung without the support of the security agencies,' an ANC source in the security establishment told me. That was Mbeki's mistake: when he went to Polokwane, he had lost the support of significant players in the security cluster. And Zuma wasn't going to make the same mistake.

Although it is understandable for a president to want to appoint trusted individuals to the top positions in the justice and security cluster, these people have to be qualified and able to do their jobs. For safety and justice to flourish, it is paramount for the public to trust these institutions and the individuals at their heads. On this score Zuma failed dismally, and three years after his inauguration, the NPA, the SAPS and the SSA were in complete disarray.

22

The appointment of Advocate Menzi Simelane as head of the NPA
will go down in history as one of the biggest blunders by a South
African president.

With the NPA still reeling from the spy tapes saga and the controversial removal of Advocate Vusi Pikoli from office (after the
Ginwala inquiry had cleared him), Simelane was parachuted into
the NPA by Zuma with a clear mandate. 'He said he was a political animal and that it's common knowledge he is a member of the
party [the ANC] that put the president into power. He said he was
deployed by the party to this position and that part of his task was
to implement the ANC's vision for the NPA,' a senior NPA employee
told me after Simelane addressed staff at the NPA's head office in
Pretoria during the first week of his arrival in October 2009.[1]

A week later, Simelane met prosecutors at the NPA's Johannesburg
office and allegedly told them that political interference would not
be tolerated. 'But he said we should be sensitive when dealing with
political cases because the NPA is also part of government,' I was
told by a prosecutor who attended the meeting.

*   *   *

Zuma had first appointed Simelane as a deputy NDPP. Less than two months later, Zuma promoted him to the position of national director. Simelane's appointment came as a shock to prosecutors in the NPA and the legal fraternity, not least because he was slammed by the final report of the Ginwala inquiry into Pikoli's fitness. Pikoli was sacked by caretaker president Kgalema Motlanthe in December 2008, even after Ginwala had cleared him of any wrongdoing.

As director-general of Justice, Simelane had been the state's main witness in its case against Pikoli. Former Speaker of Parliament Frene Ginwala's report heavily criticised his evidence to the commission, his withholding of documents and his 'irregular' conduct in drafting a letter to Pikoli on behalf of former Justice minister Brigitte Mabandla, instructing him to cease the imminent arrest of former police chief Jackie Selebi. 'In general his conduct left much to be desired. His testimony was contradictory and without basis in fact or in law,' the report commented.

Simelane's evidence before the Ginwala inquiry showed his disregard for the independence of the NPA on at least two levels. The first was the letter to Pikoli, which Simelane testified didn't mean to convey an instruction from the Justice minister to the head of the NPA not to arrest Selebi. The letter to Pikoli, which Simelane drafted, read: 'I must be satisfied that indeed the public interest will be served should you go ahead with the intended course of action. Until I have satisfied myself that sufficient evidence exists [for the arrest and charging of Selebi], you shall not pursue the route that you have taken steps to pursue.'

Ginwala accepted Pikoli's version, that it was an instruction to cease the arrest of Selebi until Mabandla was satisfied. But assuming Simelane's version was correct – that it was not an instruction – the letter was 'reckless to say the least' Ginwala found. '[Simelane] should have been acutely aware of the constitutional protection afforded to the NPA to conduct its work without fear, favour or prejudice. The contents of the letter were tantamount to executive interference with the prosecutorial independence of the NPA, which is recognised as a serious offence in the [NPA] Act,' the final report read.

The second level of Simelane's disregard for the NPA's independence was shown when he attempted to conceal a legal opinion from the Ginwala inquiry that advised him to concern himself only with the NPA's finances as director-general of Justice. The state accused Pikoli of not properly accounting to the Justice department about the affairs of the NPA. He and Simelane had differed over who had final authority over the NPA: Simelane said it was him, as director-general of Justice; Pikoli claimed it was the NDPP.

When asked, during his evidence before the Ginwala commission, if he had ever taken legal advice on the matter, Simelane twice said 'no'. Pikoli's advocate, Wim Trengove SC, then pulled out a January 2007 legal opinion by senior counsel Vincent Maleka, addressed to Simelane, advising him that the director-general had 'no authority at all over the exercise of powers, functions and duties by functionaries of the NPA'. Maleka's opinion concluded that Simelane's only power over the NPA was to exercise responsibility for the finances of the prosecuting body.

Simelane said he didn't agree with Maleka's opinion 'in its totality'. In her final report, Ginwala lashed Simelane for ignoring Maleka's legal advice and for not sharing it with Pikoli or the commission. 'He attempted to suppress the disclosure of the information that was of significance to the work of this Enquiry. He only acknowledged the existence of these legal opinions when they were presented to him by Advocate Pikoli's legal representatives during his cross-examination ... I must also state that I have found the conduct of [Simelane] highly irregular,' Ginwala wrote. 'His failure to include all the relevant material at his disposal in the original submission by government was not consonant with the responsibilities of a senior state official furnishing information to an investigative enquiry established by the president. He had a duty to place all relevant information before the Enquiry. His testimony before the Enquiry was also not particularly helpful to me; his evidence was contradictory and I found him to be arrogant and condescending in his attitude towards Advocate Pikoli.'

Ginwala's report was publicly released in December 2008. Pikoli was fired by Motlanthe, although the commission found him to have been fit and proper for the position of NDPP. Former Justice minister Enver Surty subsequently referred Ginwala's report to the Public Service Commission (PSC) to determine what implications it had for Simelane. The PSC concluded that Simelane should face a disciplinary hearing and referred its report to Jeff Radebe, who had in the meanwhile been appointed Justice minister by Zuma. In an extraordinary move, Radebe decided that the PSC did not sufficiently hear Simelane's side of the story and gave him the opportunity to make legal representations on why he should not face a disciplinary hearing. But, even after receiving Simelane's response, the PSC stuck to its guns, saying Simelane should be disciplined.

This led to a vitriolic attack by Radebe on the Ginwala inquiry and the PSC, accusing them of not taking into account Simelane's response to the critique levelled against him. Amazingly, Radebe, the political head of the department, himself decided to clear Simelane based on the legal submissions made by Simelane's legal team on his behalf. 'I am therefore satisfied that the decision not to subject Advocate Simelane to a disciplinary hearing [as proposed by Simelane's legal team] is correct, as there is no reliable evidence of misconduct which justifies a disciplinary inquiry. Furthermore, I am confident that as a cabinet member responsible for the administration of justice, I will continue to have a healthy professional relationship with the NPA founded on the provisions of the Constitution and the law,' Radebe announced at a press conference shortly after Zuma appointed Simelane as NDPP, effectively chucking the Ginwala and PSC reports into the dustbin.[2]

In the meantime, the DA had lodged court papers challenging Zuma's appointment of Simelane as NDPP. The party argued that Zuma had ignored the legal requirement of 'fit and proper' when he appointed Simelane, and quoted extensively from Ginwala's report. The party added three extra reasons to its barrage of legal arguments as to why Simelane was not 'fit and proper' to lead the NPA:
• The Justice department had received consecutive qualified audits from the Auditor-General while Simelane was director-general.

- In a case brought by Pretoria Portland Cement (PPC) against the Competition Commission (while Simelane headed the commission), the Supreme Court of Appeal found that Simelane had abused his powers by gaining access to the company's premises in a dishonest way.
- The Constitutional Court criticised Simelane's actions in the case brought by businessman Hugh Glenister to save the existence of the Scorpions. As director-general of Justice, Simelane submitted an affidavit in the case, but the court found he did not respond 'fully, frankly and openly'.[3]

Simelane caused consternation at the NPA, shortly after he assumed office, by effectively shutting down the national office of the Specialised Commercial Crimes Unit (SCCU) and delegating the unit's functions to provincial offices; by threatening to do the same with the Asset Forfeiture Unit (AFU), and by representing the state in court in high-profile matters in spite of his lack of prosecutorial experience.

The DA's case was heard in the North Gauteng High Court in September 2010. Advocate Nazeer Cassim SC, representing Zuma, told the court that the president 'relied on a very senior minister [Radebe] who said this [Simelane] is a man of integrity. He did not interrogate the minister. He accepted it.'[4] Cassim also argued that the test for 'fit and proper' was a subjective one and that Zuma based his decision to appoint Simelane on his 'personal value system'. The DA criticised Radebe for not fully briefing Zuma on Ginwala's findings against Simelane and the PSC's recommendation that he face a disciplinary hearing.

On 10 November 2010, Judge Pieter van der Byl dismissed the DA's application for Zuma's appointment of Simelane to be overturned because there was no prescribed process to determine what 'fit and proper' means. Van der Byl ruled: 'In the absence of any prescribed process, I am unable to hold that the process followed was irrational as the president's aim was, as is apparent from his answering affidavit, to determine whether Mr Simelane was a fit and proper person for appointment as envisaged in the Constitution and the [National Prosecuting Authority] Act. I am accordingly unpersuaded that it has been shown on the probabilities that Mr Simelane is not a fit and proper person for appointment.'[5]

The DA lodged an appeal against the judgment and Simelane continued to serve as NDPP. I interviewed Simelane in his office in August 2011. He looked relaxed and told me he had recently joined Twitter, where he interacts with a significant number of followers on legal matters. Simelane spoke passionately about the so-called Amigos cases, in which ANC politicians and civil servants in KwaZulu-Natal and the Northern Cape had been charged with accepting bribes from Uruguayan businessman Gaston Savoi in exchange for awarding multimillion-rand tenders for water purification plants to his Intaka company. Simelane personally appeared as prosecutor in these cases, and was committed to seeing them through. (Ironically, in August 2012, while Simelane was on extended leave, the NPA withdrew corruption charges against KwaZulu-Natal ANC politicians Peggy Nkonyeni and Mike Mabuyakhulu in the Intaka case. Both are seen as close allies of Zuma.)

I asked Simelane whether he was worried about the DA's appeal against Judge Van der Byl's ruling. 'No, it doesn't bother me. It never did. I understand their position. I don't agree with them; it's not something I dedicate my time to. I just do my work the best way I can,' he replied.

On 31 October 2011, the Supreme Court of Appeal in Bloemfontein heard the DA's appeal. A full bench of judges, led by Judge Mahomed Navsa, grilled Zuma's lawyer, Advocate Cassim, on why the president had merely accepted Radebe's motivation before appointing Simelane. 'If the president had concerns ... shouldn't he have looked at the Ginwala case himself? The SCA said unkind things [about Simelane in a previous case], he [Zuma] didn't read it. He must interrogate these matters himself?' Navsa asked. Cassim replied: 'The minister [Radebe] assured him [Zuma] there isn't substance to the complaint', to which Judge John Heher responded: 'How can that possibly be discharging your duty to determine fitness?'

171

On 1 December 2011, the SCA set aside Zuma's appointment of Simelane as NDPP. The ruling was as brutal as they get, and flayed Zuma and Radebe for not properly assessing Simelane's candidature.

The SCA accepted that there existed no prescribed process to determine the fitness of a candidate for the position of NDPP. It highlighted the Constitutional Court's Certification judgment, which stated that the NPA must exercise its functions without fear, favour or prejudice. The court criticised Zuma for telling Radebe he had 'firm views' on appointing Simelane before he received Radebe's input. Legislation 'does not allow for a firm view before a consideration of the qualities referred to therein'. Zuma's justification for appointing Simelane was: 'Absent any evidence to the contrary I have no basis to conclude that he is not fit and proper.' But, said the SCA, 'this is a wrong approach'. Zuma did not disclose exactly why he asked for Radebe's input. Both of them considered the Ginwala report irrelevant, based on the 'rigid view' that Ginwala's commission was concerned with Pikoli's fitness, not Simelane. Zuma and Radebe 'wrongly discounted' Surty's concerns about the Ginwala report and its impact on Simelane. They were 'too easily dismissive' of the PSC's finding, that Simelane should face a disciplinary hearing.

The SCA found that the Ginwala report's findings were 'directly relevant' to Simelane's appointment. 'They bring his integrity directly into question.' Zuma and Radebe 'both made material errors of fact and law in the process leading up to the appointment of Mr Simelane'. By ignoring Ginwala's findings, Zuma 'misconstrued his powers and acted irrationally'.

On this basis alone, the SCA found, the application by the DA should succeed. Judge Navsa reminded Zuma that even he was constrained by the country's laws, particularly with an appointment as important as that of the NDPP. The court ruled:

> No-one is above the law and everyone is subject to the Constitution and the law. The legislative and executive arms of government are bound by legal prescripts. Accountability, responsiveness and openness are constitutional watchwords. It

can rightly be said that the individuals that occupy positions in organs of state or who are part of constitutional institutions are transient but that constitutional mechanisms, institutions and values endure. To ensure a functional, accountable constitutional democracy the drafters of our Constitution placed limits on the exercise of power. Institutions and office bearers must work within the law and must be accountable. Put simply, ours is a government of laws and not of men or women.

The court used unforgiving language to criticise Zuma's approach to the matter: 'I accept that the President must have a multitude of daily duties and is a very busy man. However when he is dealing with an office as important as that of the NDPP, which is integral to the rule of law and to our success as a democracy, then time should be taken to get it right,' Judge Navsa ruled.

The court dismissed Zuma's argument that a decision of fitness is a subjective one. 'It is clear that the President did not undertake a proper enquiry of whether the objective requirements of [the NPA Act] were satisfied. On the available evidence the President could in any event not have reached a conclusion favourable to Mr Simelane, as there were too many unresolved questions concerning his integrity and experience.'

The court also rejected Zuma's point that he, because he is the people's choice, could make a value judgement on the fitness of the candidate for NDPP. Implicit in that argument is the belief that a court cannot scrutinise the president's exercise of a value judgement. Navsa quoted former Chief Justice Ismail Mahomed to counter this point:

That argument is, I think, based on a demonstrable fallacy. The legislature has no mandate to make a law which transgresses the powers vesting in it in terms of the Constitution. Its mandate is to make only those laws permitted by the Constitution and to defer to the judgment of the court, in any conflict generated by an enactment challenged on constitutional grounds. If it does make laws which transgress its constitutional mandate or if it refuses to defer to the judgment of the court on any challenge to such laws, it is in breach of its own mandate. The court has a constitutional right and duty to say so and it protects the very essence of a constitutional democracy when it does. A democratic legislature does not have the option to ignore, defy or subvert the court. It has only two constitutionally permissible alternatives, it must either accept its judgment or seek an appropriate constitutional amendment if this can be done without subverting the basic foundations of the Constitution itself.

In May 2012, Radebe and Simelane appealed to the Constitutional Court to have the SCA's order overturned. Significantly, Zuma didn't appeal, indicating an unwillingness to fight for Simelane's reinstatement. In his place, Zuma appointed Advocate Nomgcobo Jiba as acting NDPP. Jiba, of course, was the other person whose career had been saved by the crime intelligence spy tapes that got Zuma off the hook.

On 5 October 2012 Justice Zak Yacoob, on behalf of the Constitutional Court, ruled that Zuma's appointment of Simelane was indeed irrational and had to be set aside. 'Dishonesty is inconsistent with the conscientiousness and integrity required for the proper execution of the responsibilities of the NDPP,' Yacoob said. 'Dishonesty is dishonesty, wherever it occurs. And it is much worse when the person who had been dishonest is a senior government employee who gave evidence under oath. Although not a court, the Ginwala Commission was about as important a non-judicial fact-finding forum as can be imagined,' Yacoob ruled. The court didn't spare Radebe who, according to the ruling, advised Zuma to 'ignore' Ginwala's comments about Simelane.

23

In July 2009, less than two months after his inauguration as president of South Africa, Jacob Zuma and his Cabinet made two crucial appointments to the embattled South African Police Service: Bhekokwakhe Hamilton Cele as National Police Commissioner and Richard Naggie Mdluli as head of the Crime Intelligence Division. At the time, the SAPS was an organisation in tatters: Jackie Selebi was about to go on trial for corruption (in October 2009); Selebi's deputies refused to believe that he was guilty and some of them continued to stonewall efforts by the Scorpions to get to the bottom of the dirt; the acting head of crime intelligence, Mulangi Mphego, was on trial for defeating the ends of justice relating to Selebi's case;[1] and the crime rate wasn't dropping as it should.

Zuma needed to appoint a strong, clean and independent-minded police chief who would not get dragged into political battles, would inspire a disheartened police force, and would bring down crime. So he appointed Bheki Cele, a colourful ANC politician from KwaZulu-Natal with a penchant for Panama hats, who had been serving as MEC for Transport, Safety and Liaison since 2004. Announcing their new appointment, the ANC said: 'With Bheki Cele at the helm of the police, we believe that they will be able to discharge this responsibility with vigour and determination. Cele has been in the forefront of fighting crime in KwaZulu-Natal ... Since his appointment as the MEC, Bheki Cele defended the weak in KwaZulu-Natal Province which saw him being thrown into the deep end of the taxi conflict and pioneering the initiative "Catching Crime on the Highway". He is also behind the "Zero Tolerance to 100% compliance in KwaZulu-Natal" for all road traffic laws.'

Before being appointed police chief, Cele had gained a reputation as a hard-nosed politician who worked closely with senior police officers in KwaZulu-Natal to fight fire with fire. He had specifically focused on violent crimes and taxi wars in the province. Cele became known as a crime-fighter, but his fame also opened him up to accusations of bias in the police's battle against crime syndicates.

*　*　*

Cele's appointment was coupled with the remilitarisation of the police by Zuma and his Police minister, Nathi Mthethwa. Out went the name 'Department of Safety and Security'; Zuma returned to the apartheid-era designation 'Department of Police' and the military ranks used under the previous regime. Suddenly all commissioners were generals. This move was heavily criticised by the biggest police union, the Police and Prisons Civil Rights Union (Popcru), who said that implementing a military rank system in the police was un-ANC. 'We further view this kind of system as a way of reversing the already started process of transforming SAPS from the culture of brutalising the community to the one that offers a safety and security and to the citizens of South Africa as a whole,' the union wrote to the governing party, who ignored the caution.

Cele started his new job with a bang. Shortly after his appointment, he lobbied for a change of legislation that would allow police officers to 'shoot to kill' without worrying 'what happens after that'.[2] Cele's argument was that criminals are often better armed than the police and that the police should fight fire with fire. In conflict situations, criminals are ready to shoot, but police had to 'arrest their minds, thinking is this right or is it wrong? Police must think about what is in front of them and do the job, or else they get killed.'[3]

Cele's rhetoric fitted with the refrain introduced by former Deputy Minister of Safety and Security, Susan Shabangu, in April 2008. Addressing a group of police officials, she said: 'You must kill the bastards if they threaten you or the community. You must not worry about the regulations – that is my responsibility. Your responsibility is to serve and protect – I want no warning shots. You have one shot and it must be a kill shot.' Shabangu was appointed by Zuma as Minister of Mineral Resources.

But Zuma and the new political bosses of the police, minister Nathi Mthethwa and his deputy, Fikile Mbalula (who was appointed Sports minister in November 2010), continued the message after they came into power. At a meeting of police station commanders in September 2009, Zuma said: 'Criminals don't take an oath to do warning shots. If you take a gun out to me, that intent is more than clear, the next thing the criminal is going to shoot at me. That intent is very clear. My thinking is once a criminal takes out their gun the intent is clear … police must then act to protect themselves and the innocents.'[4]

Mthethwa pushed through an amendment to the Criminal Procedure Act that allowed the police to use deadly force, and had the support of his president. 'We have an abnormal criminal problem in South Africa. We must therefore apply extraordinary measures,' said Zuma. Addressing reporters in Parliament on the amendments to the Act, Mbalula said: 'We cannot say to the police, retreat. We cannot say to South Africans, despair. Our job is to give people hope. Yes. Shoot the bastards. Hard-nut-to-crack, incorrigible bastards.'[5]

It was clear that the Zuma government's strategy to fight crime was to declare open war on criminals, with Cele as general-in-chief. This simplistic approach to policing fitted with the Zuma administration's lack of clear policy on key matters during its first three years in office. Crime in South Africa is a much bigger problem than something that could be solved by using deadly force. Although the government has often admitted that solving the country's crime problem should start with interventions on a socio-economic level, a clear policy or action plan on how this should be done was nowhere to be seen.

Cele's shoot-to-kill rhetoric found fertile ground with a crime-weary nation, but also led to a huge public outcry after incidents of police brutality and innocent bystanders being fatally wounded by the police. Olga Kekana, Jeanette Odendaal and Andries Tatane were only three of the many victims of trigger-happy police, probably encouraged by their political masters' new solution to solving crime. On 16 August 2012, heavily armed policemen shot and killed 34 striking miners at Lonmin's Marikana mine in the North West. By then, Cele had left the police, but the legacy of shoot-to-kill tragically lived on through the actions of these officers, who clearly had no plan, strategy or training to deal with this type of violence.

Statistics confirmed a spike in police violence. The Independent Complaints Directorate (ICD), the police watchdog body, reported an increase in the number of assault investigations against police officers between 2001/02 (255 cases) and 2009/10 (920 cases). Cases of attempted murder went up from 43 to 325 in the same period, and the ICD was investigating 524 police murders in 2009/10, compared to 281 cases four years earlier. KwaZulu-Natal, where Cele had served as police MEC before being appointed police chief, contributed most to the rise in fatal shootings: from 75 cases in 2005/06 to 205 in 2009/10, an increase of 173% in five years.

But it was not his heavy-handed approach to crime that led to Cele's downfall; Zuma seemingly had no problem with that. On 1 August 2010, the *Sunday Times* revealed that Cele had been involved in procuring a new head office for the SAPS in Pretoria at a cost of R500 million. The building in question, known as Middestad, belonged to businessman Roux Shabangu, and the transaction had not been put out for public tender. Cele denied any wrongdoing, saying he had only been involved in a needs assessment exercise, and that he had relied on his legal advisers and deputies to explain to him how the procurement process worked. What followed were two years of political instability and infighting in the SAPS and the Department of Public Works, which controls all government infrastructure requirements. The saga claimed the careers of two Public Works ministers, Geoff Doidge and Gwen Mahlangu-Nkabinde, two directors-general of Public Works and that of Cele.

Shortly after the *Sunday Times* exposé, opposition parties complained to Public Protector Thuli Madonsela about Shabangu's business dealings with the SAPS, which also included another expensive leasing agreement in Durban. Although she had no powers to institute criminal prosecutions, Madonsela's office had filled the vacuum left by the Scorpions in the Zuma era – at least in the public eye. She became the first port of call for disgruntled whistleblowers and those fed up with corruption in government, to the extent that her office was drowning in work. A case like the Shabangu/Cele building deal should ordinarily have been investigated by a law enforcement agency, to determine whether there was any criminal behaviour. The purpose of Madonsela's office is to monitor whether government does its job, not to investigate corruption. But with the Hawks yet to find their feet in the SAPS, and being part of the SAPS – then under Cele's control – Madonsela's investigation became the focal point of the unfolding scandal.

Shortly after details of the deal were revealed, Madonsela asked then Public Works minister Geoff Doidge to put the deal on hold, pending an investigation into its legality. Doidge obliged. What followed was a most extraordinary series of events. Doidge and his director-general, Siviwe Dongwana, appointed their own legal team to scrutinise the deal. In October 2010, Cele was informed by Public Works that the deal was illegal and had to be cancelled. At the end of that month, Zuma fired Doidge as minister (he was later posted to Sri Lanka as ambassador) and appointed Gwen Mahlangu-Nkabinde in his place. Barely a few days into her new job, Mahlangu-Nkabinde obtained another legal opinion, this time from the office of the state attorney, contradicting two opinions by private advocates. On 11 November, she reinstated the lease with Shabangu's company and a month later suspended Dongwana for insubordination.

It was clear that Zuma's removal of Doidge had the effect of reactivating Shabangu's R500 million deal with the state. Would Zuma

179

have any motive to protect the deal? Here's where it gets interesting. After the *Sunday Times* broke the story in August 2010, Shabangu's lawyer was quoted as saying her client was a good friend of Zuma's. For ten months, almost every media report that was published on the matter labelled Shabangu as 'Zuma's friend'. Nobody made a noise, objected to the description or threatened to burn newspapers. It was only in June 2011 that the media-shy Shabangu called a press conference at which he announced, 'I am not Zuma's friend'. He also said that his lawyer, who had said he was, had been fired.

Zuma waited another two months before publicly denying that Shabangu was his friend. Maybe it had something to do with his appointment of the cantankerous Mac Maharaj as his new spokesperson, but on 2 August 2011 – a year after the *Sunday Times* first stated that Shabangu was Zuma's friend – the president issued a statement, claiming he 'barely knows Mr Shabangu and any statement to the contrary is false'. Maharaj, on Zuma's behalf, also dismissed the theory that Doidge had been removed to rescue Shabangu's deal as an 'urban legend ... The rumours are without foundation and it is disappointing that some newsrooms have published or broadcast the rumours as fact, without even checking with the Presidency.'

If it was indeed the case that Zuma 'barely knew' Shabangu, why would he have waited twelve months to set the record straight? In those twelve months Madonsela and investigative journalists had portrayed Shabangu as a dodgy businessman – surely not someone Zuma would have wanted to be associated with?

*   *   *

In February 2011, Madonsela released her report, titled 'Against the Rules'. She slammed Cele for 'improper and unlawful' actions. Cele, she said, had used the 2010 FIFA World Cup as an excuse to circumvent proper procedures when he argued that the police's communications team had to be urgently relocated. She also revealed that the Middestad building had been offered previously to the police by an unknown business entity at a rate of R85 a square metre, but the SAPS had opted to sign with Shabangu at R110 a square metre. Madonsela asked Mthethwa to take the appropriate steps against Cele, and for Cabinet to consider taking action against Mahlangu-Nkabinde for allowing the transaction to proceed despite lawyers advising her to the contrary.

Meanwhile, Mahlangu-Nkabinde had announced a moratorium on all tenders in her department and asked the court to rule on the legality of the Shabangu lease. In July 2011, Madonsela released her report into another police building lease deal with Shabangu, this time for a building in Durban. She again singled out Cele and Mahlangu-Nkabinde for improper and unlawful actions, urging Zuma to act against them. She had harsh words for Mahlangu-Nkabinde, who, Madonsela said, had refused to cooperate with her investigation. 'The president should consider taking action against the Minister of Public Works for her actions referred to in this report and the report on the procurement of the lease of the Middestad building. I'm not prescribing to the president what to do, but I expect him to do the right thing,' Madonsela said.

After more than three months of silence from Zuma, the president fired Mahlangu-Nkabinde on 24 October 2011 and suspended Cele pending the outcome of a commission of inquiry into his role in the leasing saga. In his second major Cabinet reshuffle, Zuma also got rid of Cooperative Governance and Traditional Affairs minister Sicelo Shiceka, who had been severely criticised by Madonsela for maladministration a month before. On the same day, Zuma announced an inquiry into the Arms Deal and appointed Lieutenant-General Nhlanhla Mkhwanazi as the acting head of police.

On 12 June 2012, Zuma fired Cele after receiving a report from Judge Jakes Moloi, who chaired the inquiry into the police chief's fitness. Moloi's commission found that Cele was 'dishonest' and tried to 'mislead' Zuma by denying he had personally identified Shabangu's two buildings.[6] Cele was determined to secure Shabangu's buildings for the police, Moloi found. He further suggested that Zuma institute a criminal probe into Shabangu's relationships – with Cele and with

Public Works officials. 'It is recommended that these relationships be referred to competent authorities for further investigation ... on account of the board's lack of powers to subpoena witnesses or conduct searches and seizures.' Evidence before the commission 'proved abundantly that there was a questionable relationship' between Cele, Shabangu and Public Works officials that had to be probed further.[7] Cele vowed to fight back, and has launched legal proceedings against Moloi's report. He further suggested that there was a sinister motive behind his axing, driven by ministers in Zuma's Cabinet. After announcing his sacking, Zuma said of Cele: 'General Cele still has a lot to contribute to the country given his experience and commitment to making South Africa a better place for all each day.' The president didn't comment on Moloi's recommendation that criminal charges be preferred against Cele, Shabangu and Public Works officials.

Following his axing, the ANC in KwaZulu-Natal said the disgraced top cop still had a political future in his home province. Willies Mchunu, the deputy provincial ANC chair, also cautioned ANC members not to have 'untoward' feelings towards Zuma for firing Cele, as he was carrying out his duties as South African president. Moloi's findings about Cele did not make him 'unacceptable' to the ANC, Mchunu said.[8]

Despite Moloi's detailed findings about Cele's irregular conduct, questions remain about who exactly introduced Shabangu to the embattled police chief, and if Shabangu was indeed a friend of the president. Initially Cele was quoted as saying he had met Shabangu at the lavish March 2010 wedding of IT businessman Robert Gumede. But, before the Moloi inquiry, Cele testified that he had met Shabangu at police headquarters during an official meeting about the lease. Asked to explain the discrepancy, Cele's spokesperson told me: 'The gathering you refer to was, as you correctly mention, Robert Gumede's wedding. As a guest, it would be foolhardy to assume that General Bheki Cele knew everyone at the wedding and that he would remember everyone he would have been introduced to. To assume that he would use the wedding to discuss his work, or, in this case, the lease, is far-fetched and devoid of logic.'[9]

Will Zuma give effect to Moloi's recommendation that the police investigate the Cele-Shabangu relationship, a probe that might involve his own links to the men? Probably not.

Julius

'Now our phones are being listened to. When you greet on the phone, then you must greet Mdluli.'

24

The appointment of Richard Mdluli as head of the Crime Intelligence Division – the police unit that is supposed to infiltrate criminal syndicates and prevent crime before it happens – took place without much fanfare. A terse statement issued on 7 July 2009 announced his arrival at police headquarters: 'Top management of the South African Police Service would like to congratulate Commissioner Richard Mdluli on his appointment as Divisional Commissioner of the police's Crime Intelligence Division with effect from 1 July 2009. Prior to this appointment, Commissioner Mdluli (51 years) was a Deputy Provincial Commissioner in Gauteng.'

The statement gave a brief history of Mdluli's policing experience: 'Mdluli joined the police in August 1979 and was immediately placed in the detective environment. He worked his way up through the ranks as an investigator, detective branch commander and also served as an officer in crime intelligence. He is a competent leader, able to motivate members under his command and lead by example as an experienced investigator.' Acting police chief Tim Williams was quoted as praising Mdluli for proving 'himself to be an invaluable asset to the South African Police Service and I have no doubt that he will lead the Crime Intelligence Division with dedication, commitment and integrity'.

Mdluli replaced Mulangi Mphego, a trusted confidant of Jackie Selebi who had acted as crime intelligence head after Rayman Lalla was promoted to become a Deputy National Commissioner in charge of detectives.

What Williams didn't say at the time – but got off his chest in an interview with *City Press* two years later – was that Mdluli's appointment had been a political one. Not one police officer was part of the panel that interviewed Mdluli; the panel consisted exclusively of politicians that were known to be close to Zuma. And so the red flags went up: why were Zuma and Police minister Nathi Mthethwa so insistent on having Mdluli as their head of crime intelligence?

Shortly after his appointment in July 2009, the *Sowetan* published an article linking Mdluli to the murder of Vosloorus resident Oupa Ramogibe in 1999. 'The integrity of the newly appointed national head of crime intelligence Richard Mdluli has come into question, hardly a week after his appointment. The Ramogibe family in Vosloorus on the East Rand claims Mdluli featured prominently in the last days of their son, Oupa Abel Ramogibe,' the newspaper reported.[1]

In an interview with the newspaper, Sophia Ramogibe, Oupa's mother, claimed that Mdluli and her son were both in love with Tshidi Buthelezi, a woman from Vosloorus, and that the police intimidated Oupa after he married Tshidi. Mdluli, Sophia Ramogibe claimed, came to look for her son and said 'there will be mourning' in their family if he didn't report to the police. After surviving an attempted hit on his life, Oupa reported the incident to the Vosloorus police station.

'After arriving at the police station Oupa was taken to the scene of his ambush,' the newspaper reported. According to Oupa's brother, Mohau, the police's version of events is that while Oupa was busy pointing out the scene to them, 'someone came from nowhere, drew a gun from the holster of the investigating officer, shot and killed Oupa. The man then ran to an awaiting Golf, dropped the gun and fled. The police did nothing when all these things were happening.'[2]

Mdluli refused to comment on the article, and managed to keep a low profile in his new position. But, as he grew anxious about the possibility of being arrested, he turned to the man who had used crime intelligence spy tapes to get off the hook: Jacob Zuma.

Knowing Zuma's susceptibility to a good conspiracy, Mdluli was allegedly central in distributing a secret Ground Coverage intelligence report to the president in October 2010.[3] Mdluli denies this. The report is subtitled 'Alleged Corruption & Related Activities KwaZulu Natal', and central to its claims is an alleged meeting of Zuma's opponents in Estcourt, KwaZulu-Natal, supposedly to concoct a plot to unseat him at Mangaung. Ranjeni Munusamy, the former journalist-turned-Zuma-spokesperson-turned-journalist, reported 'unconfirmed allegations' in the *Daily Maverick* that Mdluli had delivered the report to the presidential residence in Pretoria. 'The report was allegedly given to Zuma via one of his bodyguards.'[4]

The 22-page report was the latest example of intelligence operatives attempting to influence ANC politics through the leaking of false information or half-truths into the public domain. Mbeki had the Browse Mole report, Motlanthe the hoax emails and Zuma the Ground Coverage report. We had indeed become a paranoid, spy nation. It was further reported that the report was compiled and 'faked' by private intelligence gatherers and sold for R200 000 before it was passed on to Mdluli.[5]

Mdluli is directly linked to the report through his signature, which appears on each page under the words 'Declassified 2010-11-24'. In an interview more than a year after the report had publicly been linked to him, Mdluli for the first time claimed that his signature on the document was forged. 'That ground intelligence report is bullshit. It never came from me,' he told the *Mail & Guardian* after the report had been thoroughly discredited in public.[6] He later claimed it was sourced by a senior politician.

The report is an amateurish attempt at an intelligence summary, and is soaked with spelling and factual errors. It starts out on a sombre note: 'Corruption of the tender processes and the receiving and payment of bribes is having a devastating effect on the moral authority of Government and the rule of law. Despite the knowledge of widespread corruption at the highest levels of Government, it appears that certain individuals are above the law as they are therefore untouchable.' And someone paid R200 000 for this!

The report then quickly degenerates into political bashing of Human Settlements minister Tokyo Sexwale and his 'Mvela Group' that allegedly met at a bed and breakfast in Estcourt (of all places). Despite the fact that Zuma, according to the document, was supposed to be the guest speaker, 'but due to unforeseen circumstances he did not avail himself', the purpose of the meeting was to 'discuss plans on what methods were to be employed to put pressure on President Zuma to step down from the Presidency or to create conditions that would lead to his "recall" by the ANC'. Apart from Sexwale, the so-called Mvela Group, according to the report, consisted of the following people: KwaZulu-Natal premier Zweli Mkhize; former Communications minister Siphiwe Nyanda; Sports minister Fikile Mbalula; former ANC Youth League president Julius Malema; Tony Yengeni; North West premier Thandi Modise; Justice minister Jeff Radebe; ANC treasurer-general Mathews Phosa; former ANC Western Cape leader Mcebisi Skwatsha; Arts and Culture minister Paul Mashatile; former Economic Development deputy minister Enoch Godongwana; Limpopo premier Cassel Mathale; then police chief Bheki Cele; Mpumalanga premier David Mabuza and Social Development minister Bathabile Dlamini.

The group's main targets, according to the document, were Zuma, ANC secretary-general Gwede Mantashe, SACP general secretary Blade Nzimande and ANC KwaZulu-Natal deputy chair Willies Mchunu. The group worked with a 'highly sophisticated rainbow nation criminal underworld,' the report reads.

I was reliably told that Zuma was deeply concerned about the report, and that it had had a direct impact on his relationships with people like Sexwale, Malema and Cele. In May 2012, Zuma told Parliament that he hadn't seen the report.[7] This was contradicted by media reports quoting sources close to Zuma. 'The hunters have become the hunted,' reported *The Sunday Independent* in April 2011:[8] 'There are increasing concerns that Zuma, who was briefed on the report much earlier, had allegedly believed a large portion of the report to be true, sparking concerns about what he planned to do to protect himself from those he viewed as seeking to oust him at the ANC elective conference next year. One of Zuma's aides said: "The president knew a long time ago about the report. He is a security person [he has intelligence background]. I do not know what he is going to do − but he is a politician and will not go down without fighting."' Zuma's then spokesperson Zizi Kodwa didn't deny that the president had seen the report, but said: 'We don't comment on intelligence briefings that the president gets from time to time as head of state.'

Despite the report allegedly having been provided to Zuma at the end of 2010, it only became public after Mdluli's arrest and subsequent bail hearing in March 2011.

On 11 November 2010, Mdluli wrote a 'top secret' letter to Zuma to complain about the 'campaign' against him. The letter was also addressed to Mthethwa, Cwele, Cele and Advocate Faith Radebe, the Inspector-General of Intelligence. At the time, senior Hawks investigators were brought in from Cape Town to investigate the murder charge against Mdluli, something he would have been aware of. He starts the letter by accusing the late Mpumalanga provincial police commissioner, Afrika Khumalo, of steering the campaign against him through intelligence gathering about the 'love triangle'. Ironically, Khumalo played a crucial role in Mdluli's rise through the ranks of the SAPS, having recommended him to take over as deputy police chief in Gauteng when he (Khumalo) was promoted to Mpumalanga. Mdluli said one of the reasons for the campaign against him was because 'I have not been involved in the "struggle"'.

Mdluli refers to an investigation done by the Limpopo deputy police chief, Major-General Benny Ntlemeza, into allegations that he was the victim of a conspiracy led by Khumalo. A copy of Ntlemeza's report was attached to Zuma's letter. Ntlemeza found that 'it is clear that there was a plot within the Crime Intelligence environment to prevent [Mdluli] who was then the Deputy Provincial Commissioner of Gauteng from being appointed as the Head of

Crime Intelligence'. He fingers Khumalo and two crime intelligence inspectors in Gauteng for digging up dirt on Mdluli, which led to the publication of the *Sowetan* article. Mdluli says he gave copies of the report to Lieutenant General Anwa Dramat, head of the Hawks, and Major General Joey Mabasa, former head of crime intelligence in Gauteng.

Mdluli 'categorically' told Zuma he was 'never involved in this "love triangle"'. The men who said they would remove him from his position, Mdluli claimed, were 'the very same members involved in negative campaigning at the ANC conference in Polokwane ... they were in the camp of the former president [Mbeki] and are now trying to take control of the intelligence environment within the police by devious tactics'.

Mdluli also told Zuma about his links to the ANC. 'Colonel [Nkosana] Ximba [a close ally of Mdluli who is also implicated in Ramogibe's murder] is an active member of the ANC and during the struggle was a leader of one of the Self Defence Units under MKVA. He was also a bodyguard for Mrs Winnie Mandela and former minister Steve Tswete [sic]. I worked closely with them during the apartheid era, especially during the riots. Colonel Ximba also played an important role in the Polokwane conference and also during the president's trying times with his engagement with the NPA.' He later wrote: 'I must also at this stage state that although I might not have gone outside and actively involved [sic] in the struggle, I was active in many other areas. I was, and am still, a loyal ANC member.'

Throughout the letter, Mdluli cleverly dropped teasers that were sure to grab Zuma's attention. 'The question now arises,' he wrote, 'what and how do they want to use the intelligence environment to affect the 2012 build up to ANC conference. With this in mind I have for the past few months tightened on expenditures, especially remuneration for sources with a view to ensuring that funds are not abused for ulterior motives related to the 2012 build up to the ANC conference.'

It is not clear if Ximba, who goes by the nickname 'Killer', was indeed involved in Zuma's campaign in Polokwane and his trials for rape and corruption, or if Mdluli was merely grandstanding. A former Umkhonto we Sizwe (MK) member told me Mdluli was definitely not involved in the liberation struggle but may have done 'a few favours for the ANC during the pre-1994 violence against Inkatha on the East Rand'.[9] Ximba, he said, was too young to have played a key role in MK, but has been close to Luthuli House in recent years.

On 31 March 2011, Mdluli handed himself over to police at the Boksburg Magistrate's Court for allegedly kidnapping and killing Oupa Ramogibe, the man with whom he shared a lover. Ximba and court orderly Samuel Dlomo were arrested along with Mdluli, and the three were charged with intimidation, three counts of kidnapping, two counts of assault with intent to do grievous bodily harm, murder, attempted murder, conspiracy to commit murder, and defeating and/or obstructing the course of justice. A day later, crime intelligence officer Mtunzi-Omhle Mthembeni Mtunzi was added as the fourth accused in the case.

The Sunday after Mdluli's arrest, former acting police chief Tim Williams told *City Press* that Mdluli's appointment was 'completely unusual' and 'not regular'. Williams, who was head of the SAPS at the time, spilled the beans about the 'political' process that was followed to get Mdluli into the job. Mthethwa 'instructed' him that a 'special' ministerial committee consisting of him (Mthethwa), State Security minister Siyabonga Cwele, Public Enterprises minister (then deputy Home Affairs minister) Malusi Gigaba and Mineral Resources minister Susan Shabangu would interview the candidates – Mphego, the incumbent, and Mdluli.

Williams said it was 'unknown' for a ministerial panel to hijack the interviewing process of a divisional commissioner. 'The normal process would involve the commissioner, deputy national commissioners and the deputy minister,' he said.[10] There were 'a lot of arguments about this between myself and the minister [Mthethwa]. I was completely opposed to it. They couldn't give me a reason why there was such a special panel to appoint an officer. I asked for reasons why he was appointed differently and they wouldn't give me any reasons,' Williams said, confirming that Mdluli's was a political appointment. Not 'one public servant was on the panel'. Ultimately, Williams said, Mdluli was appointed by Mthethwa – very likely with the blessing of Zuma.

Dr Johan Burger, a senior researcher at the Institute for Security Studies (ISS), commented that Mdluli's appointment 'was a clear case of political interference and a political appointment in which the normal procedures of the police were completely ignored. If a panel of ministers was involved it would be an exception to the rule. It is unacceptable. It sends only one message: that politicians want to ensure that a person who is politically acceptable to them is appointed. Then it would seem the head of crime intelligence was appointed not for policing purposes, but for other purposes.'[11]

Mthethwa's spokesperson commented that Mdluli's appointment was not unusual and that ultimately Cabinet had the final say in terms of the appointment. But this was not true. The ISS later pointed out that Mdluli's appointment was 'irregular' in terms of the SAPS Act, which requires the National Police Commissioner (Williams at the time) to appoint deputy and divisional commissioners. This didn't cost Mdluli his job, but indicated an eagerness on the part of his political masters to have him in this strategic position.

25

'The arrest of Crime Intelligence boss Richard Mdluli has lifted the lid on a ferocious political tug-of-war raging in the ANC and the government in the run-up to the 2012 ANC elective conference,' *The Sunday Independent* reported on 10 April 2011, ten days after Mdluli handed himself over to the police. Under the headline 'The ANC's succession war', the newspaper revealed the contents of the Ground Coverage intelligence report and said it emanated from a 'covert intelligence investigation' into Cele, supposedly by Mdluli. The report 'makes sensational claims that the commissioner [Cele] has ditched President Jacob Zuma in favour of the future ANC leadership of Human Settlements minister and ANC national executive committee member Tokyo Sexwale'.[1]

Although I was initially sceptical about the impact the report – badly written, incoherent and riddled with errors – would have on the ANC, it soon became clear that those in power, particularly Zuma, took it seriously. Was there a meeting in Estcourt that Zuma knew about? Did the report fill in gaps he had in his intelligence on what the ANC in KwaZulu-Natal was up to? Or did the report merely play into his paranoia, which we saw before Polokwane, that someone was out to get him?

The one thing the report strongly suggested was that the ANC

KwaZulu-Natal lobby around Zuma was no longer as strong as it was before Polokwane. Cele, a powerful power broker on the province's South Coast, was apparently making overtures to the broad anti-Zuma camp. Firing him as police chief would not have gone down well with Cele, whom I was told believed that Zuma had neglected him and that he was worth much more to the ANC. Zuma could, in any case, not go into an ANC elective conference without the support of the police chief. If the report had achieved one thing, it was probably in sowing the seeds of division between Zuma and Cele.

The president would not have been surprised by reports that Sexwale had presidential ambitions. Sexwale was born with presidential ambitions and has never been shy about his belief in his own leadership qualities. What was interesting, however, were reports that he had made inroads in lobbying staunch Zuma supporters such as Mkhize, Yengeni and Mabuza. Was this true, or not? Who knows? In a battle for power, truth is often the first victim. Zuma's non-response to the Ground Coverage intelligence report was probably more telling than the few words he said about it. There was no commission of inquiry (like Mbeki appointed with the Browse Mole report), no official police investigation or even a firm statement from Luthuli House about the party's view of the document. The loudest criticism of the report came from Sexwale himself, who publicly announced he would institute legal action against Mdluli, and subsequently reported the spy boss to Public Protector Thuli Madonsela.

It is, at the same time, amazing and frightening how a badly written intelligence report, the author of which is unknown, that makes serious allegations against senior politicians could be successfully fed into structures of power to the extent that it is accepted as the truth. Because of the country's past, the ANC would understandably be susceptible to reports of *impimpis* in its midst – turncoats working with third forces to overthrow Zuma's leadership at Mangaung. But, almost twenty years after the advent of democracy, you would have expected the state and its intelligence agencies to have the capacity to distinguish between genuine intelligence and bullshit.

But let's get back to Richard Mdluli. Although he denies it, it was widely reported at the time that the Ground Coverage report was distributed around the time of his bail hearing. His name became intrinsically linked to the report and, until twelve months later, Mdluli didn't distance himself from reports that he was either the author or main distributor of the document. This raised a number of interesting questions, seen in the light of his 'political' appointment. What was Mdluli's true role in crime intelligence? Did he keep checks on Zuma's opponents and their movements? If so, was he asked to do this, or did he volunteer? And what was his relationship with the president? Did it go further than the president knowing about his role in procuring the spy tapes that got Zuma off the hook?

The *Mail & Guardian* reported that Mdluli's arrest had set off a propaganda war. 'Mdluli is likely to bring out things on other people. This could make the fight between the police and the Scorpions look like a crèche picnic by comparison,' they quoted a highly placed security source as saying.[2]

On 20 April 2011, Mdluli was granted bail in the Boksburg Magistrate's Court, and on 8 May Cele suspended him as head of crime intelligence. In the interim, more agents working under Mdluli came forward to tell the Hawks about alleged fraud and corruption in crime intelligence, involving Mdluli. His suspension had the effect that whistleblowers were confident enough to spill the beans on years of alleged rampant abuse of a secret (police) service 'slush fund'.

This led to Mdluli's arrest five months later on charges of fraud and corruption. On 21 September 2011, he and Colonel Heine Barnard, also a senior crime intelligence official, appeared in the Pretoria Commercial Crimes Court after arrest warrants for them were issued. The charges related to the trading-in of Mdluli's personal BMW vehicle by Barnard and the purchase of two new BMWs with crime intelligence money to cover the shortfall on Mdluli's car. Both new BMWs were for the use of Mdluli and his wife, Theresa Lyons, an undercover crime intelligence agent in Cape Town. Relatively simple charges, one would think. Not if your name is Lawrence Mrwebi.

26

Three crucial things happened between October and November 2011 that shed some light on Mdluli's level of influence over the powers that be. Firstly, Zuma suspended Cele as police chief on 24 October as a result of the setting up of the Moloi inquiry into his conduct during the Roux Shabangu leasing scandal. In Cele's place, Zuma appointed Major General Nhlanhla 'Lucky' Mkhwanazi, head of the police task force, as acting National Police Commissioner. Secondly, Zuma appointed Advocate Lawrence Mrwebi as head of the Specialised Commercial Crimes Unit (SCCU) on 26 October – effectively making him the top prosecutor in the country in charge of corruption and fraud cases. And, thirdly, Mdluli wrote another letter to Zuma, dated 3 November, complaining again about the 'conspiracy' against him and making some ambiguous offers to the president.

Mkhwanazi's appointment came as a surprise, as he was not one of Cele's deputies. The 38-year-old made it clear that he was not going to play politics and was a policeman through and through. Mrwebi's appointment was even stranger. Like Jiba, he had been suspended by the NPA following the arrest of Advocate Gerrie Nel. Mrwebi was also in the NPA's bad books after his affidavit about a private meeting of Scorpions bosses ended up in Jackie Selebi's court case. But, like Jiba, Mrwebi had quietly returned to the NPA after intervention by Jeff Radebe, and had been deployed to the Director of Public Prosecutions's office in Pretoria. Mrwebi disappeared off the radar for a while — because of a falling-out between him and Menzi Simelane, I was told. Menzi Simelane was the NDPP at the time. Shortly after his appointment as head of the NPA, Simelane restructured the SCCU, effectively taking all the powers of the unit to the regional DPP offices all over South Africa. Whereas the national head of the SCCU previously had powers to intervene in commercial crimes cases, it was now up to all the regional directors of public prosecutions to oversee their own SCCU units.

But this all changed again when Zuma appointed Mrwebi as national head of the SCCU. And soon after his appointment, Mrwebi showed his willingness and zest to interfere in prominent corruption prosecutions.

My first interaction with Mrwebi was shortly after Jiba's appointment in January 2011. I wrote an article for *City Press* about Jiba's alleged role in her husband's disciplinary hearing at the NPA. Mrwebi sent me a furious email message, accusing me of siding with Gerrie Nel because I am white. A few months later, during an indaba of senior NPA managers in Johannesburg, and after *City Press* had been at the forefront of exposing the mishandling of the Mdluli matter, Mrwebi stood up during a discussion of the NPA's bad public image and accused me and *City Press* editor, Ferial Haffajee, of being racists. 'We just sat there and shook our heads,' I was told by a number of NPA employees who attended the event. Haffajee and I wrote a letter to Jiba, asking why Mrwebi referred to us as racists in front of the country's top prosecutors and whether she would be taking any action against him. We received no response.

One of the first things Mrwebi did after taking office was to ask the prosecutor in charge of Mdluli's fraud case, Advocate Glynnis Breytenbach, to provide him with a report on why the charges should not be dropped. This followed representations made by Mdluli's lawyer, Ike Motloung, to Mrwebi. I got hold of the representations in early 2012 and published the details in *City Press*.

Much like Zuma did when he was on trial, Mdluli relied almost exclusively on a conspiracy theory to have the charges against him dropped. The theory went something like this: there is a group of powerful policemen in the SAPS who didn't want him to become head of crime intelligence. They instituted an undercover investigation to find dirt on him and subsequently charged him with murder and fraud. In the representations, Mdluli names Cele and private investigator Paul O'Sullivan as the main drivers behind this conspiracy. O'Sullivan was a key whistleblower in the Scorpions' case against Selebi and also assisted the Hawks in their investigation of Czech fugitive Radovan Krejcir.

Project Libambe Lingashoni – translated by Mdluli's lawyer as 'let us wage a relentless campaign to see to it that he does not survive' – has as its aim to get Mdluli out of the police, he claimed. In the fraud case, Mdluli presented almost no evidence to challenge the charges against him, but relied solely on the conspiracy theory. 'Our instructions are that Mdluli's arrest is a continuation of the dirty tricks and manoeuvrings relating to the contestation and jostling for the position of head of crime intelligence. What has triggered this particular case is the realisation that the Johannesburg [murder] case is not sustainable against Mdluli,' the representations read. Cele, Mdluli argued, was abusing his power and authority to keep him out of the police. The case showed 'sheer desperation on the part of some in the top brass of the police and their cohorts to get rid of our client by hook or crook'.

Addressing the charges, Motloung, Mdluli's lawyer, wrote that Heine Barnard is the person responsible for the purchasing of vehicles in crime intelligence and he is the one who should be charged. The Hawks, he claimed, were trying to pressurise Barnard to implicate Mdluli and to say he was acting under Mdluli's instructions (when he purchased the BMWs).

On 14 December 2011, the NPA withdrew fraud and corruption charges against Mdluli – on Mrwebi's instructions. It emerged later that Breytenbach and Advocate Sibongile Mzinyathi, director of public prosecutions for Pretoria, had strongly opposed Mrwebi's decision, but had been overruled by him. In a later Labour Court application by Breytenbach against the NPA, it emerged that Mrwebi had used different reasoning – not even mentioned by Mdluli or his lawyers in their representations – to drop the charges. The Hawks, Mrwebi said, were not entitled to investigate cases of fraud and corruption against intelligence operatives like Mdluli and Barnard. This, he said, should have been done by the Inspector-General of Intelligence (IGI), Advocate Faith Radebe.

The Constitution provides for the IGI to carry out civilian oversight of the intelligence services, including crime intelligence, the SSA and military intelligence. She does not perform criminal investigations with the aim of prosecuting anyone, but reports to Parliament on her investigations.

Mrwebi's withdrawal of the Mdluli fraud case, against the wishes of the prosecutors involved in the matter, immediately raised red flags. Why did he go out of his way, so soon after being appointed by Zuma, to have the charges against Mdluli dropped? Was he asked, or told, to do so?

Unbeknown to the prosecution or to the public, Mdluli had written another letter to Zuma, pleading his case. On 3 November 2011, Mdluli addressed a letter to Zuma, Mthethwa and Mkhwanazi. Both Zuma and Mthethwa later claimed not to have received the letter. The letter was another sign of Mdluli's efforts to ingratiate himself with the president and his campaign to be elected for a second term as ANC president.

In the letter, Mdluli claimed that there was a conspiracy against him, driven by Cele, Gauteng police boss Mzwandile Petros, Hawks boss Anwa Dramat and head of detectives Godfrey Lebeya. He further stated: 'It is alleged that I support the minister of police and the president of the country. In the event that I come back to work I will assist the president to succeed next year.'

I specifically asked Mdluli's spokesperson to explain whether that sentence meant that he had offered to assist Zuma in his campaign to be re-elected at Mangaung. Although the sentence is potentially ambiguous, Mdluli refused to distance himself from the interpretation that the statement meant he was offering to assist Zuma in his campaign. Sources who saw the letter agreed that its purpose was to cosy up to Zuma. 'It gives you a clue why he is being protected,' one source said.[1]

Also in the letter were claims that Mdluli had received three affidavits 'regarding a conspiracy against me', and that the goal of the conspiracy was to replace him with former crime intelligence head Rayman Lalla 'or another person'. Mdluli further requested Zuma and the other recipients to suspend all disciplinary action against him until his criminal cases have been finalised.

Mdluli later admitted to writing the letter, saying he was making the executive aware 'of a plot to oust him'. 'But, I'm told it never reached the President and that's why now it's being looked at and let's respect that and see what's going to come out,' he told the SABC.[2]

The timing and contents of the letter became incredibly significant in light of the actions that succeeded it, not least that both criminal cases and disciplinary against Mdluli were controversially withdrawn.

At the beginning of 2012, there were increasing noises from the SAPS that Zuma wanted to appoint Mdluli as national police commissioner. As perplexing as it was to understand why the president would want to appoint as head of the police someone who was implicated in a murder and fraud case, there were more and more signs that Mdluli was receiving high-level political support and protection. Security sources from within the ANC were surprised that Zuma was seemingly promoting someone with no struggle credentials.

*   *   *

On 1 February, Breytenbach received a notice of intention to suspend her from the NPA, supposedly for abusing her powers in the fraud investigation against Imperial Crown Trading – the mining firm linked to Zuma and Motlanthe through the president's son and Motlanthe's lover. But Breytenbach's supporters said that this was a red herring and that the real reason for the NPA's disciplinary action against her was her insistence that fraud and corruption charges be reinstated against Mdluli. She was formally suspended by Jiba on 30 April, a week after Breytenbach had handed Jiba a hard-hitting memorandum on why Mrwebi's decision not to prosecute Mdluli should be overturned.

On 2 February, the NPA announced that it had withdrawn charges of murder and kidnapping against Mdluli and his co-accused and that the matter would be referred to a formal inquest. Advocate Andrew Chauke, the Director of Public Prosecutions in Johannesburg, had also received representations from Mdluli's lawyers and decided the matter could be 'best ventilated through a formal inquest before it can go to trial'.

Suddenly, Mdluli was one step away from being reinstated in his job, with the disciplinary charges against him the only remaining hurdle.

27

Mdluli's protection by top brass in the NPA became increasingly clear as more information was revealed about the 'special treatment' he received. In March 2012, I reported that the NPA had 'abandoned' a legal opinion sourced from a senior counsel on the merits of the murder case against Mdluli.

Advocate Andrew Chauke, head of prosecutions in Johannesburg, asked Advocate Modise Khoza SC, a private counsel at the Johannesburg Bar, to advise him whether Mdluli had a murder case to answer or not. I was reliably told by three independent sources that Khoza advised Chauke not to drop the charges against Mdluli. When I confronted Chauke about this, he was clearly uncomfortable with the conversation and changed his story throughout the interview.

Initially, Chauke denied having sourced a legal opinion from Khoza, but then said he did secure funding from the NPA to ask Khoza for his view, but 'abandoned' the opinion because 'in the interim, after reconsidering, I decided to go with my decision. I will consider the opinion when I get it'. Chauke claimed he had not received Khoza's opinion at the time of referring the murder case to a judicial inquest. 'His opinion is still going to help me going forward, the inquest is ongoing, it is not final,' Chauke told me.[1]

On 18 March, *City Press* revealed the extent of the fraud and corruption claims against Mdluli – and it was much more than the purchase of two BMWs for him and his wife. We published details from a secret 13-page report by senior crime intelligence generals Chris de Kock and Mark Hankel, which they submitted to Advocate Faith Radebe, the IGI, in November 2011.[2] In the report, De Kock and Hankel claimed that:

- Mdluli's family members were appointed to the crime intelligence agent programme without performing any undercover operations.
- Mdluli allegedly abused covert state vehicles that he was not entitled to use.
- A crime intelligence whistleblower was abducted by other crime intelligence operatives.
- A 'prominent person' from KwaZulu-Natal was allegedly placed in crime intelligence to influence Cele.
- Mdluli 'abused' a travel agent in Durban, with he and his family travelling more than 50 times at the state's cost.
- Various safe houses were rented by the police for the sole use of Mdluli and his family.
- Mdluli had a 'constant need for cash'.
- Two journalists were allegedly paid – one R100 000 to write a positive story about the police and the other R50 000 not to publish a story about a senior policeman.
- Evidence was uncovered from which it appears that crime intelligence 'sought to influence political processes in KwaZulu-Natal through the deployment of a select few covert intelligence fieldworkers' in the province. This included 'buying influence and access'.

De Kock and Hankel advised Radebe that there was a 'concerted effort from within crime intelligence ... to derail the probe' (by the Hawks). The same Hawks detectives who had taken over the Ramogibe murder investigation had since opened a probe into allegations of the large-scale looting of crime intelligence funds.

The report blew the lid off the Hawks' probe into crime intelligence and revealed that the alleged plundering of the R200 million-strong secret service fund was much more severe than was originally thought.

In the same week, I learned that the IGI had informed the police that Mrwebi's reasoning for withdrawing fraud and corruption charges against Mdluli was 'inaccurate and legally flawed'. After being informed of the NPA's decision to withdraw the case and refer it to the IGI's office, Lieutenant General Anwa Dramat, head of the Hawks, referred the matter to the IGI, with Mrwebi's opinion on why the SAPS should not be involved in the matter.

In a letter addressed to Mkhwanazi on 19 March, Radebe stated that she had received Mrwebi's memorandum on why her office, rather than the Hawks, should investigate the corruption claims against Mdluli. 'The mandate of the IGI does not extend to criminal investigations which are court driven and neither can the IGI assist the police in conducting criminal investigations. The mandate of criminal investigations rests solely with the police,' Radebe wrote. 'As such we are [of] the opinion the reasons advanced by the NPA in support of the withdrawal of the criminal charges are inaccurate and legally flawed. We therefore recommend that this matter be referred back to the NPA for the institution of the criminal charges.'

Mrwebi responded aggressively to Radebe's letter, which came to him via Dramat's office. 'I wish to advise that the office of the Inspector General of Intelligence has no oversight functions and powers of review with regard to prosecutorial decisions,' he wrote to Dramat. 'I also wish to remind that the NPA is an independent institution and prosecutorial decisions are its sole prerogative. The view of the IGI, following your solicitation of her opinion on the NPA decision on the matter, based on a document which the police or anybody else were not even legally entitled to possess, is for your consumption and does not affect the decision taken on the matter. The NPA took a principled and considered decision on this matter without fear, favour or prejudice, as it is required to do in terms of the law. That decision stands and this matter is closed,' Mrwebi wrote.

The Mdluli matter would test the strength and independence of the criminal justice system, and it became increasingly clear that, with Mrwebi in office, chances were slim for Mdluli to be criminally charged. Add to that Mdluli's prior relationship with Jiba – the acting NPA chief whose career he had saved by providing her with the crime intelligence spy tapes – and it became clear that something extraordinary had to happen if he was to be recharged. Only one man stood between Mdluli and his reinstatement: acting police chief Nhlanhla Mkhwanazi.

Only a few months into the job, those working with Mkhwanazi spoke highly of him and his work ethic. 'He's a policeman through and through. Clean, straightforward, no-nonsense,' I was told. So what happened next must have come as a huge shock for him. In the days after *City Press* published details of Advocate Radebe's refusal to take over the Mdluli fraud case, Radebe was put under 'massive pressure' by 'senior ministers' to withdraw the letter.[5] I was told that Radebe, a political appointee, was 'traumatised to the point of crying'. She apparently asked Mkhwanazi to hand back the letter she wrote, but he refused.

This led to Police minister Mthethwa calling an urgent meeting between Radebe, Mkhwanazi and himself in Pretoria. A source with inside knowledge of the meeting told me that the minister 'ordered' Mkhwanazi at the meeting to lift Mdluli's suspension and told Radebe to withdraw her letter. Radebe told Mthethwa at the meeting she had already requested Mkhwanazi to give back the letter after receiving a call from 'number one' – presumably Zuma – but that he (Mkhwanazi) refused. The young police chief told Mthethwa he would not lift Mdluli's suspension and would rather quit than be forced to do so. The tension was sky-high, and Mthethwa told Mkhwanazi that, as he hadn't appointed him, only Zuma could accept his resignation.

Under protest, Mkhwanazi lifted Mdluli's suspension but insisted that his name should not be associated with the decision. On 27 March, the SAPS released a short press statement, saying only that a 'decision was taken to lift the suspension of Mdluli ... concurrently'. It didn't say who had taken the decision.

Mthethwa denied ordering Mkhwanazi to do this, and Zuma's spokesperson, Mac Maharaj, denied that the president was in any way involved in pressurising Radebe to withdraw her report. A week later, we revealed that R200 000 had been paid from the secret 'slush fund' under Mdluli's control to upgrade security at Mthethwa's private residence at KwaMbonambi.

Mdluli's stunning return to the police, against all odds, proved to me that he had protection higher than that of the Police minister.

* * *

A series of events followed Mdluli's reappointment, and led ultimately to his suspension from the police for a second time. Although hard, exhausting and at times dangerous, the events of May and June 2012 convinced me that an active civil society, tenacious media and a strong and independent judiciary would always trump dirty, underhanded politics.

- On 1 May, Mdluli appeared with Zuma at a Cosatu Workers' Day rally in Botshabelo, outside Bloemfontein. The head of crime intelligence, whose job it is to infiltrate crime syndicates, said he attended 'as part of my duty as a police officer'.
- On 6 May, *City Press* revealed the contents of Mdluli's November 2011 'pledge' to Zuma – that he would assist the president to succeed at Mangaung.
- On 9 May, Mthethwa announced in Parliament that Mdluli would be removed from his position at crime intelligence and be moved to another portfolio pending an investigation by the State Law Advisor into his claims of a conspiracy against him, contained in his November 2011 letter to Zuma.
- On 13 May, *City Press* reported that former ANC activists had started speaking out about Mdluli's past as an apartheid-era Security Branch policeman. Mdluli denied being part of the feared 'SB' unit.

- On 27 May, Mkhwanazi suspended Mdluli again for his alleged involvement in plundering the secret service fund. This time Mdluli had none of the political protection he had previously enjoyed, and analysts said this was proof that Zuma had 'dropped' him.
- On 6 June, following an urgent application brought by civil society groups Freedom Under Law, Corruption Watch and the Social Justice Coalition, Judge Ephraim Makgoba of the North Gauteng High Court granted an interim interdict barring Mdluli from performing any policing functions, pending the resolution of the allegations against him. The charges Mdluli faced – murder, defeating the ends of justice, fraud and money laundering – were serious criminal acts 'which go to the fabric of public order and security', Makgoba ruled. It was 'unconscionable' for him to return to the police until the matter was resolved.

On 6 July, a task team that investigated Mdluli's claims of a conspiracy against him by senior policemen found that no such conspiracy existed. Mdluli's evidence could not be corroborated.

At the time of writing, Mdluli was challenging his suspension from the police in the Labour Court. The NPA's disciplinary hearing against Advocate Glynnis Breytenbach was moving at a snail's pace after two consecutive chairpersons had had to withdraw because of complaints by the NPA.

28

On 28 May 2012, I was invited to address a public seminar at Khayelitsha's Look Out Hill, organised by civil society groups Ndifuna Ukwazi (dare to know) and the Social Justice Coalition, led by activist Zackie Achmat. The seminar was attended by over 200 Khayelitsha residents who were concerned about the state of our police, the NPA and the country.

'I'm afraid I'm not here to bring you good news,' I started my address. 'Today, South Africa's law enforcement capabilities are in a shambles. We have no police commissioner. We have no national director of public prosecutions. We have no head of crime intelligence. We have no head of the National Intelligence Agency. We have no head of the South African Secret Service. And we have no head of the corruption-busting Special Investigating Unit. Which leads me to my next question: why is the government allowing this patently unsustainable situation to persist and what damage is being done to the fabric of our country when we cannot sleep safe?'

During a question-and-answer session, the anger and frustration of the residents were palpable. In the same township, incidents of necklacings had increased during 2012, and premier Helen Zille had appointed a commission of inquiry to investigate the state of the Khayelitsha police. These were the people at the coalface of the shambles in our criminal justice system, I thought. 'How do we solve this problem of the police?' a woman asked me. I told her that I didn't know, but that I did know the fish rots from the head and that it was up to organisations like theirs to make a difference, to make their voices heard.

Nine days later, Achmat was present when Judge Makgoba interdicted Mdluli from performing any policing duties pending the final resolution of the case against him. The Social Justice Coalition had joined the matter as an applicant and had submitted affidavits to court, outlining the demoralising effect cases like that of Mdluli have on policing in their township. The people of Khayelitsha had spoken up.

29

To tell the story of the dramatic arrival and departure of former judge Willem Heath as head of the Special Investigating Unit (SIU) at the end of 2011, we have to start with the firing by Zuma of Willie Hofmeyr as head of the SIU.

On 29 November 2011, Zuma announced that Hofmeyr would be replaced by Heath as head of the SIU. Hofmeyr had been wearing two hats – that of SIU head and head of the Asset Forfeiture Unit – for ten years, so it came as a surprise when the official reason given for his removal was to allow him to focus on his AFU work. This was nonsense-spin, and nobody who knew anything about Zuma or the working of the criminal justice system believed it.

Something else had happened. I don't know the real reason behind Zuma's decision, but I have my suspicions, which are shared by those in the know. Like most of Zuma's decisions, it goes back to his power battles within the ANC, this time involving Tokyo Sexwale and Lindiwe Sisulu.

In mid-2011, Sisulu and her supporters in the ANC – she is ANC royalty and regarded as one of the future leaders of the party – became increasingly annoyed by Sexwale's 'war on corruption' as Zuma's Human Settlements minister. Sisulu, who had been Sexwale's predecessor in the portfolio, saw his constant corruption comments as an attack on her term in office.

At the beginning of July 2011, Sexwale, flanked by Hofmeyr, stood up in Parliament and delivered a blistering attack on former SIU project manager Vanessa Somiah and the chief executive of the National Homebuilders Registrations Council (NHBRC), Sipho Mashinini. Somiah originally oversaw the SIU's investigation into the NHBRC, ordered by Sexwale, but was later employed by the council as head of investigations. The SIU's probe targeted Mashinini and the council's former chairperson, Granny Seape – a close ally of Sisulu.

Sexwale effectively accused Somiah and Mashinini of collusion and of 'whitewashing' the investigation. Somiah told me there was nothing untoward about her investigation and that the only issue raised with her by Hofmeyr was why she didn't interview Sisulu. Mashinini, who was suspended by the council at the time of writing, slammed Sexwale in an interview I did with him: 'Sexwale has not visited the NHBRC for the past 24 months. When he came in [as minister] he demolished all Sisulu's houses and took out full-page advertisements ... Tokyo wants to send a message that people are doing bad things and he is the good one,' he told *City Press*.[1]

A rumour began to do the rounds, to the effect that Zuma believed Hofmeyr had sided with Sexwale in the ANC's leadership battle and was using the SIU's housing probes as ways of promoting Sexwale's anti-corruption stance. This theory was popular among sources close to Hofmeyr and Sexwale. Nothing else really made sense. Hofmeyr had had major fallouts with the National Education Health and Allied Workers' Union (Nehawu) over the unionisation of the SIU, but this had been coming along for years and couldn't be the thing that moved Zuma to fire him. The other possibility was that Zuma wanted to let sleeping spy tapes lie – and that he blamed Hofmeyr for bringing the matter back into the public domain through the CCMA case of his former deputy at the SIU, Faiek Davids. In September 2011, the CCMA had ruled that what Hofmeyr heard on the spy tapes, in the presence of Zuma's lawyer, Michael Hulley, couldn't be used against Davids and that the recordings had been obtained illegally.

It would be a sad irony if the spy tapes led to Hofmeyr's departure from the SIU, as he was the chief opponent within the NPA of prosecuting Zuma, in light of what he had heard on the tapes. Said a senior security services source: 'Willie expected much more from the Zuma presidency. He played his part in the tapes saga and then thought he would become head of the Hawks, which he didn't. He must be a very bitter man.'

30

Zuma's appointment of Advocate Willem Heath (66) as the new head of the SIU was a strange, but not entirely surprising, move by the president. Heath was part of the bigger team that worked tirelessly to get Zuma off the corruption hook − another person in the ever-growing list of Zuma supporters who were rewarded after he came into power (in November 2011, Zuma appointed Michael Hulley, his private lawyer, with a background in criminal law, as the president's second legal adviser).

Once the darling of corruption-fighting in the country, Heath's career took a strange detour after he resigned as a judge in 2001. As the first head of the SIU, Heath made a name for himself as corruption-buster in the Eastern Cape, where he and his team probed large-scale corruption in local government. The SIU initially started as a tribunal, but became a proper state entity after the government realised the value of reclaiming money lost through fraud or corruption in civil proceedings.

But it was only after Patricia de Lille blew the whistle on the Arms Deal and provided Heath and the SIU with her evidence that he moved into the national spotlight. A thorn in the side of government, Heath lobbied hard to be part of the joint Arms Deal investigations team, but was left out at the last minute after intervention

by Zuma and Mbeki. The infamous January 2001 letter, written by
Mbeki but signed by Zuma, to Scopa chairperson Gavin Woods, excluded the so-called Heath unit from the Arms Deal probe on the
grounds that the Constitutional Court had ruled the SIU could not
be headed by a judge. This was spurious reasoning. Arms Deal experts have theorised that the true reason behind the SIU's exclusion
was that the unit had the powers to cancel the Arms Deal contracts.

After Heath resigned as SIU head and as a judge, he started Heath
Forensic Investigators, a private investigations firm whose clients included controversial mining boss Brett Kebble and Zuma. The once
respected corruption-fighter quickly gained a bad reputation among
his peers, who saw him as a 'hired gun'. Heath had to take on any
work, they said, because of his financial troubles. In 2009, Justice
minister Jeff Radebe hired Heath as his full-time special legal adviser. Heath resigned from this position when Zuma appointed him
as SIU boss in November 2011.

*   *   *

In the days after his appointment, I called Heath to request an interview. He was still being briefed by Hofmeyr, the outgoing SIU
head, and introduced to his new colleagues. Heath agreed to meet
at the guesthouse he was staying at in Pretoria (he was by then a
Capetonian).

City Press photographer Herman Verwey accompanied me to
meet Heath and his young assistant at the lush guesthouse. Heath
look relaxed in an open-collar shirt, but I could also see he had aged
since the last time I saw him, during his testimony at the Schabir
Shaik trial in 2004. I had a list of prepared questions, but nothing
could prepare me for the bombshell Heath was about to drop. I had
brought a voice recorder with me, and asked Heath if he was happy
for me to tape the interview, to which he agreed.

I started to discuss how his career had come full circle — from
starting the SIU in 1996 under Nelson Mandela to returning to the

214

unit in 2011 under a Zuma presidency. 'While Mandela was still the president, we had free rein. We just investigated anything that was referred to us. The atmosphere changed when Mbeki came into power,' Heath said, hinting at his absolute disdain for the former president. I wanted to know more. These excerpts are from the verbatim interview published in *City Press* on 4 December 2011, under the headline 'Inside Heath's world'.

Why?
Heath: Initially because of the sensitive cases we investigated ... when it came too close to him and other people, obviously they didn't like it.

Which cases?
Heath: The sensitive cases at that stage were as far as housing was concerned. The department of health spent a lot of money that never reached poor people. Because of his [Mbeki's] response, some of the ministers also became hesitant. During the beginning phases of the Arms Deal, I had some interviews with Mbeki. I had some information he didn't like and that was just the final straw.

It was not only Mbeki who didn't want you in the Arms Deal investigation, Zuma also said you should be excluded ...
Heath: That was Mbeki's line. Because I would still meet with members of the NWC [the ANC's national working committee] and NEC [national executive committee], and they were supportive and many of them were surprised by the SIU being stopped. That was Mbeki's brainchild — to stop our involvement.

But Zuma supported it ...
Heath: Initially I had no contact with him [Zuma] in those years. So he was, I'm guessing, probably responding to the sort of approach Mbeki had followed. As deputy president he had very little option but to go that route. Later, of course, I had regular contact

with him. Then, of course, he was most unhappy about the fact that the SIU was not involved in the investigation. And as I predicted at the time the National Prosecuting Authority, public protector and auditor-general did not come to light with any official or real discoveries during the investigations and their report was neutral.

Why were only Schabir Shaik and Tony Yengeni prosecuted for the Arms Deal?
Heath: They were sacrificed. It was easy to sacrifice them. And then, of course, Mbeki initiated Zuma's prosecution – not only as far as the corruption charges were concerned, but also on the rape case.

I listened to the recording of my interview with Heath over and over again, and could hear myself stutter for a moment, asking Heath 'is that what you're saying?' He responded in the affirmative. I asked him if he had any proof of Mbeki telling the NPA what to do.

Heath: He dictated to the NPA what decisions they had to take. I can't disclose the evidence to you, but generally there was no doubt he had a strong say in those decisions; yet the NPA was supposed to be completely independent.

Was the rape case a setup?
Heath: It was a setup. There was no evidence. And that is what Judge Willem van der Merwe found eventually. Obviously there was a sexual relationship, but on the evidence that was given in court, the lady spent the night there.

I realised that I had to come back to Mbeki and why Heath so readily implicated the former president in criminal behaviour. But I had to take another angle.

What do you think of the latest Arms Deal commission?
Heath: At this point in time, what is left of the documents? Of the evidence? Of the witnesses? After how many years – 13 years, I

think. It's still a good thing that they've appointed a commission of inquiry. Obviously one would like them to investigate that. At least it will bring out allegations that I think the people of South Africa should know about. [In 2001, Heath resigned as a judge after Mbeki had refused to grant him early retirement.]

What effect did this have on you and your belief in our democracy?
Heath: I didn't lose my confidence and belief in a new democracy, but because of Mbeki's refusal [to grant him early retirement], I had to resign. I retained no benefits as a judge. I walked out a pauper and had to start from scratch. By that time I would have difficulty going back to the bench. I moved to Cape Town to start a new career. I had to start from scratch.

When did you get involved in Zuma's case?
Heath: He called us in 2005 and we then had the first meeting with him. He contacted us personally. We had several meetings with him.

What did he want from you?
Heath: At that stage there were all the rumours about the corruption case. Following that, of course, the rape case – we also had discussions about constitutional matters not involving corruption.

What exactly did he want from you?
Heath: He wanted to have discussions with us. Initially it was about various constitutional matters, of which I can't disclose the details, and eventually we were advising him on the corruption and rape cases, although we were not part of the legal team.

What kind of advice?
Heath: Well, he discussed the facts with us, of the rape case, and we had to express views as far as the possibility of a conviction was concerned.

Was his lawyer involved in these discussions?
Heath: No, no ... they were separate and mostly secret meetings.

Did you ask Zuma why he was seeking a second opinion?
Heath: I think because of our track record of conducting serious research as far as any matter we become involved in. So it wasn't only because of my expertise as a lawyer, but also backed up by a proper analysis of the evidence.

Did you investigate the complainant in the rape trial?
Heath: No, obviously I was not entitled to do that because they're state witnesses. But on the evidence, the information that was available, we considered that.

What was your advice on the rape case?
Heath: I told him at the outset it was impossible to convict him of rape. This simply because it was consensual and eventually that's what the judge also found. That was a critical component as far as the judge was concerned.

What was the nature of your relationship with him?
Heath: It was a client-adviser relationship. After that there was the corruption case, but eventually the ANC took over and I was consulting them.

How did the relationship change?
Heath: They contacted me. So I can't say and don't know if he made any recommendations. But the initiative was taken by members of the NEC.

Was Lindiwe Sisulu the person who contacted you?
Heath: Yes.

Now I was ready to go back to Mbeki's so-called meddling in Zuma's trials. I figured that this had to go back to the Zuma spy tapes, which at least implicated Bulelani Ngcuka and Leonard McCarthy in attempting to use the timing of the corruption case to negatively impact on Zuma's political career. I've never heard that Mbeki himself was taped, and, if so, those tapes weren't part of the set released by the NPA in April 2009.

Were you involved in acquiring the so-called spy tapes?
Heath: No.

When did you become aware of them?
Heath: When some material pertaining to them was handed to me a number of years ago.

By Zuma?
Heath: Well, among various other things.

Various other things?
Heath: Now you're on dangerous ground.

For the first time in the interview, Heath sounded cautious and measured his words.

You can just say if you don't want to answer.
Heath: No, I don't want to answer.

Were you ever told how these tapes landed up where they did?
Heath: I had sight of those tapes, the transcription of that, and obviously the official approach was that it was just a concoction, that it was fabricated. My view was it was based on fact, and that the people who communicated didn't realise it was going to see the light of day. I read it thoroughly and analysed it.

When was this?
Heath: At the time when those tapes surfaced. I had sight of them

219

before it became public knowledge because they were submitted to me to analyse.

This was a significant response, as it showed that Zuma and his legal team not only disclosed the recordings, made by crime intelligence, to the NPA, but also to other parties, including Heath.

Did you ask whether the tapes were legally obtained?
Heath: No, I was just given the transcription to analyse. I had no contact with the people playing roles in it.

I wanted to explore further the comfort with which Heath implicated Mbeki.

Are you bitter about the previous ANC leadership?
Heath: Obviously I was most unhappy about the way in which I was treated and that I was left destitute, so I wasn't happy with that. As far as the new ANC was concerned, they were a completely new and different group. So they approached me with such sincerity and I accepted that they were not part of the old school, and that they were entitled to get to the truth of matters. You would know that none of them played a role in the Arms Deal.

Zuma was deputy president at the time ...
Heath: I wasn't consulted by him about the Arms Deal.

You were a state witness in the Shaik trial; you contributed to his conviction.
Heath: My evidence was so neutral. I was merely asked whether we applied for a proclamation to investigate the Arms Deal.

Do you agree with the Shaik judgment?
Heath: No.

Another moment of disbelief. A former judge doubting the veracity of a ruling by three courts?

Why not?
Heath: Because I didn't think there was sufficient evidence submitted. I studied the record and was surprised that he [Judge Hilary Squires] arrived at the conclusion he did.

Do you still believe that after the Supreme Court of Appeal and Constitutional Court have confirmed the judgment?
Heath: Well, they were dependent on the record that was available, so I still don't agree with it. I had many discussions about the issue of ANC members receiving support and financial assistance. Those who had returned from exile had nothing. So it was a common culture that those who had money would support the others.

So what is your conclusion? That nobody should be prosecuted or that everybody should be prosecuted?
Heath: It was part of a culture, and friendship and camaraderie, so it was a very common thing for those who had money to support the others.

I told Heath that the state proved a quid pro quo in the Shaik trial – that Zuma, through late-night meetings with businesspeople and letters of support, assisted Shaik's companies in return for Shaik funding his lifestyle, which constituted corruption. He had no response.

Do you believe there was a conspiracy against Zuma?
Heath: Yes. I believe the NPA was given instructions to pursue the matter on that basis.

By who?
Heath: The allegations were made at the time that Mbeki had given those instructions.

I realised that Heath was now more careful with his choice of words. I threw out more bait.

To Ngcuka?
Heath: Effectively, he had to give instructions to Bulelani. But I don't have the evidence; those were the allegations. As with the rape case.

Do you believe it?
Heath: I believe that instructions were given, yes. And you will recall that when the case was withdrawn against Zuma, they conceded that the case was tainted.

But they didn't say Mbeki gave instructions?
Heath: They had to be careful in making those allegations public. I think that was just the tip of the iceberg when they made those concessions as far as the tainting of the case was concerned. I think it was much more seriously tainted than they had admitted.

This response suggested to me that Heath either had access to more spy tapes or had been told by Zuma or his associates that there was more evidence of meddling that the NPA didn't release.

The interview caused a storm, not least because it was the first time that someone in power had openly accused Mbeki of actively participating in Zuma's criminal trials. Of course, this is what Zuma's supporters have always been saying behind closed doors, but here was the newly appointed head of a government entity, effectively accusing Mbeki of criminal deeds.

Mbeki reacted with outrage and shock. Four days after the interview was published, his office released this statement:

The office of former president Thabo Mbeki has noted Advocate Willem Heath's interview in the *City Press* newspaper's edition of December 4, 2011 in which he makes defamatory and malicious allegations against the former President.

Among others, Advocate Heath alleges that 'during his tenure ... as President of the Republic', the former president 'abused his position to compromise the criminal justice system by blocking some investigations into corrupt practices and "initiated" the corruption and rape charges preferred against President Jacob Zuma by the National Directorate of Public Prosecutions'.

Former president Mbeki categorically rejects all the allegations Advocate Heath has made. They are devoid of all truth.

The allegations made by Advocate Heath are very grave, more so because they are made by the Head of the Special Investigation Unit, a critical organ of our criminal justice system and suggest illegal conduct on the part of a former head of state and government.

Although Advocate Heath, a former judge, does not seem to have much regard for the decisions of the courts (including the Constitutional Court) except those with which he agrees, it is worth emphasising that the Supreme Court of Appeal (SCA) found no basis in the allegation of political interference on the part of former president Mbeki and the then Cabinet in the corruption case of President Zuma.

Among other things, the SCA said that 'the allegations (of political interference) were ... irrelevant ... gratuitous and based on suspicion and not on fact'.

The legal representative of the Thabo Mbeki Foundation has today formally approached government to provide evidence of all the allegations made by Advocate Heath.

The office of former president Thabo Mbeki also notes comments attributed to President Zuma about Advocate Heath insofar as they may relate to the latter's comments on the former president.

In the past, former president Mbeki has drawn attention to the use of fabrications to advance particular political agendas and to divert attention from the pressing challenges of the day.

If our broad leadership at all levels of society do not address this tendency, it may become an indelible part of our political culture and make it impossible for our country to address the real challenges we face.

Since his retirement, former president Mbeki has avoided commenting on domestic politics. It is with great reluctance that he is now being forced to comment on Adv. Heath's allegations.

Mbeki's lawyers wrote to Zuma, demanding evidence for Heath's controversial claims. Zuma told Ukhozi FM that he would seek legal advice from Radebe about Heath's statements and investigate if Heath 'held any grudges against anyone'.[1] ANC NEC member Ayanda Dlodlo called for Heath to be 'called to order' and Bulelani Ngcuka said Heath believed the SIU job was his 'God-given right'. Mac Maharaj, Zuma's spokesperson, played an old trick by saying Heath's statements were made in his 'personal capacity', but that too wouldn't make the storm go away.

Finally, on 15 December, 17 days into the job, Heath resigned from the SIU. 'It became very clear that the utterances of Advocate Heath had created a perception, rightly or wrongly, that he cannot be independent in terms of helping the Special Investigating Unit,' Radebe said.

Four days after his resignation, Heath responded by saying the interview had created the impression that he was unable to head the SIU independently. 'Correct or not, the initial media coverage of an interview in which I participated left the impression that I made unqualified statements on political events which may be unbecoming of the head of the SIU. In the public domain therefore, such an impression has created much public debate and impression is often as important as fact.'

Zuma appointed Advocate Nomgcobo Jiba to act in Heath's place, but replaced her, after less than a week, with Advocate Nomvula Mokhatla, also a Deputy National Director of Public Prosecutions. The axing of Hofmeyr, Heath's resignation and the appointment of an acting head caused instability in the SIU that led to the loss of key personnel. The unit's budget was cut and Mokhatla ended a relationship with private forensic firms to outsource forensic investigators to assist the SIU in complex cases.

In early 2012, Mbeki instituted defamation proceedings against Heath, which were still pending at the time of writing. It will be a fascinating case if it goes to trial. Will Heath be able to bring the goods to back up his statements? Will Zuma and the intelligence agencies assist him if such evidence actually exists? Or will Heath, and Zuma by implication, finally be forced to climb down from their conspiracy theory that there was an Mbeki-led campaign to prevent Zuma from winning at Polokwane?

Part 3

Bad leadership

Julius

'President Jacob Zuma is a president of a faction within the ANC. They have never marched against corruption, they have never marched against crime, but they marched against *The Spear*.'

31

'Why did you guys think he would make a good president?' I ask a former Zuma confidante over coffee. The answer comes quickly. 'There's a difference in looking at someone as a victim and someone in power. We always knew JZ had fundamental weaknesses. But it's difficult to assess someone's leadership when they are completely vulnerable. They present themselves as a victim; you can see they are in desperate need of help. In that time, you don't sit back and assess a person's leadership qualities.'

It was clear from a number of people I spoke to that they almost viewed Zuma as two people: the Before Polokwane (BP) victim and the After Polokwane (AP) president. Zuma BP was charismatic, persecuted and fragile. Zuma AP is weak, indecisive and devious. 'I don't even think in his own mind the plan was for JZ to run for president. It was almost a sense of revenge, to show Mbeki "I can do it",' says the former aide. It was easy to translate popular support around his court cases into a presidential campaign. 'The campaign developed a life of its own. People had sycophantic feelings about him. The support he received through his trial eventually translated into a political campaign.'

There was 'no genius' behind the support for Zuma. Some supported him because they believed he was persecuted. The left had running battles with Mbeki and needed a Trojan horse. Others, like Brett Kebble, thought they could get rid of their own legal troubles by backing Zuma in his battles with the Scorpions. Was he the wrong guy at the right place? 'Maybe.'

As Mangaung drew closer, Zuma was making the same mistake Mbeki did. 'He's abusing the security services. He's not seeing what will happen in Mangaung,' the former aide says, suggesting Zuma might be in for a hiding.

By mid-2012, only a small group of Zuma loyalists remained from the BP era: Blade Nzimande, Gwede Mantashe, Siyabonga Cwele, Malusi Gigaba and Nathi Mthethwa. 'He needed people beholden to him, who he could control,' is the explanation for the large number of former Zuma aides and supporters who have either jumped ship or gone underground.

The unlikely president is strongest when he's a victim. With popular support dropping and the Mdluli scandal refusing to go away, Zuma needed a new cause before Mangaung. On 13 May 2012, we almost handed it to him on a silver plate.

32

It was a Thursday afternoon at the office when I suddenly heard rumblings in the newsroom; people talking, laughing, oohing. I also saw some male colleagues, hands over mouths, shaking their heads as they walked towards their desks.

The centre of attraction was Mohau Mokoena, a very funky lay-out artist at *City Press*, who was walking around with three printed pages in her hands. I went closer to have a look. Mokoena is the chief layout artist on *7*, the newspaper's arts and entertainment supplement, and she had designed three different dummy front pages for *7*, each with a different image on them. The images were artworks from satirical protest artist Brett Murray's latest exhibition, titled *Hail to the Thief II*. I inquired and was told that Ferial Haffajee, our editor, had asked Mokoena to design the three options and show them around the office. We were going to run a review by our arts writer Charl Blignaut on the return of protest art.

There were two that immediately caught my attention. The one was of the ANC's emblem, with the words 'FOR SALE' and 'SOLD' printed over it, and the other was a rip-off of a classic poster of Soviet leader Vladimir Lenin, only with Zuma's head and a large penis hanging from his trousers. There was also a classic 'Amandla!' struggle poster, with the words 'We demand Chivas, BMW's and bribes' on it.

Mokoena explained that Haffajee wanted to test the feeling in the office, and asked us to vote for the one we liked most. I thought the ANC emblem was strongest, but didn't mind the Lenin pose, although it wasn't a particularly beautiful painting. A general news-room discussion ensued, during which it emerged that a number of colleagues were strongly opposed to the Lenin painting. They thought that it degraded Zuma.

The final decision was to go with the 'Amandla!' struggle poster for the cover of 7, but to use the other images on the inside spread. There was never a discussion about covering up the penis; the article was, after all, about an art exhibition, to be published in the *City Press* arts supplement.

The next day, Blignaut, ever excited, came rushing to the news desk with the news that *The Spear*, as we had learned the Lenin pose was titled, had been sold for R136 000 to a German couple. Again there was a discussion in the newsroom about using a picture of the painting on the news pages rather than in the arts supple-ment. The decision was to cover the penis with a price tag because the sight could offend certain readers. We used a teaser of the story on page 1 and a small story titled 'R136 000 for Zuma's jewels' on page 3. Blignaut quoted Murray as saying: 'I'm delighted. It wasn't the kind of work I expected to sell. It was more about an idea. I didn't think someone would want to hang it in their lounge and live with it – even though it is rather well hung.'[1]

* * *

On Sunday, the newspaper was on the street. For four days, noth-ing happened – no complaints from readers, no debates on radio and no protests. In the meantime, Haffajee left for a conference in India and we were hard at work on the next edition when ANC spokesperson Jackson Mthembu released a press statement late on Thursday afternoon. The statement, titled 'ANC outraged by Brett Murray's depiction of President Jacob Zuma', said that the ANC was 'extremely disturbed and outraged by the distasteful and indecent manner' in which Murray had depicted Zuma. 'This disgusting and unfortunate display of the president was brought to our attention by one of the media houses and we have physically confirmed this insulting depiction of the president,' wrote Mthembu, meaning someone had gone to the Goodman Gallery, the venue for Murray's exhibition, and had viewed the painting.

Mthembu announced that the ANC had instructed its lawyers to go to court to 'compel' the gallery to remove the painting from display and for *City Press* to take down the image from our website. The painting had 'dented' the 'image and dignity' of Zuma, as president of the ANC, South Africa 'and as a human being'. The ANC said that, although it believed in freedom of the press and artistic expression, 'the vulgar portrait and the dismembering of the ANC logo by Brett Murray is an abuse of freedom of artistic expression and an acute violation of our constitution, apart from being defamatory'.

We knew a storm was coming and instructed our lawyers to prepare for an urgent interdict application by the ANC. Mthembu's statement led to a vicious national debate on artistic freedom, freedom of expression and human dignity. Some asked for the painting to be destroyed while others rushed to the Goodman Gallery to see the work firsthand. I spoke to Haffajee in India, and we were both surprised at the controversy the publication of the painting had caused. We agreed in principle that it was not our duty to defend the artwork, but the publication thereof. The next day, she wrote a column that we published online, titled 'The spear of the nation stays up':

Did we think the image of President Jacob Zuma by Brett Murray was particularly beautiful to persuade us to publish it? No.

Would it be something I would hang at home? No.

There is a copy stuck on my office window, along with two others from Murray's explosively angry exhibition of satirical graphic art.

Murray, now facing a demand from the governing ANC

233

that he destroy the work, designed some of the anti-apartheid movement's most iconic resistance art.

The copies sit on the window to display a moment of compromise at *City Press*.

A group wanted the image of an 'exposed' president to lead our arts section, called 7, but too many people in our office objected on grounds that ranged from us being a family paper, to concerns about dignity and cultural values.

We put the image inside and ran a funny version on page 1, its indignity covered by a price tag.

The work was sold to a German buyer soon after the show opened for more than R130 000 and it will probably leave for good anyway, so why go to court to get it destroyed?

Why would you want to destroy art in the first place?

Our Constitution explicitly protects artistic expression as a subset of free expression, to which its detractors will respond as they have all week: they draw the line at art that impugns presidential dignity.

But I've learnt that the commitment to clauses like free expression (be it in art or journalism) is never going to be tested by still lifes of bowls of flowers or by home decor magazines.

It is always going to be tested by art that pushes boundaries and journalism that upsets holy cows, which is why our clever founders enshrined the right in our Constitution.

They knew our artists and journalists would, if we stayed true to the founding South African DNA of questioning and truth-saying, need protection.

In the past week — and in the one to come — we will hear again this clash of free expression and dignity.

Inevitably, race will be drawn into it: only a black president would be depicted like this, the race brigade will drone.

Inevitably, sexuality will be drawn into it: it is the stereotype of the black man and the uncontrollable appetite, they will wail.

We have been here before when Zapiro did his series on

Justice being raped by the president and his gang.

Making good headway in the investigation into the melt-down in the police service – Mdluligate – this debate is not a distraction we at *City Press* have courted.

City Press covered an art exhibition, an interesting and re-markable exhibition that marks a renaissance in protest art, which we are tracking.

To ask us now, as the ANC has done, to take down an image from our website is to ask us to participate in an act of censor-ship. As journalists worth our salt, we can't. Besides, the horse has bolted. We published on Sunday.

My own objection is personal and I state it so, for I do not expect all my colleagues to accept it. Ours is a sexually aware, satirically sussed and progressive country.

At the same time, we are a traditional society with a presi-dent who is most well known for his many marriages.

Our identity is not as simple as the cultural chauvinists and dignity dogmatists like to make out. Ours is, by design, a live and let live world.

I'm tired of the people who desire to kill ideas of which they do not approve. Besides, our morality and good practice is selective.

The man driving this latest nail into the ANC's commitment to free expression is Jackson Mthembu, who was recently ar-rested for drunk driving at 7am on a busy highway.

He is no paragon of virtue and neither is our president, who has done more to impugn his own dignity than any artist ever could.

But mostly, I will not have my colleagues take down that image because the march away from progressive politics to pa-triarchal conservatism is everywhere.

It is there in the Traditional Courts Bill, which seeks to re-turn rural women to servitude; it is there in a governing party MP, who seeks to strip gay people of their right to love; it is there in the draft Protection of State Information Act, which seeks to pull a securocrat's dragnet over the free flow of news and information.

It is there in the march of polygamy; there in the push-back on quotas for women politicians and there in the people who want art pulled down because they do not like its message.

We are Mzansi after all, not Afghanistan, where they bulleted the Buddhas of Bamiyan because the art did not conform to what the rulers believed it should be.

Late on Friday night, we received the ANC's court papers. Significantly, we saw that Zuma himself was the first applicant and had deposed to the founding affidavit. The ANC was the second applicant. Until then, Zuma had not said a word on the matter or announced that he would personally try to interdict the Goodman Gallery and *City Press*.

On Saturday, at our last news diary meeting for the week, the team decided to lead with what Zuma had said in his affidavit. We devoted almost the entire front-page lead story to Zuma's affidavit and the support he had received from his children – who had also joined the matter as an applicant – his Cabinet colleagues, the ANC and Menzi Simelane, the NPA head who Zuma had placed on extended leave. Simelane was the first person to mention the idea of a *City Press* boycott when he tweeted: 'Those who are offended by the depiction of the president's private parts must boycott City Press.'

In his affidavit, Zuma said he was 'shocked and felt personally offended and violated' when he saw a copy of Murray's painting. The work, he said, depicted him as a 'philanderer, a womaniser and one with no respect'. A continued display of *The Spear* would impugn his dignity 'in the eyes of all who see it', Zuma wrote. Zuma's daughter Gugu released a statement on behalf of his children that described the painting as vulgar and lacking humanity. 'It seeks to take away our father's dignity, and destroy his true character and stature as a man, a father, and a leader of the ANC and South African society at large,' the children wrote.

In the same article, we quoted renowned poet and cultural activist Mongane Wally Serote, who said the painting was trivial and distasteful, and not deserving of the attention it was getting.[2] 'We are making something trivial important. We are blowing it out of proportion. Whatever inspired that art was completely mediocre and distasteful. We have a country where there are very important things that must be addressed. For example, we should be asking how we inspire people to build a diverse South African nation,' Serote said.

On the Sunday morning, *City Press* executive editor Fikile-Ntsikelelo Moya and I met with our legal team to prepare for the interdict application, scheduled for Thursday 24 May. We discussed a number of legal strategies, including our constitutionally enshrined freedom of expression and that it was reasonable and lawful to publish Murray's uncensored painting in our arts section.

The next morning (Monday 21 May), the episode took a new and depressing turn when I received a call informing me that a classifications team of the Film and Publication Board (FPB) had arrived at the Goodman Gallery to inspect *The Spear*. I rushed to the gallery, but arrived too late to see what the country's democratic censors looked like. The FPB confirmed that they had received complaints from 'the public' and were looking at censoring the artwork. This was an unprecedented step for the country's censor board, whose members spend most of their time watching pornographic films to decide what classification they should receive. When we asked for a list of artworks classified by the board since 1994, they couldn't provide us with one. FPB spokesperson Prince Ndamase said he could not recall a case.[3] We found one case in 1998, when an exhibition by artist Mark Hipper was classified 18N because it contained naked images of children, but nothing comparable to *The Spear*.

A threat of classification is one of the harshest penalties a newspaper can face. We realised that if the FPB hastily classified *The Spear*, we would be forced to remove the image from our website as it would only be allowed to be displayed on age-restricted websites. This would effectively also make Zuma's case against us irrelevant, as that was exactly the order he had asked for. So our lawyers proceeded

237

to write to the board, asking them to afford us an opportunity to make representations before they classified *The Spear*.

On the same day as the FPB's inspection, Tselane Tambo, daughter of the late ANC president Oliver Tambo, tweeted that she had little sympathy for Zuma: 'So the Pres JZ has had his portrait painted and he doesn't like it. Do the poor enjoy poverty? Do the unemployed enjoy hopelessness? Do those who can't get housing enjoy homelessness? He must get over it. No one is having a good time. He should inspire the reverence he craves. This portrait is what he inspired. Shame neh!'[4]

The ANC's and Zuma's case was set down for hearing on Tuesday 22 May before Judge Fayeeza Kathree-Setiloane of the South Gauteng High Court in Johannesburg.

On the same day, the self-proclaimed spokesperson for one of South Africa's largest churches, the Nazareth Baptist Church – also known as the Shembe church – asked for Murray to be stoned to death. Enoch Mthembu was quoted as saying: 'This man has insulted the entire nation and he deserves to be stoned to death. What he did clearly shows his racist upbringing because art does not allow people to insult others. This is an attack on the culture of the majority, the black people of South Africa. With our culture we are allowed to marry many women. And white people must understand that and tolerate our culture as we do theirs. We are not like some of them who prefer prostitutes as they regard women as sex objects.'[5] A month later, Mthembu was forced to apologise and withdraw his statements by the South Gauteng High Court after Murray successfully obtained an interdict against him, prohibiting Mthembu from inciting violence.

Zuma's supporters continued to be vocal in their condemnation of *The Spear*, with ANC secretary-general Gwede Mantashe saying the painting was racist: 'We have not outgrown racism in the 18 years of democracy. I can tell you, if you depict a white politician in that form the outcry will be totally different.'[6]

* * *

The courtroom was packed with mostly Zuma supporters as all the parties appeared before Judge Kathree-Setiloane. She informed us that Gauteng Judge President Bernard Ngoepe had decided that the case should be heard by a full bench of judges – three in the High Court – and that the matter would reconvene two days later.

We returned to the office to prepare for Thursday's hearing. As I got into my car, I received an SMS saying 'Spear defaced'. I switched on the radio and there it was: two men, one black and one white, had entered the Goodman Gallery, at about the same time as we were appearing before Kathree-Setiloane, and took out cans of paint, with which they defaced the painting. The first man, later identified as East Rand resident Barend la Grange, took out a small can of red paint and painted two large 'X' symbols over Zuma's face and genitalia. The second man, Tzaneen taxi driver Louis Mabokela, had a can of black paint and used his hands to smear the painting. Both were arrested by a security guard working for the gallery; the guard manhandled Mabokela and threw him to the floor.

La Grange said he didn't like Zuma, but was 'against the way he was portrayed'. Mabokela had travelled from Tzaneen to smear *The Spear*. 'It's an insult. He is a parent,' the 25-year-old said after appearing in court.[7] The two men were still facing charges for malicious damage to property, and the security guard for assault.

Later that afternoon, our lawyers received a call from the FPB, informing us that we would have to appear before the board that night if we wanted to make representations on the classification of *The Spear*. It was clear to me that the FPB had been instructed, or had decided of its own volition, to finalise this matter as quickly as possible.

We jumped into our cars and rushed to the FPB's plush Centurion offices, where we quickly caucused outside the boardroom with Advocate Steven Budlender, who was representing us in the case. In the boardroom, we were met with the smell of hot Nando's chicken and the sight of a smiling Yoliswa Makhasi, the board's chief executive officer. As we entered, I heard Makhasi say to Haffajee, who had returned from India that morning, that she followed her on

Twitter. It would be interesting to see what the country's censor-in-chief tweeted about, I thought, and searched for her account. I found Makhasi's account, and was shocked to see that she had already expressed her views about *The Spear* – the same matter she now wanted to adjudicate. I quickly printed out a timeline of Makhasi's tweets and gave it to Budlender, who read it out.

On 18 May, Makhasi responded to a tweet by Talk Radio 702 host Redi Tlhabi, who was responding to a message by political analyst Eusebius McKaiser. McKaiser had tweeted: 'lame that @eNews shows depiction with genitalia blurred as if it is porn', to which Tlhabi responded: 'If u saw penis everyday of yr life, u'd be ok with it☺'. Makhasi's response was: 'enews is watched by kids and sensitive viewers, that was a sensible thing to do!'

On 21 May, Makhasi announced on Twitter: 'The FPB sent its Classifiers to the Godman [sic] Art Gallery today to classify the image, we will make our findings public in due course.' Curiously, Makhasi didn't say that they would inspect the painting to decide if it should be classified, but stated as a fact that the work would be classified.

That morning, Tuesday 22 May, Makhasi shared with her followers the media's concern about an FPB classification. 'The Spear is taking a new turn; FPB getting lots of letters from lawyer representing some newspapers gagging it from publicizing the … Classification decision. Its interesting how media is sensitive to being gagged and yet so quick to want to gag others.'

Budlender argued that Makhasi could not be part of the hearing as she had clearly expressed a view on *The Spear* in public. She subsequently recused herself from the hearing, and later that night deleted her Twitter account. The rest of the hearing was just as bizarre as the start. It was never clear exactly who we appeared in front of. The 'board' consisted of six FPB employees, two private individuals and two lawyers, who did most of the talking. At the end of a lot of toing and froing, the board's chief operating officer, Mmapula Fisha, who was now the chair, revealed that a classification committee had not yet been appointed to view and classify *The Spear*. Supposedly, an FPB delegation had visited the Goodman Gallery the previous day to 'classify' the painting. It remained a mystery who exactly had done the inspection.

The hearing was postponed for a week, which gave us a day to prepare for Zuma's court challenge.

The next day, 23 May, all the parties were required to file heads of argument to the court. The gallery, represented by Advocate David Unterhalter SC, said that his client, Murray, other practising artists and fine art academics who had filed affidavits in support all understood 'the work as a symbolic and metaphorical satire'.[8] 'They have testified that, like it or loathe it, *The Spear* has made an important contribution to the milieu in which they work. *The Spear* has been a catalyst for the type of deliberation that characterises and is indeed the lifeblood of a democracy,' Unterhalter's papers read.

Attached to the gallery's court papers were supporting affidavits by artists, including William Kentridge and Senzeni Marasela. 'Penises, in the age of Aids when explicit sex education for primary school children is de rigueur, are a dime a dozen. Much of Aids education has been to break down traditional taboos of children being shielded from adult sexuality,' the internationally renowned Kentridge wrote in his affidavit. 'There is nothing shocking in the specifics of the image. The shock is in the metaphor – Lenin and the penis meeting President Zuma ... the themes and symbolism employed by Brett Murray in his work are typical of the themes and visual language employed by many fine artists in Africa, Asia, Australasia, Europe and the Americas. It is a global, modern language.' Murray's overt depiction is in line with a 'change in attitude towards a public discussion of political power and the sexuality that accompanies power'.[9]

Murray 'made no attempt to make an image of President Zuma as a private man with a personal life. The genitals in the image are worn like the coat of Lenin – almost as a badge of office. It may be an incorrect summing up of the president but it is not an illegitimate subject to address,' said Kentridge. He encouraged a debate on power, sex and their depictions. 'Both the work of the artist and the controversy his work arouses are to be welcomed for this. The metaphorics of the emperor's clothes reappears.'

Marasela, a former artist in residence at the Iziko South African National Gallery, took issue with the fact that the public display of male genitalia was labelled 'un-African and disrespectful to our culture ... We cannot assume that all black men collectively agree that they have one uniform culture that opposes public display of male genitalia, or that all black people think in any one particular way.'

In our heads of argument, *City Press* argued that Zuma's case was fatally flawed because there was no 'basis or precedent in law for a blanket ban of a work of art'. We further argued that the image had been reproduced thousands of times on websites in many countries, and that any ban would be unenforceable.

In his affidavit before court, my colleague Fikile-Ntsikelelo Moya stated that, by publishing *The Spear*, *City Press* was doing what it is 'constitutionally entitled to do' – reporting on an 'interesting and remarkable exhibition that marks a renaissance in protest art'.[10] In publishing *The Spear*, *City Press* 'neither sought to endorse nor adopt the messages conveyed by the exhibition or the portrait. Rather, we allowed the public to judge the matter for itself.' He reiterated that any takedown order would be impractical: 'The horse has long since bolted. As a direct consequence of the media statements made by the applicants and the launch of the present application, the portrait has been given widespread national and international publicity. Subsequent to the ANC media statement and because of it and the present application, the portrait is now available on at least 10 South African websites (none of which are controlled by *City Press* or Goodman Gallery) and on websites in at least 15 foreign countries ranging from Argentina and Australia to Zambia and Zimbabwe.'

With regard to Zuma's dignity, Moya said that, although the president had a right to privacy, *The Spear* 'did not disclose any private facts about him given that it derives from the artist's imagination'. Publication of the image amounted to 'legitimate criticism', as Zuma's extramarital affairs were well known.

We were going to argue that politicians and public office bearers should have a 'thicker skin ... Politicians knowingly lay themselves open to close scrutiny and forthright criticism by both journalists and the public at large, and consequently ought to display a greater degree of tolerance.'

33

On Thursday 24 May 2012, we went to court to defend the publication of *The Spear* and to keep the image on our website. The courtroom was packed with journalists and ANC supporters, and security officials had to turn people away. I spotted Duduzile and Duduzane Zuma, Jackson Mthembu, Tony Yengeni and Gwede Mantashe in the crowd. It felt a bit like being in the lion's den; it was clear that public sentiment, at least from the ANC and its supporters, was against us, despite the most brilliant legal arguments.

Judge Kathree-Setiloane was joined on the bench by judges Neels Claassen and Lucy Mailula. Zuma and the ANC were represented by Advocate Gcina Malindi SC, the Goodman Gallery by David Unterhalter, and *City Press* by Steven Budlender.

As is usual in civil cases, the applicant presents its argument first, followed by the respondents. Malindi argued that the continued publication of the image was unlawful and that the applicants were seeking a final interdict. But the bench asked him how they could rule on lawfulness in an urgent application without hearing evidence, and how it would be practically impossible for the court to monitor future publications of the image, in light of the fact that it was already widely distributed on the internet. Judge Claassen suggested that an apology might be a better remedy to ask for, as it was something that could be monitored. Malindi also conceded that the right to dignity and privacy didn't apply to the ANC or to Zuma in his capacity as president of South Africa and of the ANC, but only to Zuma the person.

Malindi clearly had a difficult time persuading the judges of his arguments, and, during the tea break, had to take new instructions from his clients about exactly what they were asking for. Before the break, Claassen had asked Malindi a question that led the advocate to break down in tears in court and for the case to be postponed indefinitely: 'Would you be making the same submission to this court, if the artist had placed the head of Mr [FW] de Klerk on that painting, instead of the president?' This was a turning point in the case, but one that was unfortunately abused by commentators on both sides.

I was there when Malindi broke down, but want to allow readers to read for themselves what preceded that emotional moment in an already tense case. This is the full, unedited transcript of the interaction that led to Malindi crying in court.

CLAASSEN J: Yes, Mr Malindi.
MR MALINDI ADDRESSES COURT (Continuation): As the court pleases, Justice Claassen, My Lord, if I may start with the last question that Your Lordship raised about what my answer would have been if the head on the statue were that of former President De Klerk. The answer appears on page 20 of our heads of argument. Basically ... [intervene]
CLAASSEN J: Paragraph?
MR MALINDI: Paragraph 3.11, My Lord
CLAASSEN J: Paragraph 3.11 is on page 19.
MR MALINDI: Oh, My Lord maybe the printing came ... As the court pleases. I used my heads as I ... not as they were ... as they were finally. I will read it out, My Lord. It is just I am just using a different version of my heads. My Lord, the short answer is that no one deserves an indignity. No matter who they are and we quote the statement by Allen Gerworth an American academic who writes about dignity as follows and

that will also be found, I believe in *The State* v *Mkwanyane* in different words.

'If inherent human dignity as the ground of human moral rights, must belong to all humans equally, then it must be a characteristic of criminals as well as saints, of cowards as well as heroes, of fools as well as sages, of mental defectives as well as mentally normal persons, of slaves as well as masters, of subjects as well as lords, of disease ridden invalids as well as athletes, of drug addicts as well persons of self control, of starving ... [indistinct] as well as well fed capitalists and so forth.'

Now that ... [intervene]

CLAASSEN J: So that would include the head of Mr De Klerk on the picture.

MR MALINDI: That would include the head of Mr De Klerk.

CLAASSEN J: Then I need to ask you why in your heads are you making a racial issue of it? If you look at page 4, paragraph 1.7.2. At 1.7.2 in the last, the middle sentence, you say:

'The fact that the majority of those with such cultural sensibilities are African and regarded as species of an inferior culture and status, is irrelevant in the objective analysis of whether or not an unlawful infringement has occurred. It is simply a relic of the dominant and pervasive Colonial mindset that has no place in our constitutional dispensation even if it parades as progressive thought.'

Where does that come? What evidence is there to say that this is a Colonial attack on the black culture of this country?

MR MALINDI: As the court pleases. What is the ... [indistinct]. Justice Mohamed what ... [indistinct]. My Lord, if I may turn to the question that my ... Your Lordship poses. The respondents have proffered evidence by experts who are themselves artists to justify art as boundless.

CLAASSEN J: Who is the 'us'?

MR MALINDI: The arts.

CLAASSEN J: Oh, the arts. Sorry. I misheard the word. Yes?

MR MALINDI: Thank you My Lord. The suggestion that runs

through the justification is that some people do not understand the nuances of fine arts and that comes from the first respondent. That when you look to a picture ... at a picture it will give you messages and it will give you directions as to how you must look at it. Mr Kentridge also gives a justification of how the works of art ought to be interpreted.

CLAASSEN J: Ja?

MR MALINDI: And throughout the justifications My Lord, there are heavy suggestions that the uneducated do not understand art. That it is a class of certain people who can appreciate art. And that therefore, art is beyond the comprehension of people who do not belong into this group of people who go to the Goodman Gallery and sit and discuss art et cetera. Now My Lord, this court will then be enjoined in the event that the court finds Section 10 rights are amenable to limitation to find that balance between that right and Section 16(1) (c). In order to come to that balance, the court is going to consider the diverse South African community as to where that balance should be struck only through the eyes of the experts that the respondents whose evidence they have provided to the court. It is not going to be through the eyes of the curator of the ... [indistinct] of Goodman Gallery who says: My only job is to allow the artists to express themselves boundlessly in whatever language they want to express themselves, even if it conveys messages of insulting other people. He says I am not entering that debate. Now My Lord, in South Africa as Your Lordship would know, we come from a history of apartheid wherein black people were oppressed and denied all the resources that the white community enjoyed. Not only are we divided in terms of the levels of education, because black people were only limited to inferior education. We also come, all of us, from legitimate cultures as white South Africans, black South Africans, we come from various religious grouping, so Your Lordship might well ask me why do you make it a religious issue, somewhere in our heads, because that religion that the diverse community of South Africa comes from, informs them how they interpret things. So race in South Africa, My Lord, coincides with the categories that our learned colleagues have set out in the categories of people that the court must consider their opinion as legitimate opinions to interpret art. Now we say My Lord ... [intervene]

CLAASSEN J: I understand that, Mr Malindi. But my problem with that argument is that we have the applicant [Zuma] and the applicant's daughter objecting to this picture, but then we also have three black persons saying that that picture is not necessarily to be interpreted as insulting. So it is black against black. Where does the racial issue now come in?

MR MALINDI: Well ... [intervene]

CLAASSEN J: It is the question of the artistic licence which this court has to weigh up against the dignity of a particular person. That has got no racial overtones, with respect.

MR MALINDI: Yes. I agree with Your Lordship that sometimes race becomes irrelevant. And race in the eyes of the three black experts who have provided affidavits, is irrelevant because they are connoisseurs of art.

CLAASSEN J: Yes.

MR MALINDI: That is how they have been recognised by the world in which they belong as artists. So for them, they are seeing art through the eyes of the elite class of South Africa.

CLAASSEN J: Hmm?

MR MALINDI: That has greater appreciation for the arts and it is ... that is not to say black people do not have great appreciation of the arts, it is the eye through which they look at the arts, at literature and everything else. We black people also have high levels of appreciation of these things, but there is an elitist approach to where rights in South Africa must be pitched and that elitist approach is we must give the most liberal interpretation to every right, without mediating the diversity of the people that former Chief Justice Mohamed talked about and I will find the quotation.

CLAASSEN J: No, I have read it.

MR MALINDI: You have read it. That in South Africa whenever we mediate any interest, we mediate any value we must know that we come from a past, we are moving towards the ultimate ideal and in order to reach that ideal, we must not force people without mediating their interests to the ultimate, because that is the ideal, that is where we are going, that is where the South African Constitution is taking us. Now, Mr Murray the artist, when making that image should have asked himself, am I going to offend if I did this? Should I have regard to many South Africans who have no appreciation of contemporary arts as there has been described, or the nuances that have been spoken to in appreciating art. Should I have regard to some religious sector that may take offence to this? And incidentally My Lord, in our replying affidavit, I do not know what page it is, we refer to a work of Mr Murray, which was not exhibited because it was the view of the gallery where he had to exhibit it, that it would offend the Muslim and Jewish community. Those are the things that every artist, every writer, every orator must take into account that their words have to be weighed in such a way that they accommodate this diversity of people. So My Lord, in short and about this work that was not exhibited, by implication that means that Mr Murray accepted that it should not be displayed. Now My Lord, it is not a racial issue. We implore the court and we implore all the people who convey messages to know and consider the diversity of South Africa. Nor cultural background, nor approach and interpretation to things must be regarded as inferior because there is a super class of people who think things must be seen in their eyes. The Constitution can only take us to that stage after negating the diverse range of thought.

CLAASSEN J: Well, I am glad you are putting it in that way, Mr Malindi, because there are uneducated and poor people of other racial backgrounds in the country as well. So if it is a racial thing, then I would deplore that fact. If it is purely an elitist thing for a select group whether they are black or white, then I understand the argument. And I can understand your argument that even an elitist group will have to take into consideration the sensibilities of the nation. Like the sensibilities of the Jewish community, or the Afrikaans community, or the Muslim community that we have had in other cases in the country. But that is not to say that it is a racial issue.

MR MALINDI: It is not a racial issue.

CLAASSEN J: Yes?

MR MALINDI: So My Lord, in order to conclude on your last words My Lord, it always makes it difficult for black people in particular, and for people who come from cultures that are regarded as inferior, to argue ... [intervene]

CLAASSEN J: No, no. I must ... I must interject there, Mr Malindi. Where is the evidence that the black culture is regarded as inferior? On what evidence must we base such a finding? Because if that is so, Mr Malindi, you would not be standing here and arguing very eloquently, this matter.

MR MALINDI: My Lord, I happened to be one of those who fortunately became ... [indistinct] enough to reach university level.

CLAASSEN J: Ja, but ... [intervene]

MR MALINDI: But My Lord, I am not going to pursue that line of thinking.

CLAASSEN J: Ja. I think that ... [intervene]

KATHREE-SETILOANE J: Sorry ... [intervene]

CLAASSEN J: That is missing the issue, Mr Malindi.

MR MALINDI: My Lord, my concluding statement on what Justice Claassen is saying.

CLAASSEN J: Yes?

MR MALINDI: Is that the difficulty as I stand here, is to be heard as if I am arguing for backtracking on the values that the Constitution says we must all have.

CLAASSEN J: Hmm?

MR MALINDI: It is not the argument of the first applicant [Zuma].

CLAASSEN J: Okay.

MR MALINDI: It is not the applicant ... the argument of the second applicant [the ANC] to the extent that they still are cited as the applicants, that we must reverse the case that we have made, we must progress but that progression must not undermine the appreciation of the diversity ... [intervene]

CLAASSEN J: We must limit ... [intervene]

MR MALINDI: Of South African society.

CLAASSEN J: We must limit the argument as to the question of dignity of an individual.

MR MALINDI: Yes.

CLAASSEN J: Whether he is black, white, pink or blue, and the artistic expression, freedom of expression of an artist, whether he is pink, white, blue or yellow. That is the really issue in this matter. Is it not?

MR MALINDI: That is so My Lord. And as I submitted ... [intervene]

CLAASSEN J: Ja. Alright.

MR MALINDI: The court is going to engage into a fine balancing act.

COURT: Yes.

MR MALINDI: In mediating between Section 10 and 16, if the court is going to enter that area. I beg your pardon ... [intervene]

CLAASSEN J: Ja. There is another matter which I should have raised with you Mr Malindi.

MR MALINDI: Yes?

CLAASSEN J: And that is are we, this court duty bound to take judicial recognition of the fact that the reports in the newspapers have now indicated that the painting has been vandalised, defaced, almost destroyed. That is has been taken down. We do not know ... we do not know if that painting can be restored and if ever it can be published again. We do not know that. If it is a case where that painting has been destroyed or vandalised to such an extent that it is worthless and cannot be exhibited again, then what are we doing here?

KATHREE-SETILOANE J: Is then the relief that you seek, not academic?

MR MALINDI: Justice Kathree-Setiloane, before I answer that question, may I just direct the court to paragraph 3.9, just that quotation in Mankwanyane, to be read together with the quotation that I read out by Allen Gerworth.

CLAASSEN J: Which paragraph of your heads is this in?

MR MALINDI: In paragraph 3.9 My Lord.

CLAASSEN J: Paragraph 3.9. Thank you. Yes?

MR MALINDI: Justice Kathree-Setiloane, the image of the first applicant [Zuma] continues to exist on the first respondent's website.

KATHREE-SETILOANE J: Hmm.

MR MALINDI: To what extent the court may take judicial notice of the fact of the vandalisation, which happened to be by two people coming from two racial different racial groups, Mr Justice Claassen. I do not know to what extent the court can take judicial notice of that fact. But the case is about the vindication of a Constitutional right. That declaration does not become academic, that pursuit of that vindication does not become academic.

KATHREE-SETILOANE J: Well, on … well you are seeking a final interdict, the interdict. You are seeking an interdict that the portrait not be exhibited, displayed, et cetera. That aspect certainly becomes academic. There is nothing to take down if it has already been taken down.

MR MALINDI: It becomes difficult, the gallery may decided that the portrait deserves its place in the gallery, with some explanation as to what had happened there. So we do not know what ultimately will happen to it. So it is not entirely academic and if there is an explanation, a plate at the bottom that says: Statue of Lenin, changed and converted into representing Mr Zuma with his genitals and vandalised on x-date, people will still view it. And I am speaking off the top of my head, and I do not think the court can … [intervene]

KATHREE-SETILOANE J: Well people will certainly still view it over the Internet.

MR MALINDI: Ja.

KATHREE-SETILOANE J: The image is ... the image is all over the Internet. Both nationally and internationally.

MR MALINDI: That is why we ... [intervene]

KATHREE-SETILOANE J: And you cannot delete that with one press of the button.

MR MALINDI: Yes. That is why we pursue the remedy that the gallery and *City Press* must be interdicted from continuing to carry the image on their sites.

CLAASSEN J: But even if that is granted, how would that stop the dissemination of that image?

MR MALINDI: As the court pleases, My Lord ... [intervene]

KATHREE-SETILOANE J: Well, how would that ... The first applicant [Zuma] contends that his right to dignity has been infringed. Now how would granting an interdict to stop the dissemination of the image repair the damage that has already been done?

MR MALINDI: Firstly ... [intervene]

KATHREE-SETILOANE J: Or the injury that he believes has already been caused to him?

MR MALINDI: Firstly the vindication of his rights, is a ... would be a huge way to ... [indistinct] his wounded feelings, his humiliation if the court says that portrait was unlawful. It is declared unlawful, it goes a long way. As to who has seen it, there is a continuation of this violation as we speak. The court's question is whether the applicant [Zuma] must be happy that another many million people would not see it. We are saying the continuation violation and once it is declared unlawful to display it or to distribute it, the first and second respondents will cease to publicise it, to ... to ... to publish it and distribute it and so on. It is ... [intervene]

MAILULA J: Ja, perhaps the ... [intervene]

KATHREE-SETILOANE J: But it is distributed.

253

MAILULA J: Perhaps maybe the question, to put it this way: There are other websites which have the portrait also. Now if that portrait is ... [indistinct] why are those websites allowed to carry on, but not the ... [indistinct].

MR MALINDI: The sensible thing for those websites to do would be to remove them once there is a declaration of unlawfulness and it would be for the applicant [Zuma] to then decide afterwards whether it takes action against those who continues to display and distribute it. The court cannot monitor a declaration. The court has to declare unlawfulness and that is almost enough for the purpose of vindicating a right.

MAILULA J: And how is that declaration now to address the publication of ... [indistinct] right and in ... [indistinct]. How does that happen?

MR MALINDI: How it will happen, My Lady it is the same way as when the court finds that a statement is defamatory.

MAILULA J: Yes?

MR MALINDI: And it orders whether it is compensation or an apology, or fashions some remedy. The existence of that statement, a defamatory statement, continues to be available to anyone who that ... who dares to access it. So if Mr Mkhize, the Premier of Kwazulu-Natal, has won a case that says a statement, a comment was defamatory it is open to me to go on the website and access the statement and read it again. It is ... but he is happy that there has been a declaration of an unlawful ... of the unlawfulness of that statement and that is what the applicant [Zuma] seeks My Lord, My Lady.

CLAASSEN J: Well, what do you say about the English authority, cited in the heads of argument of Mr Unterhalter, paragraph 106 and 107, where Lord Griffith the well known British Lord, says that:

'If the injunction ...' which is the English word for an interdict, '... had been issued the law would indeed be an ass, for it would seek to deny to our citizens the right to be informed of matters which are freely available throughout the rest of the world.'

And that is the point that my learned colleague on my right makes. Once the world can see that image, why ... how ... why should this country also not see it and in any event, how can an interdict of this court stop this country of seeing it, if they can download it from the public domain which the whole world has to see.

MR MALINDI: Well, Justice Claassen, the court is laying emphasis not at the core of what this case is about, which is a Constitutional right that is sought to be vindicated. Many South Africans are happy that 1994 came and we are free now. A lot of the things that are promised in the Constitution, have not reached many people. The right to water, access to water, sanitation, food and shelter. That does not mean in the Constitution or the law is an ass. They have been vindicated that their struggle was a just struggle.

CLAASSEN J: Well, I do not think that you have answered the question Mr Malindi, but we will leave it at that.

MR MALINDI: [Sobbing – sobbing]

CLAASSEN J: The court will adjourn.

MR MALINDI: [Sobbing loudly – sobbing louder]

I could see Malindi's face when he broke down, and I was touched by the deep pain he must have experienced before crying. Listening intensively to the interaction between him and Judge Claassen, I got the impression that Malindi felt he had to defend the legitimacy of the struggle against an ignorant white judge.

All parties agreed that it was not appropriate for the case to continue in these circumstances, and the matter was postponed indefinitely. There was a broad consensus that Zuma would have struggled to convince the court to interdict *The Spear*. From all three judges' comments to Malindi, it was clear they had no appetite for interdicting a painting that had already gone viral globally. Between the lines, I think, they suggested a solution should be found outside court. So out we went.

A few kilometres away, while addressing a conference of the

National Union of Mineworkers (NUM), SACP general secretary and Higher Education minister Blade Nzimande called for a boycott of *City Press* until we apologised to Zuma.

Outside court, while addressing a group of Zuma supporters, Jackson Mthembu chanted, 'Don't buy *City Press*, don't buy.'

34

Later in the afternoon of Thursday 24 May 2012, the ANC asked all South Africans to boycott *City Press* and to join a protest march to the Goodman Gallery the following Tuesday. '*City Press* newspaper, by continuing to exhibit the offensive painting has clearly shown its collusion to the indecent depiction of President Zuma which violates his right to human dignity,' Mthembu said in a statement. '*City Press* has therefore become a paragon of immorality, abuse and perpetrator of injustice and slander. Their refusal to remove this portrait from their website and their controlled social media is a clear indication that this newspaper does not belong to our shared democratic dispensation and values.'

It was the first time the ANC had asked for a boycott of a newspaper – or any product, for that matter – since 1994.

The boycott call did not go down well with some ANC members; some told us they would openly buy two copies of the paper. Nomfanelo Kota, press attaché at the South African mission in New York, posted on Facebook: 'I don't see what revolutionary cause will be achieved by not reading the *City Press*. The ANC taught me to be critical. Re-educate me if you want to convince me. I have never followed blindly in all my years in the ANC. I don't believe that the ANC can be threatened by newspapers, otherwise it would mean these 100 years of our movement and its values meant nothing.'[1]

On 27 May, political analyst Justice Malala wrote in the *Sunday Times* that Malindi's crying had shifted his own viewpoint on *The Spear*: 'The very centre of my being moved. I remembered a huge chunk of what I had put away in the deepest recesses of my mind. I remembered, I was forced to remember, that there is hurt, there is pain, there is anger and there is even hatred in my and my fellow black people's hearts about what has happened here. I remembered apartheid.'

Malala wrote that he was 'firmly' on the side of those who thought Zuma's court action was 'ill-advised, nonsensical and a poor pandering to one man's whim above those of our constitution ... Yet I cannot escape the raw and real pain and hurt that Malindi's breakdown in court underlined. Perhaps, in my defence of the freedoms to express oneself, the freedoms to artistic creativity, I missed something. Perhaps I – and many of the people who have been batting on this side of the field – forgot that these freedoms cannot be exercised in a vacuum.'

There was still real, unprocessed hurt in South Africa, he wrote, that we often forget about. 'Did the failure to recognise the deep wounds of our past make us miss a moment in which we could have defused *The Spear* issue, then? Could Zuma, in his anger and his shame, have decided to let the matter go – or was his and his advisers' anger so overwhelming they decided to go ahead? Could Murray have, before he raised his brush, wondered about the hurt that we all still carry inside us? Could *City Press* – despite the fact that in my and its editors' view it is absolutely within its rights to report on and keep the offending painting's picture up – have done things differently?' he asked.

He ended his piece by saying that, despite his pain, and because of our Constitution, 'the painting must stay up, and newspapers must be able to report about it without being boycotted and burnt'.

Haffajee was deeply touched by Malala's piece and decided to take down the image from our website. She sent a draft of her column 'The Spear is down – out of care and fear' to us for comment. Initially,

I was opposed to taking down the image; I agreed with Malala's conclusion that a constitutional democracy was a rough, sometimes scratchy tug-of-war, and that we always had to defend foremost our right to publish. But I also appreciated Ferial's olive-branch gesture; she saw an opportunity to defuse a tense moment and emerge the bigger person as Zuma's leadership was failing, again. And so, on Monday 28 May, *The Spear* came down.

The Spear is down – out of care and fear
Ferial Haffajee

The Spear is down. Out of care and as an olive branch to play a small role in helping turn around a tough moment, I have decided to take down the image.

When we published an art review, which featured *The Spear* as one image, I could not have anticipated that it would snowball into a moment of such absolute rage and pain. Have I been naive in this? Perhaps.

City Press is not and has never been an object of division; neither am I. I prefer to understand *City Press* as a bridge across divides, a forum for debate.

We have just turned 30 years old and have exciting plans for *City Press*, which I do not want imperiled by us being forced into the role of opposition that discomforts me. My own identity is that of critical patriot, I am a great fan of my country, and that is how I want to edit. Besides, there are really important stories we lost sight of, like the continued investigation into Lieutenant General Richard Mdluli, unemployment and the infrastructure budget.

That we are now a symbol of a nation's anger and rage is never the role of media in society. We are robust and independent, yes, but divisive and deaf, no.

There is a long history of art that has offended in South Africa, some of it the best we have ever made. You can see it here. I hope we are not crafting a society where we consign artists to still lifes and the deep symbolism of repressed artists like China's Ai Weiwei. A society where we consign journalism to a free expression constrained by the limits of fear.

This week society began the path of setting its mores on how we treat presidents in art and journalism; what is acceptable and what is not.

I hope we will reach these conclusions decently in debates, colloquiums and plenaries rather than setting them in blood or angry red paint or in orange flames snaking up from burning pages.

The other lesson in all of this is that our common national dignity is still paper-thin; that our mutual understanding across cultures and races is still a work in progress and that pain is still deep. We have not yet defined a Mzansi way of maintaining a leader's dignity while exercising a robust free speech or reached an understanding that a leader embodies the nation, no matter what we may think of him or her. Neither does it seem our leaders know that dignity and respect are earned qualities too.

We take down the image in the spirit of peacemaking – it is an olive branch. But the debate must not end here and we should all turn this into a learning moment, in the interest of all our freedoms.

Fear

Of course, the image is coming down from fear too. I'd be silly not to admit that. The atmosphere is like a tinderbox: *City Press* copies went up in flames on Saturday; I don't want any more newspapers burnt in anger.

My colleague has been removed from a huge trade union

congress and prevented from reporting – I don't want the lingering image (which in any event is viral) to stop us being able to do our core job. Our vendors are most at risk.

It was quite shocking to watch three big men of government, the SACP general secretary Blade Nzimande; the governing party's Gwede Mantashe and its spokesperson Jackson Mthembu call *City Press* all manner of names and to call for a boycott. That they have failed is neither here nor there; that they did mark a moment of inflexion in our society.

It saddens me that not one of them nor a single representative of the governing alliance sought engagement with *City Press* before seeking a High Court interdict. For any editor to respond to a threat to take down an article of journalism without putting up a fight is an unprincipled thing to do, so we've fought as much as we could. It doesn't serve *City Press* or South Africa to dig in our heels and put our fingers in our ears.

The threats and invective against the writer of the review and a couple of us in the middle of the debate have been painful and have wrought a personal cost.

In this the national pain which columnist Justice Malala spoke about is ours too. I have had my intimate body savaged by social media personalities who wanted me, I guess, to feel their own and the president's humiliation.

I have. An ANC leader from my area on Twitter started a campaign of such disinformation I had to spend much of Saturday night quelling it. He knows where I live. What will he do next? The tweet that broke this camel's back was one by [a businessman, who later said an impersonator was tweeting under his name].

He said I probably don't want the painting to come down as I need it for the long lonely nights. I presume he meant its phallus. He knows I am single. It must have taken great anger to get a man I know to be of elegance and wit to get to such a point.

I play tough tackle and expect to get intellectually whipped when I do. But this humiliation I can well live without. It's simply not worth it and I guess we have made our point and must move on.

Haffajee's column was published and the image removed the day before the ANC's planned protest march on the Goodman Gallery. Still, the party went ahead with its march, led by Nzimande, Ngoako Ramatlhodi, Yengeni and union leaders. Speaking outside the gallery, Nzimande said: 'We are saying, this insulting drawing of the president, we are saying to the Goodman Gallery, don't sell it, it must not leave this country, it must remain here, it must be destroyed once and for good. If we allow this drawing to go to this German person who has bought it, we are actually making our president the second Sarah Baartman. So this thing must not be sold, it is not worth anything, it belongs to the museum of shame in this country.'

The next day, the ANC and the Goodman Gallery announced that they had reached a settlement, which was read out by Mthembu and gallery owner Liza Essers. The settlement recognised that 'all parties have struggled to achieve the right to human dignity and culture and the freedom of expression and have a mutual desire and joint responsibility to maintain these rights as fundamental freedoms in our young democracy'. Since the painting had been defaced, it would no longer be displayed. 'With regard to giving offence to President Zuma, the Goodman Gallery and Brett Murray intended no insult to him as a private person ... The debate engendered by this work has been robust and rich and will continue, but what is clear is the real distress and hurt that this image has caused some people ... and the Gallery regrets the pain that the display of the painting has caused,' the settlement read.

On 1 June 2012, the FPB classified *The Spear* 16N.

35

After catching our breath, I realised how Zuma and his bulldogs had exploited the moment – a moment of real pain for some – for their own political point-scoring. The painting was down, both from the walls of the Goodman and from the *City Press* website, but still Mantashe and Mthembu insisted on marching. And Nzimande upped their demands: the painting must be destroyed and not leave the country.

At the end of June, a month after the storm, Haffajee spoke at the National Arts Festival in Grahamstown: 'I would not take down that image knowing what I do now,' she said, explaining how *The Spear* became Zuma's political scapegoat.

> So, *The Spear* was about corruption too. The entire theme of *Hail to the Thief*, Brett Murray's exhibition, was about the seductions of power or what the ANC calls the sins of incumbency.
>
> There's a fist raised in *Amandla*, slammed down in repression. The ANC For Sale and Sold. The bastardisation of the epic struggle posters. At *City Press*, we went through an ethical decision-making process about putting the image as a cover of the arts section or making it an inside story. Not running the image was never a consideration – it was, after all, reproduction not production.

We have a long history of art that has troubled power…

When the SACP leader Blade Nzimande stood up at the NUM conference and made the first boycott call against *City Press*, I felt my freedom being constrained. Later that day, the ANC's Jackson Mthembu did the same thing. What many don't know is that the ANC and the Presidency realised their case was weak and they played a large part in getting the urgent interdict hearing postponed to immediately take to the streets to call for a boycott. We were played.

Don't Buy *City Press*, Don't Buy

We laugh now, but then, I felt the future. When next a political scapegoat is needed to hang a political campaign on, then the media will be fair game, especially if you are big and black, which *City Press* is. We almost became the focal point of a presidential campaign. Two days later the paper was burnt in a march led by one of the first ladies and attended by the political and business glitterati. Three days later it was boycotted. Then I took the image down because its publication and dissemination had opened up a deep and collective woundedness, a dignity as fragile as a piece of dove-shaped origami. It was, I said at the time, an olive branch extended in citizenship.

But also because I didn't want *City Press* burnt. Or myself insulted. And so, my freedom died a little, taken by my own hand.

But also by the hand of the Film and Publications Board. If I were you, I'd ask for a tax refund for what this body has become. It is meant to protect children from harmful content, but in that week, I saw it morph into a political handmaiden. In about 20 hours of hearings, the screeching limitations of cadre deployment were writ loud.

From the CEO, to the spokesperson, to the classifiers whose names you cannot know, their minds were made up long before the hearing we insisted upon.

Spear 16N

This was a predetermined outcome which had almost nothing to do with protecting children. It was done to satisfy the political masters. I felt my freedom evaporate as I realised that this is how it happens: you hollow out institutions, stack them with automatons, call them deployed cadres, politicise the bureaucracy, create an enemy and mount a populist cause. Achieving freedom took decades and it took thousands of lives, but it takes very little to kill it.

I saw it in action at a set of parliamentary hearings on transformation in the print industry, again where, abetted by ideologically hidebound academics and government minstrels, the committee fired the next shot across the bow of free expression. If you stack the institution with cadres, close the space for independent thinkers and mount a populist cause, you inevitably harm freedom.

The upshot of all this is that I am a changed person. Less a child of Mandela's generation, more a freedom of expression fundamentalist. I would not take down that image knowing what I do now. I would smash into a wall and probably get fired. Let the ANC claim a proper scalp. This fundamentalism is not terribly healthy; no fundamentalism ever is. But through this and other episodes in the years of freedom, I've come to understand that this lifeblood is so easily and quickly undermined that you have to be extremely vigilant to protect its fragility which like our dignity is also like origami, paper-thin.

On 7 October 2012 the Film and Publication Appeal Tribunal, under chairmanship of Professor Karthy Govender, set aside *The Spear*'s 16N classification and ruled that the work was not pornographic or a depiction of sexual conduct.

36

One of the most harrowing examples of the breakdown of moral leadership in Zuma's ANC was the sad tale of the assassination of a man who gave his whole life and being to the movement. Moss Phakoe, a former ANC councillor and union organiser in the North West town of Rustenburg, was 52 years old when he was gunned down in his modest driveway after putting up posters for the ANC in March 2009. In July 2012, former Rustenburg mayor Matthew Wolmarans and his bodyguard, Enoch Matshaba, were convicted for Phakoe's murder and sentenced to 20 years and life imprisonment, respectively.

What upset me most about Phakoe's story was not the gruesome fact that ANC cadres have resorted to murder. It was the sad story of how Phakoe and his fellow comrade and councillor, Alfred Motsi, desperately tried, without success, to expose Wolmarans' alleged corruption in the ANC. I wrote an opinion piece for *City Press*, under the headline 'A political solution that killed', detailing Motsi's evidence, given in the North West High Court, of how he and Phakoe were turned away by several senior ANC leaders, including Zuma himself, when they begged for the rot in Rustenburg to be dealt with.

The corruption case against Wolmarans essentially concerned the outsourcing of the management of Rustenburg Kloof, a picturesque state-owned holiday lodge that my family and I used to visit when I was a kid. Phakoe and Motsi compiled a dossier on what they said amounted to corruption in the awarding of a tender to friends and allies of Wolmarans.

As loyal ANC cadres, the two whistleblowers decided to present their evidence to the ANC before going to the police. Firstly, they presented their case to the party's regional and provincial leadership in North West, without any effect. Then, according to Motsi's evidence, they had a meeting with ANC heavyweights Siphiwe Nyanda (Zuma's parliamentary adviser and former Communications minister) and Billy Masetlha (the former spy boss). Again, nothing happened.

Towards the end of 2008 – after Mbeki had been recalled as president – Motsi and Phakoe delivered their dossier to the offices of ANC secretary-general Gwede Mantashe and then President Kgalema Motlanthe. After not receiving any response – again – they decided to approach Zuma himself, and delivered their evidence to his Johannesburg house. He invited them to his Nkandla homestead over the 2008 Christmas period. It was at this time that Zuma's supporters were lobbying for a 'political solution' to be found for Zuma's own corruption problems.

In Nkandla, the men addressed Zuma for 'almost a whole night' to explain the case against Wolmarans. They departed, and a month later met with Zuma, Motlanthe, Mantashe and other senior ANC leaders in Potchefstroom. Motsi testified that they again presented their dossier and were told the case would be handled by Sicelo Shiceka (later the Minister of Cooperative Governance and Traditional Affairs, who was himself fingered for massive irregular expenditure by the Public Protector). Mantashe, Motsi testified, said he was a 'troublemaker'.

Eventually, Phakoe was afforded the opportunity to address Shiceka, at a meeting held in March 2009. Curiously, Wolmarans was also present, and Phakoe had to present his dossier in the presence of the man he had accused of corruption. Motsi testified that, before his friend and colleague addressed the meeting, he looked

Wolmarans in the eye and said: 'Hate me, but don't hurt me.' Two days later, Phakoe was shot dead in cold blood by Matshaba. He and Wolmarans had organised the hit.

'If ever the ANC and Zuma needed a reason corruption should be dealt with by the criminal justice system – and not through some comradely political solution behind close doors – the dead body of Moss Phakoe is that reason. Here was a whistleblower who put his life – literally – on the line to give effect to Zuma's plea in his 2009 state of the nation address for citizens to "report crime and assist the police with information to catch wrongdoers",' I later wrote.[1]

In May 2012, I interviewed Phakoe's three children in his house in Middle Street, where two of them still lived. We sat in the lounge, where a picture of Phakoe receiving an award from Thabo Mbeki and a framed certificate of a management course he had completed graced an otherwise empty wall. Karabo, Tlholo and Tshepiso Phakoe told me they didn't know about the hatred some had for 'Papa'. Tlholo is angry at the treatment his father got from the ANC.

'I have one thing to say: leaders who fail to act decisively against corruption failed a father, a brother, a friend and a comrade who was in the movement of the ANC since we were very young. It hurts us that nobody senior in the ANC has come to listen to us. It feels like Moss Phakoe was just killed and buried. Our father died in the movement; our father died in the ANC. It hurts me so bad.'[2]

Moss Phakoe's passion was 'helping people, his ANC and his God,' Tlholo says. 'My father was killed by his loyalty to the movement; he was too loyal to the movement and died for the movement.'

Outside court there were two protesting factions: those with ANC T-shirts and posters reading 'Hands off our Wollie' supporting the murderers, and a group of Cosatu supporters asking for justice.

In handing down judgment, Judge Ronnie Hendricks said Wolmarans saw Phakoe as an opponent and plotted to kill him. 'He accused you of corruption and that angered you. You employed the service of accused one [Matshaba] to eliminate the deceased. You were clever enough not to do the killing yourself.'[3] Hendricks asked for political tolerance in a democratic country.

Writing in *City Press* after Wolmarans' conviction, Cosatu general secretary Zwelinzima Vavi said the case provided 'shocking insight' into crime and corruption in South Africa.[4] 'Everything possible was done to delay the police investigation, protect the culprits and keep the truth from the people. Friends of the murderers even mobilised sycophants from the ANC to display the movement's sacred ANC symbols outside court in support of the killers. Regrettably, those who bussed in these protesters remain members and leaders of the movement,' he wrote. Vavi further said that Cosatu would ask the ANC at its Mangaung conference to endorse a motion that comrades facing 'allegations of murder, rape and corruption' be forced to step aside until they are cleared. This was significant in light of the fact that Zuma had stayed on as ANC deputy president while he was facing corruption and rape charges. Vavi wrote:

> Nepotism, patronage, corruption and greed are not only destroying the ethic of self-sacrifice and service to the people that has traditionally characterised our revolutionary movement. They are also exacerbating divisions and factionalism, which increasingly are not about ideology, but about access to tenders and contracts. Leadership contests are now less about political principles than about which faction of which individual will advance business careers and fill bank accounts. The worst problem of all is the emergence of death squads. Political killings are on the rise, in particular in Mpumalanga, KwaZulu-Natal and the Eastern Cape. If this continues, anyone who speaks out will be silenced, the entire state will be auctioned to the highest bidder and we shall be well on our way to becoming a corrupt banana republic. We owe it to Comrade Moss Phakoe's memory to take a stand and say no to corruption.

37

On 26 June 2012, President Jacob Zuma opened the ANC's policy conference at Gallagher Estate in Midrand amid growing tensions in the governing party over campaigning for leadership positions at Mangaung. The so-called Second Transition had become the hallmark of Zuma's unofficial campaign for a second term, and the concept featured prominently in Zuma's address.

For me, the biggest irony of this was that Zuma's nemesis, Julius Malema, was the original author of the theme underlying the 'Second Transition' – economic freedom in our lifetime. Here Zuma was campaigning on an idea originally punted by the young man who had become his arch-enemy!

I followed Zuma's speech on Twitter via the hashtag #ANCpolicy, primarily to see the reactions of South Africans who use the social network to comment on what the president said. Although Twitter is by no means a representative platform, it was a fascinating exercise to watch the comments as Zuma progressed with his address.

These are selected tweets that commented and reflected on the president's first unofficial campaign speech:

@Nipho_Reserved: Tired of policies RT #ANCPolicy Zuma: ANCYL proposed sending young people to other countries for skills training.

@phillipdewet: Zuma gets his loudest applause yet on land reform: 'current willing-buyer, willing-seller model must be reviewed.'

@Qhakaza: #Zuma speaks of 2nd transition as if it has been fully accepted and approved by all ANC leaders. That is quite problematic.

@LwandoMfene: We need to separate general government/@ MyANC_ policy from our incompetent/corrupt uncles&aunts occupying local government posts.

@Mabine_Seabe: Mr President, the Constitution is not a problem when it comes to Land Reform. The problem is management and implementation.

@NBikitsha: Why loud applause over change to willing buyer,willing seller? ANC has been saying this since 2005. Action is what is needed.

@arch_mpilo: I wonder who wrote this speech for Zuma ... hai he finds it difficult.

@GlorMazibuko: After the #ANCPolicy delegats will be dining themselves with the most expensive food neh?

@velvetart: Zuma's call to fight corruption met with a half-assed golf clap.

@mzwaimbeje: Mangaung must prioritise and integrity on leadership and fight corruption.

@Nxola_isLeShuff: Mangaung must promote integrity in leadership – and yes Zuma said it himself!

@LukhonaMnguni: The ANC should b discussing how 2 restructure child grants, 2 coupons&sending a portion to skuls 4 uniform&food. Mothers misuse it.

@SihleDeLaKubusa: Amazing how #ANC takes credit for

things it played no real part in … I take it the Cold Front over SA right now is by the party?

@Mabine_Seabe: Luthuli House needs to fire its speechwriter … This speech is stating the obvious. Same old stats and 'promises'.

@Tumi_Manamela: I just wish South Africans could be as hard on the President as they are on Bafana Bafana coaches.

@oliver_meth: only if Zuma delivers simple and practical strategies on governance, then I am for his second transition!

@BruceRelates: Zuma rhetoric gushing out like a burst water pipe. All this hot air should see Gallagher lift off.

@NkululekoNcana: Zuma says ANC is anti-imperialist … #ANCpolicy but some of the actions by gvt would suggest otherwise …

@Tumi_Manamela: Ag, let me go back to my work. This speech is nothing we've never heard before. *YAWN*

@RanjeniM: Europe is collapsing and taking our R2 billion and Zuma is talking about Morocco. SMH.

@Bhintsintsi: Zuma: The ANC must lead debates in society, and not just be subject of debates #ANCpolicy {Too busy dousing factional fires to do so}

@Lubanzi_Deepa: Social grants has created a dependency tendencies in South Africans, it has caused RELIEVED instead of RELEASED from poverty.

@MrBasabose: *yawns* RT #ANCPolicy Zuma: Accelerate fight against corruption.

@Lwaz_: Zuma is that preacher that doesn't do as he preaches.

@Digrobler: Then you must be first to go, Mr Zuma @ Moneyweb: ANC must cleanse itself: Zuma. Says ANC will take action.

@Liz_Setepi: There's the scary 'Amandla' lol. The singing is cherry on top. This is the Zuma I know lmao.

@MusaGumede: Good speech from the President Zuma.

@Tumi_Manamela: He giggled for 10 mins, he sang, he just fell short of dancing his butt off. That's all our president knows.

@RanjeniM: When all else fails, Mshini Wam, Mshini Wam …

@MmanalediM: #ANCpolicy: Zuma in the 2006/7 mood singing 'mshini wam' and 'nomabesidubhula siyaya'. Smell Mangaung?

The Arch

'Is this the kind of freedom people were tortured and people were maimed for? Why the heck? Why the heck did we have this Struggle? What the heck was it for?'

38

My morning begins with an 8am meeting in Sandton. The black businessman in front of me is concerned. No, he is disturbed. For many years his company has successfully done business with the democratic state. But things have gone wrong. 'Now everybody is asking for bribes, from the top to the bottom. I'm not paying; I'll rather walk away than pay. It's now just about politics. If you're not in the right faction, you can forget about tenders.'

He had high hopes for Zuma, a man of the people. 'But now you don't even get paid for services you delivered. They just say, "sorry we don't have money". But this whole thing is politicised now. If you're not in the right camp, you don't get paid.'

He's begging me to investigate a suspect deal involving senior ANC politicians. He's also scared. 'Look what's happening in KwaZulu-Natal, now they are killing people. This thing is bad.'

He is referring to the assassination of ANC Oshabeni branch leaders Dumisani Malunga and Bheko Chiliza, who were contesting a councillor's position in the Port Shepstone area. After dinner on 9 September 2012, they were shot dead while driving home. A few days later, ANC Youth League leader Sifiso Khumalo pleaded guilty to the killing and also implicated taxi boss Hle Cele, who had supported Khumalo for the councillor's position.

After the meeting I drive to the *City Press* office, where I spend the next few hours studying Public Protector Thuli Madonsela's report, 'On the Point of Tenders', into tender corruption in Limpopo, which involves Julius Malema. Her report is a shocking indictment of how the procurement system has been violated by politically connected businesspeople with no regard for service delivery. The entire system has broken down and everybody is involved: tender clerks, politicians, mid-level managers, heads of department, MECs.

In the same week, Malema addressed a press conference where he accused Zuma and his administration of plotting to assassinate him. 'If we die tomorrow, we would have been killed by Jacob Zuma and his people who do not have the interests of the people at heart. If we are illegally arrested tomorrow, we would have been arrested by Jacob Zuma and fair and free courts of law will set us free,' Malema said, shortly after being chased away by police from Marikana, the North West mining town where 34 miners were shot dead by police on 16 August during an illegal strike about wages. I go to *Wikipedia* to see if they have recorded the Marikana massacre – the biggest disgrace of Zuma's term so far – as an official entry. Under the heading 'Marikana miners' strike', I read:

> The Marikana miners' strike or Lonmin strike was a wildcat strike at a mine owned by Lonmin in the Marikana area, close to Rustenburg, South Africa. The event garnered international attention following a series of violent incidents between the South African Police Service and strikers which has resulted in the deaths of 36 mine workers, two police officers, four other unidentified persons and the injury of an additional 78 other workers and police.
>
> The shooting incident on 16 August 2012 that the press dubbed the Marikana massacre was the single most lethal use of force by South African security forces against civilians since 1960, and the end of the apartheid era. The shootings have been described as a massacre in the South African media and have been compared to Sharpeville massacre in 1960. The

276

incident also took place on the 25-year anniversary of a nation-wide South African miners' strike.

Controversy emerged after it emerged that most of the victims were shot in the back. Many victims were shot far from police lines. On 18 September a mediator announced a resolution to the conflict, stating the striking miners had accepted a 22% pay rise, a one-off payment of 2,000 rand and would return to work 20 September.

Malema, 31 years old, had become the president's enemy number one. After being kicked out of the ANC for making derogatory statements about the government of Botswana and unflattering remarks about Zuma's focus on Africa compared to that of Mbeki, the firebrand has been a thorn in Zuma's flesh. The same man who once threatened to kill for Zuma if he was prosecuted was now insulting the president on an almost daily basis, accusing Zuma of planning to kill him.

Zuma chuckled in Parliament when COPE MP Papi Kganare described Malema as a 'Polokwane political Frankenstein created by yourself to achieve your objective to become president' who had become 'uncontrollable'.[1] 'I produced no such person … not at all, so I shouldn't be blamed,' said a smiling Zuma, knowing that Kganare was dead right.

Because Zuma and his supporters made no noise when Malema vowed to kill for him before he became president. Zuma was quiet when Malema insulted journalists, opposition leaders and ANC politicians who didn't agree with him. Zuma said nothing for months when Malema was lobbying for the nationalisation of mines under the ANC banner, although it was not ANC policy. And Zuma shared a stage with Malema when the youth leader told supporters during an ANC election rally in Kimberley in May 2011 that white people should be treated as 'criminals' for stealing black people's land. The president did not rebuke him. When the media exposed Malema's involvement in state tenders in Limpopo, neither Zuma nor the ANC expressed concern or ordered a forensic investigation to be conducted. It was only after Malema started questioning Zuma's leadership that his real problems started.

* * *

Later that afternoon, I get a call for an urgent meeting. I rush to Midrand where I am told the most disturbing version of how politicians are allegedly interfering to fast-track Malema's prosecution. The irony of it, I think to myself. Five years ago, Zuma's supporters were crying foul over political interference in his prosecution. Now they are allegedly doing the same. Two days later, the state obtained a warrant for Malema's arrest. The young man immediately shouted political interference – he has learned well from Zuma. Keep on shouting, challenge the state's every move along the way, maybe lay your hands on some intercepted telephone calls and you'll be safe.

'*Umlilo wephepha*' – paper fire. That, according to Avusa editor-in-chief Mondli Makhanya, is what Zuma and his supporters hoped Julius Malema would be: something that burns out quickly. After using him as his 'rabid bulldog', Zuma now wanted to extinguish the fire as quickly as possible. 'Like a scorned spouse who got a raw deal in the divorce, his stuck record track is Jacob Zuma, Jacob Zuma, Jacob Zuma. Like the angry spouse, he wishes to do all in his power to destroy his hero-turned-nemesis,' Makhanya wrote.[2]

But Malema was using, even abusing, the massive leadership vacuum left by Jacob 'let's debate' Zuma. In the past two newsrooms I've worked in, it was a running joke that every time there was a national crisis or issue that warranted Zuma's attention, his stock reply would be 'let's debate the issue'. Of course debate is an important ingredient in a democracy as diverse as ours, but sometimes leaders need to make firm decisions, even if they are unpopular. Malema saw this weakness and started exploiting it as soon as he lost Zuma's support. Zuma then became his own worst enemy as he failed to deal swiftly and decisively with matters of national interest: Marikana, the Limpopo textbook crisis, languishing public hospitals, rampant tender corruption, dissatisfied soldiers, a criminal justice leadership crisis, a paralysed intelligence service. And without any clear explanation for his inaction, it was left to the South African public and the ANC branch members who voted him into power to speculate: was he protecting his political allies, friends and family members? Was he compromised because of his own blemished past? Didn't he care about the well-being of his country? Or did he just not have any ideas or plans how to fix what was broken?

In April 2012, Nedbank chairman Reuel Khoza ignited the wrath of the ANC when he criticised the state of leadership in the country in his annual chairperson's report. 'South Africa is widely recognised for its liberal and enlightened constitution, yet we observe the emergence of a strange breed of leaders who are determined to undermine the rule of law and override the constitution. Our political leadership's moral quotient is degenerating and we are fast losing the checks and balances that are necessary to prevent a recurrence of the past. This is not the accountable democracy for which generations suffered and fought,' Khoza wrote. He was lambasted by Zuma's loyal bulldogs: Gwede Mantashe, Nathi Mthethwa and Blade Nzimande. Nzimande wrote Khoza was part of an 'ideological third force' that feared black majority rule. But Khoza wasn't intimidated, and continued his criticism of Zuma and the ANC at a public lecture at the University of Limpopo in September. 'What makes for the kind of predictive leadership that we have now, that is only a masquerade of leadership, is the fact that it is not predicated on principle,' Khoza said.[3]

Three months before he was due to be re-elected or rejected by the ANC, Zuma took the extraordinary step of deploying the SANDF on a full-time basis to Marikana until the end of January 2013 – a month after Mangaung. It was a significant moment for a number of reasons; it was an admission that the ANC and its alliance partners had failed to control a constituency it had previously taken for granted; it was an admission that the police and intelligence services had failed to bring stability and peace to the volatile region; and it was a last, desperate show of force to reclaim control and use state machinery to show the miners, who were asking Malema and not Zuma to address them, who the boss was.

* * *

'The Emperor is naked,' wrote the author and public intellectual Njabulo Ndebele in *City Press* after the drama around *The Spear* had calmed down. He likened South Africa to Hans Christian Andersen's famous tale, 'The Emperor's New Clothes'. It was the most scathing assessment of Zuma's leadership I have read since he became ANC president in 2007: 'In the foreground to all the public statements and engineered drama he started in his bid to secure public sympathy as victim of a racist attack, President Zuma conducted himself "normally",' Ndebele wrote. 'There he was on television among school-children with one on his lap; there he was among the aged, bearing gifts to cheer their hearts; there he was announcing that Nkandla was on its way to being a city; and there he was turning the tap to "deliver" water to a woman in Hammanskraal who had written to him in desperation. The president was taking care of his people. But the Emperor is naked!'[4]

The Spear, Ndebele wrote, shook him but did not offend him: 'My capacity to be offended had been eroded cumulatively and decisively by Zuma's conduct before he became president of the ANC and president of South Africa, and ever since. Numbed by disbelief at a string of disconcerting episodes, I found myself struggling to turn numbness into outrage. *Hail to the Thief II*, Murray's exhibition, I had to admit, expressed my outrage.'

Then Ndebele turned to Zuma's handling and alleged interference in the Richard Mdluli matter and the criminal charges against the ANC's leader in the Northern Cape, John Block:

> What kind of president of a country is not ashamed to be
> known to have brought political pressure to bear on his police
> services to have serious charges of murder and fraud dropped

against an individual who does not inspire public confidence, so that this person can be reinstated as the head of crime intelligence?

Such conduct by the president is neither professionally nor morally justifiable. It does not 'promote the unity of the nation which will advance the republic,' as the Constitution enjoins.

Prior to this, the president did nothing to reassure an anxious public when John Block, chairman of the ANC in the Northern Cape and its MEC for finance, was arrested and charged with tender fraud. Hazel Jenkins, the province's premier, even stood in firm support of Block.

President Zuma comes across as being highly tolerant of criminality. In the context that criminal charges against him were unsatisfactorily withdrawn, his conduct in this respect should not be surprising. ANC party members caught on the wrong side of the law are likely to receive active support or admonitory leniency. This presents an image of the president as not being committed to upholding, defending and respecting 'the Constitution as the supreme law of the republic'.

Zuma, Ndebele wrote, didn't seem to have a clue about politicians' conflict of interest when they do business with the state. 'Is it any wonder that tender fraud has spread like a contagion across the country? The president of the republic has accorded it parliamentary tolerance.'

The import of all this permits one to ask: just how far has South Africa gone down the path towards becoming a full-blown gangster state? What about the spate of senior public appointments made, only to be challenged successfully before the courts? What about attacks, some by ministers and senior ANC party officials, on the courts and the Constitution?

Who was in control of the country, if not the ANC, Ndebele asked:

Has the ANC become an empty shell, traded on the stock market of tenderpreneurship? Hail to the thief! These questions should send a chilling message to all South Africans that it is time to begin to take their country back. The cumulative effect of it all is strongly suggestive to me: President Zuma seems eminently impeachable.

The point of his reflection was to 'point out the history of the corrosion or erosion of presidential dignity and respect as a result of consistent, even predictable, and questionable presidential conduct,' Ndebele wrote. '*The Spear* did not cause the disrespect and the loss of dignity; it simply reflected it. The Emperor is naked!'

Could the naked Emperor survive another round of trials and tribulations to clinch a second term as ANC president? I wondered. Is he the ultimate survivor, able to surmount the consequences of bad decisions, bad judgement and bad leadership choices? Or have the ANC delegates who elected him five years ago since discovered that his coat was see-through all along?

Annexures

Annexure 1

Zuma's Cabinet (2009)

1 Fired or resigned   2 Moved to another position   3 Died

PRESIDENT
Jacob Zuma

DEPUTY PRESIDENT
Kgalema Motlanthe

MINISTER OF AGRICULTURE, FORESTRY AND FISHERIES
Tina Joemat-Pettersson

DEPUTY MINISTER OF AGRICULTURE, FORESTRY AND FISHERIES
Pieter Mulder

MINISTER OF ARTS AND CULTURE
Lulu Xingwana[2]

DEPUTY MINISTER OF ARTS AND CULTURE
Paul Mashatile[2]

MINISTER OF BASIC EDUCATION
Angie Motshekga

DEPUTY MINISTER OF BASIC EDUCATION
Enver Surty

MINISTER OF COMMUNICATIONS
Siphiwe Nyanda[1]

DEPUTY MINISTER OF COMMUNICATIONS
Dina Pule[2]

MINISTER OF COOPERATIVE GOVERNANCE AND TRADITIONAL AFFAIRS
Sicelo Shiceka[1]

DEPUTY MINISTER OF COOPERATIVE GOVERNANCE AND TRADITIONAL AFFAIRS
Yunus Carrim

MINISTER OF CORRECTIONAL SERVICES
Nosiviwe Mapisa-Nqakula[2]

DEPUTY MINISTER OF CORRECTIONAL SERVICES
Hlengiwe Mkhize[2]

MINISTER OF DEFENCE AND MILITARY VETERANS
Lindiwe Sisulu[2]

DEPUTY MINISTER OF DEFENCE AND MILITARY VETERANS
Thabang Makwetla

MINISTER OF ECONOMIC DEVELOPMENT
Ebrahim Patel

DEPUTY MINISTER OF ECONOMIC DEVELOPMENT
Gwen Mahlangu-Nkabinde[1]

MINISTER OF ENERGY
Dipuo Peters

MINISTER OF FINANCE
Pravin Gordhan

DEPUTY MINISTER OF FINANCE
Nhlanhla Nene

MINISTER OF HEALTH
Dr Aaron Motsoaledi

DEPUTY MINISTER OF HEALTH
Dr Molefi Sefularo[3]

MINISTER OF HIGHER EDUCATION AND TRAINING
Dr Blade Nzimande

MINISTER OF HOME AFFAIRS
Dr Nkosazana Dlamini-Zuma

DEPUTY MINISTER OF HOME AFFAIRS
Malusi Gigaba[2]

MINISTER OF HUMAN SETTLEMENTS
Tokyo Sexwale

DEPUTY MINISTER OF HUMAN SETTLEMENTS
Zou Kota

MINISTER OF INTERNATIONAL RELATIONS AND COOPERATION
Maite Nkoana-Mashabane

DEPUTY MINISTER OF INTERNATIONAL RELATIONS AND COOPERATION (1)
Ebrahim Ismail Ebrahim

DEPUTY MINISTER OF INTERNATIONAL RELATIONS AND COOPERATION (2)
Sue van der Merwe[1]

MINISTER OF JUSTICE AND CONSTITUTIONAL DEVELOPMENT
Jeff Radebe

DEPUTY MINISTER OF JUSTICE AND CONSTITUTIONAL DEVELOPMENT
Andries Nel

MINISTER OF LABOUR
Membathisi Mdladlana[1]

MINISTER OF MINERAL RESOURCES
Susan Shabangu

MINISTER OF POLICE
Nathi Mthethwa

DEPUTY MINISTER OF POLICE
Fikile Mbalula[2]

MINISTER OF PUBLIC ENTERPRISES
Barbara Hogan[1]

DEPUTY MINISTER OF PUBLIC ENTERPRISES
Enoch Godongwana[1]

MINISTER FOR THE PUBLIC SERVICE AND ADMINISTRATION
Richard Baloyi[2]

DEPUTY MINISTER FOR THE PUBLIC SERVICE AND ADMINISTRATION
Roy Padayachie[3]

MINISTER OF PUBLIC WORKS
Geoff Doidge[1]

DEPUTY MINISTER OF PUBLIC WORKS
Hendrietta Bogopane-Zulu[2]

MINISTER OF RURAL DEVELOPMENT AND LAND REFORM
Gugile Nkwinti

DEPUTY MINISTER OF RURAL DEVELOPMENT AND LAND REFORM
Joe Phaahla[2]

MINISTER OF SCIENCE AND TECHNOLOGY
Naledi Pandor[2]

DEPUTY MINISTER OF SCIENCE AND TECHNOLOGY
Derek Hanekom

MINISTER OF SOCIAL DEVELOPMENT
Edna Molewa[2]

DEPUTY MINISTER OF SOCIAL DEVELOPMENT
Bathabile Dlamini[2]

MINISTER OF SPORT AND RECREATION
Makhenkesi Stofile[1]

DEPUTY MINISTER OF SPORT AND RECREATION
Gert Oosthuizen

MINISTER OF STATE SECURITY
Siyabonga Cwele

MINISTER IN THE PRESIDENCY (1)
National Planning Commission
Trevor Manuel

MINISTER IN THE PRESIDENCY (2)
Performance Monitoring and Evaluation as well as Administration
in the Presidency
Collins Chabane

MINISTER OF TOURISM
Marthinus van Schalkwyk

DEPUTY MINISTER OF TOURISM
Thozile Xasa

MINISTER OF TRADE AND INDUSTRY
Rob Davies

DEPUTY MINISTER OF TRADE AND INDUSTRY (1)
Thandi Tobias

DEPUTY MINISTER OF TRADE AND INDUSTRY (2)
Maria Ntuli[2]

MINISTER OF TRANSPORT
Sbu Ndebele[2]

DEPUTY MINISTER OF TRANSPORT
Jeremy Cronin[2]

MINISTER OF WATER AND ENVIRONMENTAL AFFAIRS
Buyelwa Sonjica[1]

DEPUTY MINISTER OF WATER AND ENVIRONMENTAL AFFAIRS
Rejoice Mabhudafhasi

MINISTER OF WOMEN, YOUTH, CHILDREN AND PEOPLE WITH DISABILITIES
Noluthando Mayende-Sibiya[1]

Annexure 2

David Wilson's affidavit

David Wilson states under oath in English:

1.

I am an adult male currently residing at [his address and contact details in Kuala Lumpur, Malaysia].

2.

The following statement is true and correct to the best of my knowledge and ability and sets out the broad course of events, without necessarily raising all aspects and issues and without going into all detail.

3.

I was employed in the Renong Group ('Renong') initially from 1990 to March 1994 and again from July 1995 to January 2002. I was the managing director of Renong Overseas Corporation Sdn Bhd, a wholly owned subsidiary of Renong Berhad, from July 1995 to January 2002. This company was responsible for the management of the investments and activities of Renong outside Malaysia. My working address was 3rd Floor, Wisma YPR, Lorong Kapar, Off Jalan Syed Putra, 58000 Kuala Lumpur, Malaysia and later at 14th Floor, Menara 2, Faber Towers, Jalan Desa Bahagia, Taman Desa, Off Jalan Klang Lama, 58100 Kuala Lumpur, Malaysia. Since leaving Renong I have been working as a director of Starnergy Sdn Bhd, a Malaysian project management company.

4.

Renong is a large diversified Malaysian conglomerate that owns several international hotels in Malaysia and an extensive land bank for future development. After the elections in South Africa in 1994 Renong was interested in finding similar opportunities for investment in South Africa.

5.

After investigating several potential investment opportunities in South Africa, the Hilton Hotel and the Point Development in Durban were identified as possible investments during the third quarter of 1995. In particular, the Point Development was seen as a potential empowerment project, because the land was effectively owned by the Government through Transnet, Portnet and the City of Durban.

6.

During the period August to October 1995, I and other management staff of Renong held discussions with Mzi Khumalo, the chairman of Point Waterfront Company (Pty) Ltd ('the Point Waterfront Company'), the Minister of Public Works and the Director General of the Public Works Department at which Renong outlined its ideas on how the Point Development could be implemented as an empowerment project. Subsequently, when the concept of the Point Development project had been more clearly defined, Mr Khumalo advised Renong of the names of the representatives who had been nominated to look after the empowerment interests. These names comprised Tutu Mnganga, Bheka Shezi, Moses Tembe and others, whose names I cannot presently recall, who were all residents of

Durban. I understood from Mzi Khumalo that these nominees had been endorsed and approved by the Government of South Africa, specifically from the Minister and Director General of Public Works.

7.

In the third quarter of 1995, an initial shareholders agreement was signed between Renong Overseas Corporation Sdn Bhd, representing Renong, and Secprop 60 (Pty) Ltd, a shelf company representing the empowerment interests. The shareholders agreement set out the principles upon which the shareholders were to work together to bid for and, if successful, implement the Point Development and, inter alia, described the arrangements by which Renong would provide the funding for the 49% shareholding of Secprop 60 (Pty) Ltd in the proposed development. The nominated empowerment representatives were the directors of Secprop 60 (Pty) Ltd and the company was later renamed as Vulindlela Investments (Pty) Ltd ('Vulindlela').

8.

In August 1995 a large delegation from Renong, comprising the Chairman, directors and senior management of the companies in Renong, visited South Africa. Several functions were held during this visit and I believe that I first met Mr Schabir Shaik at one of these dinners.

9.

In October 1995 the Point Waterfront Company called for proposals from interested parties in the private sector for the development of the Point. Presentations were made to the Board of the Point Waterfront Company in November 1995. Two other consortia made proposals, one of which was a consortium led by the Nkobi Group.

10.

The day before the presentation to the Point Waterfront Company, I was requested by telephone by Mr Schabir Shaik to attend a meeting in the Nkobi Group's offices in the central business district of

Durban early that evening. Mr Schabir Shaik told me that this meeting would be to Renong's benefit. When I arrived at the offices it became evident that the purpose of the meeting was to try to intimidate Renong. I had been given the impression by Mr Schabir Shaik that I would be meeting with him privately and was surprised to discover that there were about fifteen other people present, none of whom I had met before, comprising representatives from the Nkobi Group and property companies that had formed a consortium to bid for the Point Development project. Mr Schabir Shaik was the spokesperson. I believe that this was the second time I met Mr Schabir Shaik.

11.

When I confirmed that Renong intended to make a presentation to the Point Waterfront Company, Mr Schabir Shaik and others present indicated that the consortium whose members were present at the meeting was very powerful and influential and that it would not be in Renong's interests if Renong proceeded with the presentation with their current partners. He informed me that he and his consortium had extensive experience working in Durban, and if Renong worked with them everything would be fine. Mr Schabir Shaik proposed that a joint presentation should be made with his consortium. I rejected this proposal and said that Renong would not change the present arrangements. Renong went ahead with its presentation as planned, which was well received. From this point onwards Renong was, to my knowledge, the only bidder left in the picture.

12.

I kept the Chairman of Renong, Tan Sri Halim Saad, informed of progress on the Point Development and, in particular, the delays that Renong was experiencing as a result of Mr Schabir Shaik's interference and insistence that his consortium should be involved in the project. As a result of this interference and the uncertainty which it caused, it was considered necessary to obtain confirmation at a political level that the empowerment partners that had been identified were indeed acceptable. In June 1996, the Chairman asked me to draft a letter to Mr Jacob Zuma, in his capacity as national and provincial chairman of the ANC, asking for his assistance in resolving matters regarding suitable parties for Renong to work with. The letter was signed by the Chairman and I believe it was dated 8 June 1996. I do not presently possess a copy of this letter.

13.

Towards the end of June 1996 a letter, dated 10 June 1996, from Mr Schabir Shaik addressed to the Chairman of Renong, Tan Sri Halim Saad, came to my knowledge. Only after reading this letter did I become aware of a relationship between Mr Jacob Zuma and Mr Schabir Shaik.

14.

At a certain stage, I believe it was in early November 1996, the Chairman, showed me a letter that he had received from Mr Jacob Zuma, in his capacity as Minister of Economic Affairs and Tourism of Kwazulu-Natal. The letter was dated 31 October 1996, although it appeared from the contents of the penultimate paragraph that it may have been drafted some time earlier. In this letter reference is made to the letter dated 8 June 1996 sent by the Chairman to Mr Jacob Zuma. Mr Jacob Zuma assured the Chairman in this letter that he, in the aforementioned capacity, was 'extremely concerned about the development of the Point Project' and that he was keen to assist Renong 'in resolving any matter currently impeding this development'. He also mentioned that he was both the national and provincial chairperson of the ANC. He invited the Chairman or a senior member of Renong to meet with him in Durban at a time to be arranged. The Chairman instructed me to arrange a meeting with Mr Zuma through Mr Schabir Shaik and to attend on the Chairman's behalf.

15.

I had first met Mr Jacob Zuma, in his capacity as Minister of Economic

Affairs and Tourism of Kwazulu-Natal, at a black tie business function in Durban around September 1995. I was sitting at the same dinner table and was introduced to him as part of the general introductions. He struck me as being an affable and outgoing person who was confident in his ministerial role.

16.

Mr Schabir Shaik made arrangements for me, as the nominated representative of the Chairman, to meet Mr Jacob Zuma as proposed in Mr Jacob Zuma's letter. The meeting took place in the evening during the last quarter of 1996 at Mr Schabir Shaik's apartment in Durban and was attended by Mr Jacob Zuma, Mr Schabir Shaik and me.

17.

Mr Jacob Zuma was clearly uncomfortable during the meeting and I gained the clear impression from his demeanour, the substance of the meeting and the manner in which it proceeded that he was there under sufferance. He spoke in a guarded fashion and appeared to be anxious to get the meeting over with. This behaviour was in stark contrast to the impression I had of him at our previous meeting. Throughout the discussion, Mr Schabir Shaik would introduce the topics discussed, whereupon Mr Zuma would confirm and expand upon what Mr Shaik had said. He said that he was not happy with the persons nominated to represent the empowerment interests in the Point Development, although he offered no explanation for this. He proposed that Mr Schabir Shaik should be involved in the project and stressed repeatedly that he would be a good partner for the job. During the course of the discussions it became increasingly clear that Mr Jacob Zuma was acting as if Mr Schabir Shaik had some sort of hold over him. At one point Mr Jacob Zuma made mention of the support and assistance he had received from Mr Schabir Shaik. I gained the strong impression that this support and assistance was of a financial nature.

18.

I responded to Mr Jacob Zuma by emphasizing that Renong had no wish to get involved in the selection of the empowerment nominees since this was a matter for the Government of South Africa to decide. The meeting ended with no real resolution of the matter. It was our intention to continue with our existing empowerment partners unless formally advised otherwise by the Government of South Africa. Such an instruction was not forthcoming.

19.

On 20 January 1997 I sent a facsimile to Mr Schabir Shaik in respect of a meeting to be held in Durban on the 3rd, 4th or 5th of February 1997 in order to discuss the Point Development. As I recall, this was in response to a further request by Mr Schabir Shaik to meet.

20.

On 3 February 1997 at 10:10hrs the said meeting was held at the offices of the Nkobi Group in Durban. At this meeting, I indicated to Mr Schabir Shaik that Renong was not prepared to make any changes to the makeup of their empowerment partners unless and until they had the written affirmation of Mr Jacob Zuma, in his capacity as national and provincial chairman of the ANC, that he was happy with the distribution of the 49% shareholding of Vulindlela in the joint venture company carrying out the Point Development.

21.

It had always been Renong's understanding that the Government of South Africa would decide on the individuals to be nominated as the representatives of the empowerment interests. It was furthermore acknowledged, in the context of the improving relationship at the time between the ANC and the IFP in Kwazulu-Natal, that the IFP should also be involved in some capacity in the Point Development.

22.

Mr Jacob Zuma had raised no objections initially to the empowerment nominees or the involvement of Vulindlela. It was therefore a source of frustration to Renong when the nominees were subsequently queried by Mr Jacob Zuma and other parties.

23.

Mr Schabir Shaik never indicated that he was an office bearer in the ANC. He said he was a member of the ANC and frequently reiterated that people of Asian extraction were to be included in the empowerment programmes.

24.

After the difficulties that Mr Shaik had caused Renong in trying to implement the Point Development it was clear to Renong that Mr Schabir Shaik was not a suitable business partner and no further business discussions were held with him after 1997.

Annexure 3

ANC press statement

ANC calls on all South Africans to boycott buying City Press
Newspaper and to join the protest match [sic] *to the Goodman Gallery*

24 May 2012

The African National Congress (ANC) calls upon all South Africans, members of the ANC and the Alliance, to indefinitely boycott buying the City Press Newspaper. The boycott will stand until the removal of the insulting portrait of President Jacob Zuma from their website. Furthermore, we call upon all South Africans to join our protest action on Tuesday, 29 May 2012, to the Goodman Gallery in Johannesburg. Further details on the protest march will be provided in due course.

The City Press newspaper, by continuing to exhibit the offensive painting has clearly shown its collusion to the indecent depiction of President Zuma which violates his right to human dignity. The City Press has therefore become a paragon of immorality, abuse and perpetrator of injustice and slander. Their refusal to remove this portrait from their website and their controlled social media is a clear indication that this newspaper does not belong to our shared democratic dispensation and values.

This newspaper has singled itself as anti ANC, the President, our democracy and the majority of South Africans. It is our view that City Press has placed profiteering and populism before the principles enshrined in our constitution. City Press has missed an opportunity to prove to this country that they are indeed committed to our Constitution and its values.

The protest action to the Goodman gallery is aimed at further intensifying our campaign against this gallery's refusal to remove this insulting portrait from their website. Furthermore, this protest action, seeks to show our total condemnation and disdain to any form of art that is indecent, dehumanising and demeaning to any person including President Jacob Zuma.

We are also through this protest action directed at Goodman gallery, saying with one voice and our foot that nobody including, Brett Murray and the gallery has a right to 'deface' the ANC's logo and insignia.

The logo of the ANC with an inscription 'FOR SALE' and 'SOLD' has not only defaced a symbol that the ANC has intellectual property right to, but is a clear sign of attack on the ANC as an organisation.

We are therefore calling upon all South Africans, our Alliance partners, our members as well as our supporters to come not only to defend the rights of our President to be treated with human dignity but also to come and defend the African National Congress.

The ANC is humbled by the overwhelming support from all South Africans who come from all walks of life and political persuasions, who continue to support the noble call made by our constitution and reiterated by the ANC that the rights of President Zuma have been violated.

Let us continue to defend all the rights that are contained in our constitution as we believe that the right to freedom of artistic expression does not supersede other rights that are enshrined in our constitution. We will use all avenues available to us in this regard,

those avenues includes courts, protest action and boycotts of any offending party.

Issued by:
Jackson Mthembu
ANC National Spokesperson

Annexure 4

Zuma Incorporated: the business associates

These people are either directors or members of business entities linked to the Zuma empire (see graphics section).

Balmakhun, Malthidevi (Dobson Investments)
Balmakhun, Rajendra (Dobson Investments)
Bhengu, Thandazile (Wamuhle Construction)
Birshtein, Boris Joseph (Royal HTM Group)
Brauns, Jerome (Nippon Import Export SA, SA Guiding Star
    Trading, Southeast Network Construction SA)
Braverman, Jack (Royal HTM Group)
Buthelezi, Mthunzi Percyvell Xola (Izichwe Investment Holdings)
Carrim, Aslam (Isthebe Petroleum)
Charles, Karl Keegan (Tekwini Inkunzi Investment)
Chauke, Ramafole Goodenough (Imifula Development
    Corporation)
Chiti, Bwalya Stanley Kasonde (Royal HTM Group)
Cowell, Dean Anthony (Vukani Africa Events and Training)
Cox, Christopher James (Unigame)
Cox, Stephen Michael (Unigame)

De Koker, Charmaine Antoinette (Fire Raiders)
Dlamini, Celenhle Thembayena (Iningi Investments 190)
Dlamini, Joy Chantal (Nippon Import Export SA)
Dlamini, Nkosinathi (Isthebe Petroleum)
Dlamini, Thumbumuzi (Iningi Investments 190)
Dukhi, Ryan (Dobson Investments)
Fiford, Trevor Alexander (Fire Raiders)
Fraser, Deborah Marcia (Intsika Yembokodo Development Projects,
  Vuna Imbewu)
Fraser, Emily Hellen (Vuna Imbewu)
Fulbeck, Christopher John (Myriad Brokers)
Gabela, Mduduzi Trevor (Owabantu Logistics and Construction)
Garach, Surendra Bhugwanjee (Dobson Investments)
Gcabashe, Sipho Joseph (Black Target Investments, Dobson
  Investments)
Govender, Ronica (Westdawn Investments)
Gupta, Arti (Sahara Holdings)
Gupta, Atul Kumar (Sahara Holdings, Shiva Uranium)
Gupta, Chetali (Sahara Holdings)
Gupta, Rajesh Kumar 'Tony' (Afripalm Horizons, CRCC Afripalm
  Construction, Gemini Moon Trading 254, Islandsite Investments
  255, Karibu Hospitality, Mabengela Investments, Westdawn
  Investments)
Gupta, Varun (Shiva Uranium)
Harrington, Madhukant Narotham (Silvex 556)
Hlomuka, Khulani Kenridge (Khumusi Trading Enterprise,
  Masikhuza)
Hulley, Michael Andrew Thomas (Cyndara 92, Elatirex, Labat
  Africa, Meziblox, Sanchopath, Sanchophase)
Jia, Shan (CRCC Afripalm Construction)
Khoza, Duduzile Gracial (Intsika Yembokodo Development
  Projects, Vuna Imbewu)
Khoza, Mwelase Ignatius (Amahle Management Services)
Khoza, Nomsa Mavis (Mayisane Investments)
Khoza, Tsiki Princess Jabu (Intsika Yembokodo Development Projects)

Khoza, Xoliswa Lenhle (Iningi Investments 190, Mayisane
    Investments, The Zodwa Khoza Foundation)
Khuzwayo, Mthokozisi (Leading Role Trading and Projects)
Litha, Mpho (Attractive Move Invest)
Lukhele, Erick Sozabile (Mthunzy Holdings)
Luthuli, Bhekayena Wilfred (Corpclo 2790)
Mabena, Lebogang (MaNtuli Zuma J Foundation)
Mabogoane, Victor Mothswane (Bambanani Micro Business
    Network)
Madlala, Protas (Jacob G Zuma RDP Education Trust)
Madlala, Siphakamiso Michael (Izichwe Investment Holdings)
Madolo, Nokuhle (Isthebe Petroleum)
Maharaj, Krishen Praemllal (Izichwe Investment Holdings)
Mandela, Zodwa Zoyisile Gadaffi (Izichwe Investment Holdings,
    Aurora Empowerment System, Labat Africa)
Mankazana, Zwelakhe (Jacob G Zuma RDP Education Trust)
Manzi, Thamsanqa Ellenberg (Imifula Development Corporation)
Maphela, Raphael Godfrey (Wamuhle Construction)
Maphumulo, Mzingelo Goodenough (Wamuhle Construction)
Maseko, Absalom (Bambanani Micro Business Network)
Masters, Christopher Robert (Vukani Africa Events and Training)
Mathe, Baldason Thembinkosi Thintani (Jacob Zuma Foundation)
Mazibuko, Mantombi Lizzie (Khumusi Trading Enterprise)
Mbatha, Menzi Glen (Afripalm Horizons)
Mchunu, Joseph (Silvex 556)
Mdlalose, Phumlecelile Patrick (Bambanani Micro Business Network)
Mendlula, Hezekia Sibusiso (Bambanani Micro Business Network)
Mgengwane, Luyanda Valentine (MaNtuli Zuma J Foundation)
Mhlongo, Pamela Nokuzola (Bambanani Micro Business Network)
Mhlongo, Thabo Samuel (Unogwaja Investments)
Mkhize, Sibusiso Thembinkosi (Imvusa Trading 582)
Mkhize, Thandeka Lady-Fair (Masikhuza)
Mkosana, Esther Magamase (MaNtuli Zuma J Foundation)
Mncwango, Siphiwe Patrick (Khumusi Trading Enterprise,
    Masikhuza)

Mngadi, Zama Hlengiwe (Wamuhle Construction)

Modipane, Badirileng Tricia (Isthebe Foods, Ocean Crest Trading 51)

Mogano, Mogotladi Raesibe (Karibu Hospitality)

Mokwena, Mandisa Nozibele Andrea (Glenlyn Investments, Lavender Sky Investments 25, Vautrade)

Moonsamy, Ragavan (Sahara Holdings)

Msomi, Elphus Mkanyiseleni (Bambanani Micro Business Network)

Msomi, Sifiso (Jacob G Zuma RDP Education Trust)

Mthembu, Wellington Zinhle (Izichwe Investment Holdings)

Mthethwa, Phumelele Walton Aubrey (Izichwe Investment Holdings)

Mthethwa, Sello Moses (Sahara Holdings)

Mtshali, Thami (Jacob G Zuma RDP Education Trust)

Muller, Johannes Marthinus (Fire Raiders)

Mvuzi, Andile Terrence (Owabantu Logistics and Construction)

Myeni, Duduzile Cynthia (Jacob Zuma Foundation)

Mzobe, Sibusiso Lucas 'Deebo' (Masibambisane Rural Development Initiative)

Mzobe, Vusimuzi Stephen (Izichwe Investment Holdings)

Naidoo, Parmananda Anjil (Black Target Investments, Dobson Investments, Mthunzy Holdings)

Nath, Ravindra (Westdawn Investments)

Ndaba, Sophie Sefora (Attractive Move Invest)

Ngcobo, Linah Dzongweni (Intsika Yembokodo Development Projects, Vuna Imbewu)

Ngubane, Catherine Hazel Nokuthula (Cherry Moss Trade and Invest 176)

Ngubane, Sheshile Thulani Zwelihle (Aurora Empowerment System, Labat Africa)

Ngubane, Silindokuhle Innocentia Busisiwe (Aspigon 98)

Nhlenyama, Cynthia (Jacob G Zuma RDP Education Trust)

Ntombela, Faith Nozizwe Siphiwe (Glenlyn Investments)

Ntombela, Wiseman Manqoba (Flysawise)

Ntuli, Ntombifuthi Nobuhle (Heavenly Promise 85)

Nyembe, Phakamile (Heavenly Promise 85, MaNtuli Zuma J
Foundation)

Nziratimana, Jiji Thomas (Mthunzy Holdings)

Nzuza, Siphiwe Patrick (Masikhuza)

Oh, Tae Jung (Ocean Crest Trading 51)

Panchpersadh, Kajal (Dobson Investments)

Phiri, Enock Chikapa (Mthunzy Holdings)

Pilane, Molefe John (Corpclo 2790)

Prinsloo, Martie (Jacob G Zuma RDP Education Trust)

Qobose, Muziwakhe Thomas Dominic (The Zodwa Khoza
Foundation)

Ramela, Malan Samson (Flysawise)

Raphahlelo, Freddie (Jacob G Zuma RDP Education Trust)

Razak, Mahomed Saleem (Sahara Holdings)

Reddy, Privanesh (Tekwini Inkunzi Investment)

Sabelo, Goodness Nomusa (Wamuhle Construction)

Samuels, Veronica Sibongile (Isthebe Petroleum)

Sello, Bonginkosi Mangaliso Mpho (Flywise)

Shabalala, Nkululeko Handsome (Izichwe Investment Holdings)

Shabalala, Phillip Nhlakanipho (Masikhuza)

Shabalala, Sanele (Izichwe Investment Holdings)

Shange, Phumelele (Masikhuza)

Shezi, Sibusiso Moses (Heavenly Promise 85)

Shezi, Sizwe (Jacob G Zuma RDP Education Trust)

Sigxashe, Lindani (Glenlyn Investments, Lavender Sky
Investments 25, Vautrade)

Simelani, Salakuthini Mummy (Wamuhle Construction)

Simmer, Farrell Chad (Tekwini Inkunzi Investment)

Singh, Mally (Nippon Import Export SA, SA Guiding Star Trading,
Southeast Network Construction SA)

Stewart, Spencer George (Meziblox)

Tsokote, Madiba (Bambanani Micro Business Network)

Vavi, Noluthando Norah (Intsika Yembokodo Development
Projects)

Wilkinson, Craig Louis (Imifula Development Corporation)
Willet, Carmen Megan (Jacob Zuma Foundation)
Winter, Elwyn David (Unigame)
Yaka, Mvelenhle (Jacob G Zuma RDP Education Trust)
Zim, Polelo Lazarus (Afripalm Horizons, CRCC Afripalm
    Construction)
Zondo, Reginald Gugulethu (Tekwini Inkunzi Investment)
Zulu, Tholakele Rosetta (Wamuhle Construction)
Zuma, Buyenze Thembekile (Heavenly Promise 85)
Zuma, Fakazi Michael (Leading Role Trading and Projects)
Zuma, Nkosazana Bonganini (Born Free Investments 660)
Zuma, Priscilla (Isthebe Petroleum)
Zuma, Sikhumbuzo (Selby) (Dumaka Alternative Technology,
    Isthebe Construction and Engineering, Isthebe Foods, Isthebe Oil
    and Gas, Nippon Import Export SA, SA Guiding Star Trading,
    Southeast Network Construction SA)
Zuma, Trurman Michael Zakhe (Isthebe Petroleum)
Zwane, Gcini Rejoyce (Khumusi Trading Enterprise)
Zwane, Nomfundo Thobeka (Aspigon 98, Spectacular Real
    Productions)
Zwane, Nontobeko Fundiswa (Nyenyedzi Productions, Aspigon 98,
    Spectacular Real Productions)

Source: Companies and Intellectual Property Commission
(as at 26 September 2012)

Acknowledgements

I've been writing this book in my head since 2004, when I first started working on the Shaik/Zuma story. Thank you to all my editors, news editors and colleagues throughout the years who trusted me with the story and allowed me to follow Zuma wherever his legal troubles took him. A special word of thanks to Ferial Haffajee and my other *City Press* colleagues, for agreeing to let me out of the newsroom to write this book. Your support and encouragement has been unwavering. To all those journalists who have lived and breathed the Zuma story with me over the years: Stephen Grootes, Felix Dlangamandla, Paddy Harper, Sam Sole, Matuma Letsoalo, Estelle Ellis and Adri Kotzé, to name a few. Thanks for sharing your notes, wisdom and beer. My publisher, Ingeborg Pelser of Jonathan Ball Publishers, finally convinced me to set the Zuma story down on paper – thank you for being crazy and brave enough to see the project through in very little time. Thanks to my family and friends, for their undying support, belief and assistance with the book. And, finally, thanks to my beautiful wife Cecile, who remains a constant source of inspiration, advice and support.

Adriaan Basson
Johannesburg, September 2012

Notes

Chapter 1

1 *Mail & Guardian* Online, 9 May 2009.
2 *Pretoria News*, 21 November 2011.
3 *Sowetan*, 11 November 2011.
4 *Daily News*, 28 November 2011.

Chapter 2

1 Sapa, 21 July 2011.
2 *Mail & Guardian*, 4 July 2008.

Chapter 3

1 *Mail & Guardian*, 17 January 2008.
2 Sapa, 1 March 2012.
3 *Sowetan*, 16 January 2012.
4 *Sowetan*, 13 January 2012.
5 Sapa, 24 March 2010.
6 *Mail & Guardian*, 9 September 2008.
7 *Mail & Guardian*, 17 February 2012.
8 *The Star*, 29 January 2009.
9 *City Press*, 29 April 2012.
10 *The Times*, 28 April 2010.
11 *Mail & Guardian*, 12 March 2010.

Chapter 7

1 *Sunday Argus*, 26 February 2006.

Chapter 8

1 *Sunday Times*, 1 July 2012.
2 *The Star*, 4 August 2008.

Chapter 10

1 *Mail & Guardian*, 11 July 2008.
2 *Mail & Guardian*, 22 August 2008.
3 Ibid.
4 *Mail & Guardian*, 22 August 2008.

Chapter 11

1 *Mail & Guardian*, 24 January 2008.
2 *Mail & Guardian*, 19 June 2009.

Chapter 12

1 *Mail & Guardian*, 22 August 2008.

Chapter 13

1 *Mail & Guardian*, 19 January 2007.

Chapter 14

1 *Mail & Guardian*, 4 June 2010.
2 *Ibid.*
3 *City Press*, 2 October 2011.

Chapter 15

1 *Cape Times*, 16 April 2009.

Chapter 17

1 *Mail & Guardian*, 19 March 2010.
2 *Daily Mail*, 22 April 2009.
3 *Mail & Guardian*, 19 March 2010.
4 *Business Day*, 24 February 2011.
5 Sapa, 3 June 2012.

Chapter 18

1 *The Times*, 27 July 2010.
2 *Sunday Times*, 30 August 2009.
3 Ibid.
4 Fin24, 27 June 2010.
5 *Mining Weekly*, 12 October 2009.
6 *Mail & Guardian*, 16 July 2010.
7 *Ibid.*
8 *Sunday Times*, 17 April 2011.
9 *Ibid.*
10 *City Press*, 25 March 2012.
11 *Ibid.*
12 *City Press*, 23 January 2012.
13 *The Times*, 15 April 2012.
14 Sapa, 16 March 2012.
15 *The Times*, 27 July 2010.

Chapter 19

1 *Sunday Times*, 20 March 2011.
2 *Sunday Times*, 27 February 2011.
3 *Ibid.*
4 *Ibid.*
5 *Business Day*, 23 July 2010.
6 *Financial Mail*, 24 April 2009.
7 *City Press*, 6 March 2011.
8 *Ibid.*
9 *Mail & Guardian*, 16 April 2010.
10 *Business Day*, 15 December 2011.
11 *Mail & Guardian*, 13 August 2010.
12 Moneyweb, 10 August 2010.
13 *Mail & Guardian*, 13 August 2010.
14 Moneyweb, 3 October 2010.
15 *City Press*, 6 March 2011.

16 *Mail & Guardian*, 30 September 2011.
17 *City Press*, 6 March 2011.
18 *Mail & Guardian*, 3 August 2012.
19 *City Press*, 12 August 2012.
20 *Mail & Guardian*, 4 December 2009.
21 midrandgroup.blogspot.com.

Chapter 20

1 *Sunday Times*, 30 January 2010.
2 news.bbc.co.uk/2/hi/africa/ 8491375.stm, 1 February 2010.
3 *Mail & Guardian*, 3 June 2010.
4 Ibid.
5 *The Mercury*, 6 January 2011.
6 *Sowetan*, 7 June 2010.

Chapter 22

1 *Mail & Guardian*, 30 October 2009.
2 *The Witness*, 1 December 2009.
3 *Mail & Guardian*, 17 September 2010.
4 Ibid.
5 *The Witness*, 11 November 2010.

Chapter 23

1 The case against Mphego was struck off the roll in May 2010.
2 *Weekend Argus*, 1 August 2009.
3 *Ibid.*
4 Sapa, 29 September 2009.
5 Sapa, 12 November 2009.
6 *Sunday Times*, 27 May 2012.
7 *Ibid.*
8 *City Press*, 18 June 2012.
9 *City Press*, 27 February 2011.

Chapter 24

1 *Sowetan*, 10 July 2009.
2 *Ibid.*
3 *Mail & Guardian*, 23 September 2011.

4 *Daily Maverick*, 5 June 2012.
5 Sapa, 14 April 2011.
6 *Mail & Guardian*, 10 May 2012.
7 *Daily Maverick*, 23 May 2012.
8 *The Sunday Independent*, 17 April 2011.
9 *City Press*, 15 April 2012.
10 *City Press*, 3 April 2011.
11 Ibid.

Chapter 25
1 *The Sunday Independent*, 10 April 2011.
2 *Mail & Guardian*, 8 April 2011.

Chapter 26
1 *City Press*, 6 May 2012.
2 SABC, 11 May 2012.

Chapter 27
1 *City Press*, 18 March 2012.
2 *Ibid.*
3 *City Press*, 1 April 2012.

Chapter 29
1 *City Press*, 10 July 2011.

Chapter 30
1 *City Press*, 8 December 2011.

Chapter 32
1 *City Press*, 13 May 2012.
2 *City Press*, 20 May 2012.
3 *City Press*, 3 June 2012.
4 Sapa, 21 May 2012.
5 *The Times*, 22 May 2012.
6 *Ibid.*
7 *The Star*, 24 May 2012.
8 *City Press*, 23 May 2012.
9 *Ibid.*
10 *City Press*, 21 May 2012.

Chapter 34
1 *City Press*, 27 May 2012.

Chapter 36
1 *City Press*, 11 March 2012.
2 *City Press*, 13 May 2012.
3 *Sowetan*, 18 July 2012.
4 *City Press*, 22 July 2012.

Chapter 38
1 *The Star*, 14 September 2012.
2 *Sunday Times*, 9 September 2012.
3 *The Star*, 13 September 2012.
4 *City Press*, 17 June 2012.

Index

315

Operation Bad Guys 82, 83, 94
see also Scorpions
Operation Destroy Lucifer 76, 77,
81–82, 88
see also crime intelligence (police)
Pahad, Essop 149
Parekh, Jagdish 151
Patel, Ebrahim 17, 29
Phakoe, Moss 266–269
Phosa, Mathews 151, 188
Pikoli, Vusi 36, 65, 67–68, 81, 91,
166–168, 172
see also Ginwala inquiry
Polokwane conference 2, 6, 9, 17, 18, 21,
22, 31, 36, 61, 62, 68, 71, 75, 77, 81,
83, 94, 98, 99, 105, 112, 114, 115,
121, 127, 128, 138, 140, 145, 146,
190, 191, 193, 225, 229
see also African National Congress
(ANC); Zuma, Jacob
Powell, Ivor 78
Public Protector 34, 58, 179, 194, 267,
276
see also Madonsela, Thuli
Radebe, Faith 189, 199, 203, 204, 205,
206
Radebe, Jeff 8, 33, 129–130, 164, 165,
188, 197, 214, 224
and Menzi Simelane 91, 169, 170,
171–172, 174
Ramaphosa, Cyril 21
Ramatlhodi, Ngoako 25, 30–31, 32, 83,
262
Ramogibe, Oupa 186, 190, 191, 203
Reddy, Vivian 55, 135, 139
Renong Group 47, 48, 49–50, 291–298
SACP, *see* South African Communist
Party (SACP)
Sahara Computers 146, 148, 149
SAPS, *see* South African Police Service
(SAPS)
SARS, *see* South African Revenue
Service (SARS)

SCA, *see* Supreme Court of Appeal
(SCA)
Scopa (Standing Committee on Public
Accounts) 58, 214
Scorpions 1, 25, 26, 28, 31, 32, 36, 39,
58, 65, 67, 74–75, 84, 95, 107, 170,
179
Kebble investigation 77, 82, 96–97,
230
Operation Bad Guys 82, 83, 94
rivalry with police 76–77, 78, 79,
82–83, 86–89, 94, 195
Selebi investigation 81–82, 83, 87, 94,
175, 196, 198
Shaik trial 44, 49, 53
Zuma corruption charges 55, 60–61,
67, 68, 73, 98, 129
Scriven, Grant 47, 53
secret service, *see* South African Secret
Service
Section27 32, 134
Seepe, Sipho 71
Sefularo, Molefi 17
Selebi, Jackie 75, 76, 77–78, 81, 82, 83,
84, 86, 88, 113, 118, 119, 167, 186
and spy tapes 94–95
prosecuted for corruption 79, 84, 87,
89, 93–94, 101, 130, 175, 196, 198
Serote, Mongane Wally 237
Sexwale, Tokyo 18, 28–29, 154, 188,
193, 194
war on corruption 210–211
Shabangu, Roux 178, 180, 181–182, 183
and Zuma 180, 182
Shabangu, Susan 154, 177, 191, 196
Shaik, Moe 72, 96, 97, 129, 147, 165
Shaik, Schabir 1, 8, 24, 66, 72, 147, 216
corruption trial 24, 39, 44–48, 50–53,
65, 66, 67, 137, 214, 220, 221
Nkobi Group/Nkobi Investments 39,
45, 46–47, 51, 293–294, 297
Point Development 49–50, 292–298
relationship with Jacob Zuma 24, 49,